Beautiful on the Mountain

An Inspiring True Story

BEAUTIFUL
ON THE
MOUNTAIN

When there was trouble in Graves Mill,
God sent the most unlikely answer

Jeannie Light

TYNDALE
MOMENTUM

An Imprint of
Tyndale House Publishers, Inc.

B
LIGHT

For Elizabeth Baucum

How beautiful on the mountains
    are the feet of the messenger who brings good news,
the good news of peace and salvation,
    the news that the God of Israel reigns!

ISAIAH 52:7, NLT

Contents

Foreword

WHAT HAPPENS when a young woman finds herself thrown into a rural Virginia community and then is asked to reopen for them a long-disused local church? With only a few college classes in biblical subjects for preparation, Jeannie Light tells a tale of her years organizing Bible studies and worship, visiting hospitals and planning celebrations in a beautiful but remote corner of rural Virginia. As you read her stories, you learn along with her to care for and love a flock as diverse as the original Twelve. You'll be introduced to a cast of characters few novelists would have the creativity to describe as well, or as lovingly, as Jeannie does.

There are some very profound lessons in this tale. The most important is that when God throws you into the unknown, He can be trusted to guide you through the unforeseen and provide the grace for you to emerge from it a stronger Christian than when you went in. Jeannie had no idea what she was taking on when the good citizens of the hamlet of Graves Mill asked her to "do church" for them. Almost every day brought a surprise or a challenge for which the only thing she could do was lean on God with a desperate "Please help me" prayer.

The second lesson from the book is that preaching the Gospel in a community of ordinary people must be incarnated by living the

Gospel. To her own surprise, Jeannie discovered that opening the Bible among a group of strangers had the effect of opening up a new community: a community of people who laughed, joked, wept, and helped each other out in a sort of mini Kingdom of Heaven. The characters in this book are as funny, flawed, and tragic as any of us. Yet in Jeannie's story, the love of God enfolds them all, revealing how the body of Christ is supposed to function in everyday situations.

Jeannie and I served together as lay Eucharistic ministers in a dynamic church in northern Virginia for a few years in the 1990s. For at least part of this time, Jeannie was still living in the rural community and making the two-hour drive to church every week. I am ashamed to say that I did not know her very well at the time and had no idea what she was doing.

During more recent years of getting to know Jeannie well, I think I have discovered what being a true saint is like. It doesn't have much to do with ecclesiastical clothing, but it has a lot to do with pickup trucks, horse manure, crying children, weeping mothers, guffawing uncles, and ordinary people from every sector of life you could think of. It has a lot to do with praying for grace and wisdom, and with listening to people tell their unique stories. You'll laugh often as you read *Beautiful on the Mountain*, and you'll also weep with joy as you watch the way God works. Enjoy.

David Aikman
DECEMBER 2013

Introduction

AFTER FORTY YEARS of living, how many of us find ourselves where we expected to be when we were twenty? Did Abraham, growing up in the cosmopolitan city of Ur, expect to become a nomadic herdsman? Did Peter and Andrew have so much as a premonition that Jesus would call them from their fishing nets to wander the world's dusty roads? For most of us, life does not unfold according to our plans, but the Scriptures record promises that if we walk with God, He will supply our needs and there will always be enough bread for the day. Sometimes there's even butter on it. *Beautiful on the Mountain* is the record of God's faithfulness and provision for an unexpected journey in the wilderness.

In 1977 I came to Graves Mill, a tiny hamlet in the Blue Ridge Mountains of Virginia. As part of a divorce settlement, I owned a seven-hundred-acre tract of mountain land that was, as the locals said, "so poor a rabbit needed to pack a sack lunch to get through it." The parcel, once part of a mountain plantation, was a combination of rocky cliffs, wooded slopes, and about 125 acres of pasture. I was quite sure that the Lord had called me to raise sheep there, but over time I would come to realize that I had miscounted the legs.

In 1969, almost eight years before I took up residence in the mountains, the Baptist circuit closed the little church in Graves Mill.

The simple building stood empty and silent during those years, but the local residents never stopped dreaming of the day when it would once again reverberate with songs and sermons and shouts of "Amen! Preach it, brother!" I never dreamed that the little church would come to life, nor that I'd be included in the cast of characters in a tale of loggers, poachers, and the last of the mountain people, those who remembered life in the hollows before automobiles and telephones. However, living among them, I learned to care about the poor as people rather than anonymous recipients of my charitable donations. I was forced to learn to live in a community with less—much less—than in my previous life, and to learn that in God's economy, less is more when He guides the accounting. I confess that I fought the lessons every step of the way.

Many of the conversations in this book are imaginative reconstructions, but I was fortunate to have stacks of personal files, sermons, notes, and old cassette tapes from Bible studies and services, so some of the conversations are exactly as they happened. A few names have been changed to protect people's privacy. The story proceeds in episodes. There are emergencies, confrontations, visitors, and services. People arrive, play a part, and are never seen again, yet their appearance in our lives changes us and perhaps changes them as well.

It is my story, yes, but it is also the story of God's care for a little community as we journeyed together. God's ways are not ours, but for those who love Him, all things work together to bring us finally to that place where we get a glimpse of the Celestial City and see that indeed, it is beautiful on the mountain.

As Charles, a valley farmer, observed after I'd talked about heaven, "Ah, Missy, that there place sure must be beautiful, but Missy, ahhhh, th' gittin' there! Th' gittin' there!"

Jeannie Light
OCTOBER 2013

Prologue

*Historical . . . does not refer only to the bare, plain facts
of an account but to the fact plus its significance.*

RANIERO CANTALAMESSA

"I'M STAYING INDOORS TODAY!" I muttered as I reached for the door-knob. I had barely opened the cottage door when Tallis, my six-year-old Dalmatian, pushed his way past me, frantic to return to his rug in front of the fireplace. Cold winds were blowing down the valley, and we were both chilled after the round of morning chores, tending the chickens and horses. I lost no time following him inside and slammed the door shut against the raw autumn winds. I flopped down in the Boston rocker to pull off my Wellingtons and was still struggling with the first boot when the phone began to jangle.

I looked at my muddy boots. *I don't want to track muck across the floor to answer the phone.* I decided to let it ring. But as I worked at removing the boots, the green box on the wall continued to ring insistently, so I gave the left boot an energetic yank and padded in my stocking feet around the pine table to grab the receiver. It was the caseworker from the county social services.

"I'm *so* glad to get you!" she exclaimed. "Listen, I know this isn't exactly your thing, but this child has a bad neck fracture—at least, I think that's what it is—and she's in a cast. Auto accident, of course. There were a bunch of kids, probably drinking. Obviously she can't attend school, so I've been sending volunteers to help her keep up with her classes. I'm not sure how much she's learning, but it does give the mother a break. Besides, the girl is depressed and a new face provides a distraction. You see, her friend was killed in the accident, so I guess it's no wonder she's moody. Today's volunteer has the flu. Could you go down there this morning? You could teach from her composition or literature assignments, couldn't you? After all, you did teach English at the university extension, and since you're in the church business, this would be a very Christian thing to do."

She knew I couldn't refuse a request expressed in those terms.

"I'll see what I can do," I promised. "Lord, have mercy," I whispered to myself.

It was a gray morning. I had noted the low clouds above Jones Mountain, warning that the day ahead would be chilly. I'd already knocked a thin skim of ice out of the chickens' watering fountains. Tallis was huddled close to the ineffective fireplace, still recovering from being outside. The little cottage was poorly insulated, and the fireplace, rebuilt after the original house burned around it, didn't draw properly. Cozy or not, it was more inviting than a trip downriver to whatever mountaintop or hollow social services had in mind. With a sigh of reluctance, I did my best to bank the fire before changing my work jeans for a pair of decent slacks. A suit or dress might have looked more professional, but it wasn't practical.

Tallis nuzzled my knee, begging for attention. I patted the dog's head while he looked up at me mournfully, his one blue eye and one brown reflecting my mood. He had a pedigree long enough to give me an inferiority complex if I thought about it, but because his mismatched eyes made him useless for stud, his breeder had been delighted when my husband and I appeared at the kennel. She happily agreed to let us have him for a very small sum even though he was already housebroken and leash trained. When my husband and I divorced, Tallis was left with me.

Now Tallis whined as if to say, "You will let me come with you, won't you?"

"No, old pal, I'm sorry but you can't come on this trip," I said. "Later, maybe we'll get up to the mountain. Now, you be a good dog and guard the place, okay?"

Tallis's head and tail drooped, but he went obediently to his customary corner in the bedroom. I picked up a Bible, prayer book, notepad, and pens, and shrugged into my coat.

I decided against taking my little Chevette hatchback in favor of the four-wheel-drive Chevy pickup. In this backcountry, one couldn't predict the road conditions. The truck was high enough off the ground that it could clear stones and gullies impossible for the little car. Its springs were stiff, though, so I bounced my way along the river, noting the stubble where the last of the corn had been harvested at the Rhodes's farm. Behind it, the trees standing tall on German Ridge had lost their earlier blaze of fall color; today the leaves clinging to the trees were as dull as the skies above them.

I carefully rounded a blind curve. You never knew what might startle you on the narrow road. There could be slow-moving farm vehicles around the bend, horseback riders, or even stray steers. Some of the popular breeds, such as Charolais or Herefords, treat fences as if they were spiderwebs so it wasn't too surprising that their owners had trouble keeping the more adventurous animals inside their pastures.

After several miles I drove even more carefully so I wouldn't miss the turn I'd noted in the directions. At last I found the road sign and turned left into the foothills of the Blue Ridge. I had not seen this area before, and I was surprised to find so many small houses and trailers huddled in the spaces between small, ragged fields and steep, wooded hillsides.

A mile down the road, I spotted the right mailbox and turned into the faint track on one side of a weedy yard. The house appeared to be one of the resettlement houses that the federal government had built in the 1930s, when Shenandoah National Park was created. At the time, the feds moved the mountain people out of the hollows into these cracker boxes. I was never certain which little bungalows actually belonged to that lot, but I could find out in a matter of minutes at the tiny post office in the hamlet of Graves Mill. All the locals knew exactly when almost every dwelling in the parish had been built and by whom.

Whatever its origin, this little place was no more than a small box with a bit of porch tacked on. I collected my Bible and climbed slowly out of the truck. As I carefully picked my way along the rutted drive, I studied the house. The paint, which may have been white sometime in its history, was peeling, and a rust-coated hand pump stood in the yard. *Probably no indoor plumbing.* Indeed, as I stepped closer, I spotted an outhouse at the end of a well-worn path. I crossed the rickety porch and knocked, praying for wisdom.

The woman who peered at me through the narrow window in the door could have been sixty, but she might have been forty or even younger. Women aged quickly up here; men who had been hardscrabble farmers in the days before tractors were now day laborers, and their wives were far from pampered. Apparently deciding that I was not a threat, she slowly opened the door, pushing a strand of gray hair behind her ear while staring at me suspiciously.

"The social worker called me," I explained. "She said your daughter needed help with her schoolwork."

The woman's eyes went blank, her face expressionless. "This way," she said.

I followed her inside, noticing that the pattern was nearly worn away on the cracked kitchen linoleum. The pungent smell of cooked cabbage and smoked pork hung heavy in the hot, steamy room. A wood-burning stove crouched beside a box of kindling. *What would it be like to spend one's entire life confined within these walls? What measure of God's grace would suffice to sustain someone in this place?*

What measure of God's grace would suffice to sustain *me* if He called me to continue living and working in these hills? I never had any desire to be a missionary and certainly never imagined myself making this kind of visit. To be perfectly honest, I was scared.

CHAPTER I

HEADWATERS: ROME, JULY 4, 1976

It cannot be stated definitely what the call of God is to, because His
call is to be in comradeship with Himself for His own purposes,
and the test is to believe that God knows what He is after.

OSWALD CHAMBERS

SOMEONE SAID that obedience is a long walk in the same direction. It is one step at a time, one day at a time. We take wrong turns; we lose our way. There are no maps, but we follow a Voice—the Word—and love propels us onward.

For me, it all began in Rome.

My godparents had advised me to take a trip to Europe in the summer of 1976 because my ten-year marriage into a well-known Midwestern family was in serious trouble. At breakfast several months earlier, my husband, Harvey, had announced that he was very unhappy.

"Perhaps you should see a counselor," I said, feeling helpless.

"Maybe," he replied, looking woebegone.

"I can go and stay with Mama-san for a few days," I suggested, hoping that might help.

Frances Lee Lull, known to all her close friends as Mama-san, had taken me under her wing years before. I was certain she would be a wise counselor and that her kindness would bring some comfort to my fear and hurt.

"Don't do that!" Harvey exclaimed. "Think of the gossip! I don't want rumors on the county grapevine that we're having any trouble!"

"If I am away, you'll have time to think," I replied, pushing my breakfast aside. Food was the last thing I wanted at the moment.

I did pack an overnight case and drove to Springhill, Mama-san's farm, to see her. She took one look at me and showed me to the guest room. Harvey did call a counselor, a man reputed to be the best Charlottesville, Virginia, offered. In a few days he was enrolled in a transactional analysis group. When I told our pastor about the type of counseling my husband was receiving, he wasn't happy. In fact, he told me that being a part of those groups almost always led to divorce. After talking with Pastor Hall, I returned home and shared his warning with Harvey, then asked him to go with me to see our pastor.

He politely refused. He was delighted with the analysis program and was sure it was exactly what he needed.

"What is it?" I wanted to know.

He rubbed his temple. "Families have 'hot potatoes,'" he explained carefully. "These are issues they can't resolve so they pass them on to the next generation. Our marriage is a 'hot potato.'"

I stared at him in shock and disbelief. "Well, can I join that group?" I refrained from observing that it seemed to me that divorce, rather than marriage, might be the "hot potato."

"I need to do this alone," Harvey replied.

I was more than a little afraid of whatever transactional analysis might be and didn't push the issue, but when I told him my plans to move back home from Mama-san's, he was not pleased.

Soon, according to neighborhood gossip, he was involved with a member of the analysis circle, a local girl who also happened to be one of my friends. I knew her well; I trusted my husband's integrity and could not believe there was any substance to the rumors. However, the two were working together on a committee planning the county's celebration for the US Bicentennial, so it was awkward. My godparents thought the trip to Europe would spare me the embarrassment of the occasion, grant me a clearer perspective, and provide my husband space for reflection and a change of heart.

I didn't have any better ideas for what to do about my failing marriage, so I took their advice. And since I'd never visited Italy, I planned to spend two weeks in Rome after visiting old friends in Sweden. The itinerary for the summer also included time at L'Abri (the Christian retreat in Switzerland founded by Francis and Edith Schaeffer), the Salzburg International Arts Festival in Austria, and a few days in Germany with a friend from college days. In all, I would spend just over two months abroad.

Like most tourists in Italy, I tried to take in as much as possible in a short amount of time. I saw Michelangelo's *Pietà*, stood transfixed before Raphael's magnificent works, and trekked through the basilicas of St. Peter's and St. John Lateran. I walked and walked the ancient cobbled streets and city squares. Whenever I found a church, I would stop to pray. The most comfortable and comforting places were the small parish churches where no American tourists ever ventured, where elderly local matrons knelt in silence, heads covered with black veils. I was silent too. I had no specific petitions except a heart's cry for peace and direction. Sometimes despite my best efforts, I'd visualize my three-story Southern plantation house sitting behind its clipped boxwood hedges and Mary Helen, my beloved housekeeper and friend, standing in the doorway, smiling broadly.

On the Fourth of July, Pope Paul VI had promised a 1:00 p.m. audience for Americans abroad. The summer sun was almost directly overhead when I joined the motley lot congregated in St. Peter's Square. There were some turned collars and habits here and there scattered in the crowd, but the majority of those gathered were American tourists or businesspeople who happened to be in Rome that day. Most, like me, wore sandals and bright permanent-press shirts. Some held small American flags.

Although I wasn't a Roman Catholic, I had decided to join the faithful. I admired this pope's efforts to reach multitudes professing no religion at all, as well as those adhering to non-Christian faiths. I'd read of his efforts to internationalize the Roman Curia (the governing body of the Catholic church) and of his untiring work for peace. I recalled his visit to the United Nations in New York in 1965—the first papal visit to the Western Hemisphere—and his often-controversial efforts to implement the work of the Second Vatican Council. The truth was, though, that I was alone in the city, homesick, and scared, and I wanted to do something to celebrate the Bicentennial. An audience with the pope seemed the best available choice. At least I'd be with other Americans on this special day.

I arrived early. To my surprise, several hundred people had already gathered. I worked my way through the crowd until I was fairly close to the balcony where the pope was supposed to address us. I searched the faces of those around me; they showed no trace of the usual Independence Day exuberance. Even the small children seemed subdued. A towheaded boy who looked to be about eight years old carried his little American flag as proudly as if he were leading a regiment. His two sisters, perhaps five and three years of age, giggled and whispered in the parents' shadows, but even they were surprisingly still for such small children.

I wonder what Joe and Mary Temple are doing this morning? Joe and Mary Temple Fray were my godparents and the linchpins of my life back home in Madison County, Virginia. I was certain they would be celebrating with their family today. Remembering the time difference, I realized it was much too early for festivities yet. Perhaps Joe was just waking up. *No, he's probably outside feeding his chickens or checking his big garden for bugs or late peas. And Mary Temple's in her sunny kitchen preparing breakfast.*

The Frays were prominent members of my church and leaders in the county's social life and politics as well as personal friends. They traced their history back to Madison's original German settlers who built the historic Lutheran church in 1740. Through the centuries, their descendants had been known for honesty and for their contributions to the good of the community.

As a boy, Joe's ambition was to be a dairy farmer, but when the county elected him treasurer, it was the beginning of a lifelong adventure serving the country people he loved. An old-timer once told me Joe was the only honest politician he'd ever seen on two legs, and I believed him. Joe was a young treasurer when the Great Depression devastated the country in the thirties, hard years when Virginia struggled with drought as well as the Depression. Terrible fires roared across the desiccated mountain forestlands. Wells and springs ran dry. Cash was as scarce as hen's teeth, but when a man couldn't find the change to pay his taxes, Joe would travel out to see him and his wife. They'd talk over the situation, and Joe would find some way through the crisis so the family could keep their home. Needless to say, he was well loved and respected in the community, and I was proud to be his and Mary Temple's godchild.

The way that happened was quite unconventional. I had attended the Episcopal church since college and never expected to be part of a Lutheran church. However, the Episcopal church was planning to issue a new prayer book and I, like many others, disliked the changes. The revisions sounded flat and awkward compared to the old prayer book's melodious King James English. One of my friends recommended that my husband and I visit Hebron Lutheran Church, situated several miles outside Madison, Virginia, sitting like a small gem in its lush green valley. Harvey liked the hitching rails, the frescoed ceiling, and the friendly congregation, so we continued to attend Sunday services, and eventually we met Joe and Mary Temple.

A few months later my mother was diagnosed with liver cancer, and after a brief struggle with the malignancy, she asked if she could come live with me in Virginia. Harvey was working at the naval hospital in Bethesda, Maryland, and had an apartment in the city. I lived in a rented country cottage with little electric wiring and no telephone. With the owner's permission, I set about making improvements so that the house would be comfortable for my mother and hired Mary Helen to help me care for her. Mary Helen was with me the morning that Mother died, peacefully, just a few days after arriving from Michigan. Joe and Mary Temple heard of Mother's passing and came to comfort me. After that, I was firmly committed to the Lutheran parish, though I missed the liturgy of my former church and still used the 1928 Episcopal *Book of Common Prayer* at home.

I became Joe and Mary Temple's godchild for the simple reason that I never was baptized as a child. My father's rather Victorian reasoning was, "Never mind baptizing the girls. When they get married, they'll just take their husband's denomination anyway." My parents insisted on plenty of religious education—I memorized Scripture, went to Sunday school, and joined the youth group— but baptism wasn't part of the program. Once I began attending Hebron, I became active in the church's life, even teaching catechism to thirteen-year-olds.

That is, I did until Pastor Hall discovered I wasn't baptized. He was horrified. He tried to explain the theology, and though I didn't completely understand what he said, I agreed to have water poured over my head. Joe and Mary Temple were delighted to "present me" for baptism. They proudly took their places beside me and promised "to bring up this child to lead a godly life." Ever after, Joe said the one thing wrong with the ceremony was that he couldn't hold the "baby." They did, however, take their promises seriously and from that day forward made me part of the family.

As I stood in St. Peter's Square and thought about them, I was tempted to weep, but I could almost hear Mary Temple's words of encouragement, "Now you just buck up. Things are never as bad as we think they're going to be." She would be looking at me with those kindly eyes behind the spectacles and ever so slightly incline her queenly head of snow-white hair. She was always erect, always a Southern lady. I straightened my shoulders. I wouldn't let her down, not if I could help it.

The pope hadn't appeared yet. I turned around slowly, admiring St. Peter's Square and marveling that I was there. What a long way I'd traveled since my childhood! My father, a third-generation Michigan farmer who had worked the land his family cleared early in the 1800s, died when I was twelve. My mother, a professional violinist, had a nervous breakdown, so my only sibling, a younger sister, and I went to live with an aunt and uncle. That is, I lived with them during the school year; summers, I worked for local families as a live-in house-keeper and mother's helper.

By strict self-discipline and intense study, I managed to finish high school in three years, doing well enough to earn multiple schol-arships that covered my entire tuition to Kalamazoo College. Once there, I worked for room and board, books, and life's little necessities. I earned a bachelor's degree in English literature, a Phi Beta Kappa key, and a Woodrow Wilson Fellowship, allowing me to attend the graduate school of my choice.

I chose the University of Virginia not only because it was an excellent school but because my mother's family had been southern and some of my earliest memories were of the family gathered in my grandmother's parlor on Sunday afternoons, telling stories of the South and the Blue Ridge Mountains. In nine months, I finished my master's degree in nineteenth-century English literature with honors, and one success capping another, I "married well," as my little Victorian grandmother would have put it.

Feet shuffled on the cobblestones. I looked around at the crowd, but the pope still hadn't appeared. I longed for a distraction from the thoughts floating up unbidden. *I'm sure Doctor isn't pleased with the mess his son and I are making of our lives.* I shuddered. I had come to know and love my husband's family while I was a student at Kalamazoo. In fact, the family had endowed the college's scholarships for study abroad and I had received one, spending the summer between my sophomore and junior years in France. The following summer I came to work for the family as a live-in cook. Soon they were my very dear friends, and to my surprise, father, mother, and sons treated me as if I belonged among them. Because I missed my own father and mother and the stability of the old home farm, I snuggled into their kindness like a cat on a warm hearth.

Harvey was the youngest of the four boys. During the time I lived with the family, we met only briefly because he was either traveling or studying at Yale. When I returned to Michigan on my first Christmas break from graduate study in Virginia, the two oldest brothers were married and the third busy with his own life, leaving the "little brother" at a loss for something to do. I was idle, too, so Harvey and I took long walks through the snow and flirted over a desultory chess game. I returned to Virginia and my classes; he went back to Northwestern University in Evanston, Illinois, where he'd transferred from Yale. To my surprise, he wrote fairly often. The letters were friendly, and I was flattered with the attention.

Then came the telephone call from his mother. I don't remember the words, but the news shook my world to its very core. She and Doctor, as we called him, had separated and were getting a divorce. After I hung up the phone, I began sobbing so loudly that a friend across the hall rushed to see what had happened. Somehow the divorce was worse than a death in the family. The safe harbor I had cherished against the unknowns of the years ahead was utterly demolished.

June came and my graduation was only days away. My family was proud of my accomplishments, but none of them planned to celebrate the occasion with me. I understood; it was summer and harvesttime at the farm, and Virginia was a long way from Michigan, but I was deeply disappointed. Then I received a letter from Harvey. *He was coming!* I was nearly overwhelmed with gratitude and excitement.

Once I had my diploma in hand, he asked if we could spend a day or two hiking the Appalachian Trail in the Blue Ridge Mountains just west of Charlottesville. I hesitated. A little voice in the back of my mind whispered that this wasn't wise, but after all, this was my "brother," so I finally said yes. I knew parts of the trail in that section quite well since it was my usual escape from study and the fevers of the academic world, and I was happy to share my familiar haunts with "family." Besides, he had come from Michigan to Virginia for my graduation.

Harvey came well prepared with camping gear; I had quilts. He slept in his sleeping bag. I slept in my quilts. However, when he kissed me good-night I realized that this relationship wasn't likely to remain exactly fraternal, though it did remain chaste during those days in the wilderness. We both loved the out-of-doors and the adventure of exploring wild places, but I suspect that during those two days on the trail we paid more attention to one another than to the flora and fauna around us. I know that was true of me. I remember his blond hair blowing in the wind more vividly than I recall the campsite.

When Harvey left for summer school in Oregon, absence made our hearts grow fonder and the friendship became a whirlwind courtship. I had a summer job as a hostess in one of the mountain lodges in Shenandoah National Park, but at the last minute the oldest brother in the family asked me to work with him as a reporter and writer for the Kalamazoo city magazine he owned and edited. I loved the family, I loved writing, and if the truth were known, I was a little homesick. After some debate and several telephone calls from the family, I agreed to come.

Most of that summer Harvey was in Oregon, but just before the fall semester began at Northwestern, he returned to Michigan for a few days. He had ridden his motorcycle back from the coast, and I first saw him when he roared up to the magazine office, found me, and took me for a ride. He had kept a diary of his adventures and let me read some of it. We talked about his trip. We spent some days with Doctor at his big Christmas tree farm in the country, walking the trails and watching the ducks on the pond there. We also spent time with Harvey's mother at her lake house, and we clung to one another like two shipwrecked sailors. We were both heartbroken and disoriented in the aftermath of the family's disintegration.

I went back to Virginia with a rock on my ring finger big enough to dazzle my fellow scholars at the university. I don't even recall when Harvey proposed or exactly how it came about, but the engagement seemed somehow inevitable.

While we were excellent friends, in many ways we were ill matched. I was working on a PhD in eighteenth-century English literature; he was just beginning his junior year at Northwestern and thought he'd like to be a biology major. I had earned my way through life; he came from old-family money. He'd grown up with servants;

I had been one. Neither of us really knew much about the other or about what we wanted to become. I had been so busy climbing the academic ladder that I hadn't taken time to learn much about living. I knew I enjoyed writing and expected to become an English professor so I could afford to write poetry, something I had wanted to do since age six. My fiancé wasn't at all certain what he wanted to do or be. He loved being outdoors riding his motorcycle or his bicycle—one summer he had ridden a bicycle from Oregon to Michigan. He also enjoyed astronomy. His father had built an observatory for him on the highest point of their farm, and when Harvey was home he spent a lot of time there gazing at the stars.

Back in Virginia, I had more time to think. Distanced from the grief and uncertainty of the family breakdown, I decided that marriage was not wise for either of us. For several weeks I didn't sleep well and had trouble concentrating on my studies. Finally I gathered all the courage I had and called him to break off the engagement. It was a simple, matter-of-fact conversation, and I thought that was the end of it. It wasn't.

In the dead of winter, Harvey got on his motorcycle, leaving exams, term papers, and his academic future behind him and headed for Charlottesville through the mountains of West Virginia. His mother was frantic with worry. I was equally alarmed. He called me collect from the road almost every day, detailing his difficulties with ice and snow. By the time he arrived, my roommate was thoroughly sick of the whole drama, and I was willing to do anything to end the tensions. At least if we were married, there would be a common future and we'd find our way together.

We were married in early June 1965 in my aunt's living room. It was a simple ceremony; I wore a long white dress and my aunt and uncle were proud and happy. I was twenty-four years old and my husband was about two years younger. I left the academic world behind me and began a new life as a married woman.

After an adventurous honeymoon driving across the United States to Oregon and back in a Rambler, we arrived at Northwestern. Because money was not a problem, we found a pleasant apartment in Evanston, bought fairly good furniture, unpacked the wedding china, and settled into life together. Harvey was on academic probation, probably because of too many fraternity parties topped off with his madcap ride to Virginia to stop me from breaking the engagement. I worked with him on his studies, trying to keep him focused, and he did well. When his biology class had field trips, I traveled with him. I enjoyed these times together, and I was glad to help with the academic work.

I was lonely, though. I no longer knew who I was or what kind of woman I wanted to become. I found a job in Northwestern's rare book department assisting the acquisitions staff, the sort of position offered to women whose husbands were studying at the university. I was bored. I missed the challenges of the academic world. I attended a local Episcopal church by myself on Sunday mornings. Harvey used that time to sleep, study, or catch up with fraternity friends. I don't think I ever stayed for a coffee hour after a service. I was too unsure of myself to venture out on my own, and besides, I did not like big-city living. I was accustomed to smaller cities, country roads, and fresh air. Even a trip or two to hear the Chicago Symphony didn't fill the void.

I tried hard to be a good wife, though. I kept the apartment meticulously clean. I cooked gourmet meals, and Harvey often invited one of his close friends to come for dinner. As the months passed, I gained weight. One day my husband surprised me by coming home early. I was embroidering a pillowcase, and when I looked up from my embroidery hoop, Harvey exclaimed, "I plucked a Virginia wildflower and it's wilting before my eyes."

I didn't know how to respond, and he did not continue the conversation.

When Harvey graduated the following year, we moved to Maine. On the basis of his senior year's grades, my husband had been accepted into the University of Maine's graduate program in ecology. I was very proud of him. As for me, I was hired to teach freshman English for the university's extension program. I breathed a sigh of relief. We bought a house in the country, and I was back in the academic world. Together, we attended the local Episcopal church.

That year was merely a short interlude. The United States was mired in the Vietnam War at the time, and although Harvey was exempt from military service because he was in school, he feared that the academic exemption policy might be discontinued, leaving him vulnerable to the draft. So, rather than taking a chance on a military "invitation," he joined the navy in the spring of 1967. When Harvey went off to boot camp in June, I didn't know what to do with myself, although I knew I did not want to endure another Maine winter, this time alone.

We talked it over and decided to sell the house in Maine. I packed our belongings and headed back to Virginia. I resumed my interrupted studies and taught English at the University of Virginia Extension in Madison County, about thirty miles north of Charlottesville in the Virginia piedmont. The next year, I moved from my apartment near the university to a small rented cottage in the country, outside historic Madison and about a hundred miles south of Washington, DC.

After basic training, my husband was sent to Indonesia, where he assisted with biological research on animal-borne infectious diseases in Vietnam. It was never clear exactly why the navy was doing this research, but it offered a fine position for a neophyte ecologist and allowed him to finish his master's degree thesis long distance. Harvey liked Madison County, so eventually we bought some land and a historic house about five miles from town.

We called it Luxmont, Light's hill—*lux* (Latin for "light") and *mont* (Latin for "mountain" or "hill"). The seven-room pre–Civil War house commanded a magnificent view of the Blue Ridge Mountains. With the help of a Charlottesville company specializing in early American houses, I renovated and restored the mansion, adding a third floor, which accommodated two more guest rooms and baths.

I think I was hoping that working together on the house in Madison County would help heal our marriage. But Harvey had more tours to complete in the navy, first in Indonesia and later in Bethesda, Maryland. After my mother's death I moved to Luxmont, repairing the additional buildings and managing the farm. When Harvey was in the States, he'd come to Luxmont on the weekends.

With my husband's blessing and Joe Fray's help and guidance, I began a breeding program to establish a good herd of Hereford cattle. I planned to live the Virginia dream. I'd scrambled up the hard way during the first decades of my life, but I was sure the rest of the journey would be smooth climbing. It was a long way from the life I'd planned—writing poetry and teaching literature—but I was convinced I could conquer any challenge with a combination of sheer intelligence, will, and discipline.

Except, it seemed, my marriage. For some strange reason, informed intelligence doesn't always fix relationships. What my "informed intelligence" didn't grasp was that during our ten years of marriage, Harvey and I had spent relatively little time together—he'd gone into the military before we had actually forged a common identity. People need to stay in the same room long enough to accomplish that. We had been together in Evanston, Illinois, and in Maine, but after that, he had been in Vietnam, Indonesia, or Bethesda, Maryland, while I had roamed the Virginia byways. We were almost strangers when he returned to civilian life at Luxmont. Harvey tried to become a farmer, taking over the land, herd, and crop management. He enjoyed the exercise, but otherwise he was not a happy man. I was left to manage the house, and without the challenges of farm management, I was bored and unhappy too. We were trying to live the plantation dream, and it wasn't enough. We didn't have a serious common goal. We didn't even know how to pray together to find one.

We really don't know how to be married, I thought sadly, remembering.

The crowd awaiting the pope was moving restlessly, but no one left the square. I shuffled my feet and shrugged my tense shoulders. *What will Mary Helen and Dan be doing today?* I wondered. *Will they go to Madison for the inevitable parade? Will Mary Helen make potato salad and have a big watermelon?* My whole body ached, longing to see her, to be enfolded in one of her mama-hugs. Mary Helen had been the constant in my life through my mother's last days, my husband's various naval assignments, and my early and lonely years at Luxmont. I wanted to be home, wanted to see the broad pastures stretching toward the horizon, wanted to ride my horse, wanted to walk outside with Dan, who had become my farm manager, to look over the Herefords. I longed to look out my kitchen window to see the Blue Ridge Mountains, hazy in the distance. Was the world I'd known irrevocably shattered?

The gentle murmur of the expectant crowd lapped against the venerable walls surrounding the square. The pope! The small, white-robed figure standing on the balcony about ten feet above us seemed very close, surprisingly vulnerable. In the brilliant summer sunlight, he appeared to glow with a supernatural radiance. Palpable waves of reverence, awe, and wonder filled St. Peter's Square. Even the noisy Roman traffic seemed to recede into quietness.

Then the pope began to speak. Even now, thirty years later, I remember the quality of his voice, though I don't remember whether he spoke in English or Italian because Something was happening.

Something I cannot explain and can hardly describe, except to say that like Paul on the Damascus Road, I knew: *God is real.*

The sunlight was very bright, yes, but the light around me seemed to flash to a blinding intensity. Unlike Paul, I heard no voice, but I was devastatingly aware of my pride, my self-indulgence, and my faithlessness. I heard myself whispering, "Lord Jesus, please take my life and use it according to Your purposes. Please. It's not much and it's a mess, but it's all I have to give You."

I have no idea how long I stood there, but when I could see again, the pope's hands were raised in blessing and dismissal. I looked down at my feet, surprised to see that the stones were wet. *What?* It hadn't rained . . . With a start, I realized the cobbles were shining with my tears.

I left Rome a week later, traveling to northern Italy, Austria, Switzerland, and Germany. I was like a child learning to walk. My travel plans hadn't changed, but the whole world looked different. Where I had seen problems, I now saw Providence. I was still confused and fearful, but now I had a deep sense of God's faithful presence. During my flight from Frankfurt to West Berlin, a nasty storm tossed the plane like a toy. The passengers clung to their seats, faces as white as their knuckles. Even the flight attendants were terrified. I was frightened, too, yet in the midst of the storm I knew a peace I'd never guessed possible. Those few moments in St. Peter's Square taught me that God is real, but I wanted to know more. I wanted to know *Him* the way I had known Him as a child.

When I was eight years old, I gave my life to Christ during a country revival service, and through my early years, I never doubted the Bible or that Jesus heard my prayers. I felt secure through all the trials and changes of my childhood, and I trusted that all those hymns and Sunday school lessons and sermons were the gospel truth. When a young Methodist preacher came to our small town just out of seminary and proclaimed that the Virgin Birth was a myth, I simply dismissed him as an unbeliever. It wasn't until my college years and exposure to scientific cynicism that I questioned the Bible's authority. I wanted to be an "intellectual," and gradually my confidence in God's guidance faded, though at the time I didn't even notice what had happened. But in St. Peter's Square I had tasted Something that promised I could be whole, could set my feet on solid ground—a Living Truth.

When I returned to the plantation, Harvey promptly moved out, informing me that he would file for a divorce as soon as the Virginia laws allowed. No-fault divorce had just been legalized; after a year's separation, he could file and I could do nothing to stop it. With Mary Helen and Dan's help, I was left to manage the cattle, the fifteen hundred acres of Virginia piedmont and mountain farmland, and the division and dissolution of a southern dream.

I had no idea that the Lord would answer my prayers for His nearer presence by sending me into the wilderness, just as He did with the Israelites. He brought His people out of Egypt in about four months, but it took forty years of testing and teaching to get Egypt out of them. Although faith comes by hearing the Word, it's on the pilgrims' way that we finally learn to trust.

CHAPTER 2

CHARLES'S PROPOSAL

God moves in a mysterious way His wonders to perform.

WILLIAM COWPER

DAN APPEARED IN the plantation house kitchen just a few minutes before eight on an early spring morning about six months after my return from Europe.

"You ready?" he asked. "We's a-goin' to the mountain farm today, ain't we?"

I nodded. "That's the plan."

"I'se got the truck loaded. You drivin' the Jeep t'day?"

"Yes, Dan. I'd ride with you, but I'd better pick up the mail in town after we finish. If you can drive the pickup and come back here to check on the cattle and off-load the gear, that would be a big help."

Luxmont Farms was comprised of three tracts of land, none of them contiguous. A half mile north of the plantation house lay a tract of three hundred and fifty acres now ready for corn planting. We'd already finished vaccinating the new calves and had plowed the bottomland at the home farm, another three hundred and fifty acres of broad pastures where the cattle grazed. With those chores completed, we had a day or so to turn our attention to the third tract, about seven hundred acres of mountain land twelve miles to the west. We seldom worked there because a neighboring farmer held the grazing rights. Aside from occasionally spraying for thistles or spreading fertilizer on the meadows, the land hadn't required our attention.

Dan had been farm manager since we'd bought the home place eight years earlier. During those years, he and I had come to know each other's ways so well that we didn't need to talk much unless I did something stupid with the farm machinery. I understood pasture management. I could generally diagnose cattle problems, but tractor maintenance remained a challenging mystery. Fortunately, Dan was a wizard with a wrench.

Dan stepped outside to the back stoop, lifting his battered gray cap to let the breeze comb his black woolly head. He looked out across the pastures toward the mountains spread out in a blue panorama on the western horizon. The bottomland along Elk Run lay in a rich brown streak between the new green of the hill pastures. Dan's pause wasn't like him; he was usually off to the next task as soon as we agreed on the day's work.

"'Bout time for gettin' that corn in," he murmured. I knew Dan was ambivalent about the trip up into the hills. It was almost planting time and only a few weeks until the first hay-cutting in late April or early May. I knew that wasn't what was on his mind, though. We were both wondering if I'd be doing any of these things with him this year. Under the terms of the proposed property settlement, I would keep the mountain land while my husband retained the home farm and north tract. Dan and Mary Helen lived on the home farm and would stay on there.

Fear stabbed the middle of my stomach. *How can I possibly manage that mountain farm without Dan's help?* Even fencing in that rough territory was, to say the least, challenging. Charles Jenkins, who leased the land for grazing, was fond of saying that after God finished creating the earth, He scraped the rocks left in His wheelbarrow out into Kinsey Hollow. Rocks there certainly were, on the surface of the land and under it too. Driving a fence post amid the boulders was more art and intuition than skill, and for that reason, as well as for the value of the pastures, Charles had kept his lease not only on my land, but also on my godfather's land adjoining it on the west side. It saved keeping up fences between the tracts. *So how could I maintain fences and live and thrive on those seven hundred craggy acres?*

There was no time to think about those things this morning, and besides, although I had occasional doubts, most of the time I was absurdly confident that I was supposed to live on that mountain farm. I shoved my old straw hat down over my pigtails and followed Dan to the toolshed to see if we needed to add anything else to the equipment he'd loaded in the pickup bed: barbed wire, fence stretchers, nails, hammers, clips, and stakes. I'd forgotten my leather gloves, a necessity for working with barbed wire. I ran back to the house, grabbed them from the top shelf in the entryway closet, and hurried to the three-car garage for my Jeep. Seeing the empty bay next to it where my husband's car would have been, hit me momentarily with a stab of hurt and fear. I shook it off, started the Jeep, and turned toward the winding road leading to the mountains.

I knew the route well, so I drove on autopilot until I reached Wolftown, where the road forked to the right, curving within several yards of the Wolftown Mercantile general store. After passing a few houses, the macadam strip narrowed as it threaded its way north up the Rapidan River Valley. German Ridge guards the land to the east; Flat Top Ridge rises on the west side of the road. I passed one of the old Kite home places, sold several years earlier to the McDanolds, a family from northern Virginia. A few of their big white Charolais cattle grazed a field close to the main house, and I recalled that Charles had snorted in disdain when he mentioned "them furrin' cows ol' McDanolds an' his boy Skip done trucked inter this here valley." Later, when he realized the cows produced big calves that put on weight rapidly, bringing good prices in the market, Charles was more favorable to the "furrin'" invasion.

As the vehicles nosed their way up the Rapidan River Valley, I was forced to pay more attention to the road, not risking more than a glance at the scenery. I'd been told that the men who'd laid the road had put down a log base, forming a corduroy track. Later, gravel and macadam were added, but whatever its origins, the road hadn't been laid smoothly. "Better get used to the bumps," I said out loud. "Before long, this bumpy trail will be your only way home."

Finally I reached Graves Mill, or at least what remained of the hamlet. A series of weathered buildings, paint long faded, sagged bleakly along the road. *What a lonely, sad place!* The vacant store windows, some of them broken, seemed to mourn a time when people streamed out of the hills to purchase their coffee, sugar, flour, and muslin. I knew that in the community's heyday, the engines came chugging and whistling up the old logging railroad, bringing mail and prosperity to these now-abandoned emporiums. The train brought goods into the little town, and when it steamed out, it carried not only lumber, but also meat, apples, chestnuts, and other local produce downriver, connecting the people of the hollow with faraway markets. Those had been the glory days, but inevitably, when the primeval timber was logged out, the company moved to other slopes, and the railroad could not survive, transporting only local produce and supplies.

The road forked again, the right fork following the Rapidan River up into Shenandoah National Park and the left climbing up toward Thoroughfare Mountain. The post office lay just across a bridge on the right-hand fork, and beyond that a couple of farms filled the land up to the edge of the national park. I followed the left fork, which curved within a few yards of the old Baptist meetinghouse, a plain, white-shingled, tin-roofed building. It was basically a box with a roof; there was no steeple. This unassuming structure occupied a narrow strip of land bounded by the road at the front and Dolly Seekford's neat pasture fences behind the church. I hardly noticed it as I passed.

Across from the church, the old Jenkins house, like most Virginia farmhouses of its time, sat in the middle of the property. Nestled in a grove of trees at the end of a long driveway, it was hidden away in summer, but today the house and sheds were visible because the surrounding trees were only beginning to show leaves. Charles's parents were deceased, and the big old Victorian house stood vacant. Charles preferred his smaller white bungalow set against the steep slopes of Jones Mountain. He'd moved there with his young family when his parents were in the big house, and stayed in the bungalow even after his parents died. The old house was drafty in winter and needed more upkeep than rocky fields and pastures could support. Charles's two sons had no taste for farming and left the valley after high school graduation. Charles's wife left him several years after that, and without a woman's hand at the helm, the big house was not only too expensive to maintain, it was beyond Charles's domestic capabilities.

Charles's rocky spread lay along a lower ridge of Jones Mountain, next to the mountain farm where Dan and I planned to work that morning. The farm was familiarly known as the old Kinsey place. I'd decided to call it Jehovah Jireh, meaning "The Lord Will Provide." Apt though the name might have been, in some secret corner of my mind I knew it was pretentious, an attempt to tell the world how smart and educated I was. No one, in all the years I was there, ever called it anything but the old Kinsey place.

My land shared fence lines with Charles's land on the east, and on the west side with my godfather's tract known as the Fray place or the "other half of the Kinsey place." I knew that old Buck Hawkins, Dolly Seekford's father, had once rented the land from the last of the Kinseys. He'd herded sheep up Canterbury Hollow and even in the high meadows on the other side of the ridge, below Bear Church. Although most farmers had abandoned sheep farming earlier in the century, I was determined to become a shepherd. This spring day I was confident that the sheep farm I intended to run there would prosper.

The idea had come to me in a flash of inspiration, but I had attempted to think it through carefully. Herefords, Angus, and shorthorns—beef cattle—did well in the hills and were less vulnerable than sheep to disease and predators, but wool and lamb chops were popular once again, so a few farmers had returned to raising the animals. I'd talked with some of them and learned they were doing well. Besides, cattle were large animals and I knew I'd have difficulty managing them alone. I thought I could herd sheep and maybe even do some of the vet work. Furthermore, I knew from my conversations with shepherds down in the lower counties that the drainage on the Kinsey place would be excellent for sheep. Of course, there was the fence building, but I'd find a way to do that somehow.

Even more important to me was the encouragement I'd received from Virginia Polytechnic Institute. I'd sent off soil samples for analysis so I'd know how much lime and fertilizer to order for the pastures. I had acquired textbooks on sheep farming and had been reading a stack of manuals on everything from constructing a sheep-dipping trough to putting together a hayrack. The fact that I lacked any good land for raising the quality of grass needed for this visionary hay only vaguely concerned me. I thought that perhaps I could rent a strip of good land across the road. I was, in fact, more self-assured than I should have been, though I did have some qualms now and then. So did Dan.

"I guess it ain't a bad place t'live," he'd said during an earlier excursion. "But I don' like it, you goin' way up here on this scrubby place you calls a farm. Don' like it 't'all."

"I'll be okay, Dan," I'd replied gently. "It is the way it is. Well, there *are* those snakes . . ." I shivered, remembering. Rattlesnakes lived in the rocks and caves high up on the mountain, but they didn't always stay at high altitudes. I'd just purchased a .44 Magnum revolver that could fire either bear or snake shot. I had never considered exactly what I would do if a bear happened to be coming at me when I had the gun loaded with snake shot. *Meeting a snake is more likely than meeting a bear, but bears are fond of mutton.*

Just above Charles's place the macadamized road became a gravel track. I stirred up a cloud of dust with the Jeep, and Dan slowed the pickup, lengthening the distance between us for the quarter mile to the farm gate. I jumped out, unlocked the padlock, and drove the Jeep through Kinsey Run, then waited for Dan to close the gate and cross. The run, tumbling and rippling across the rocks, guarded the road frontage almost as if it were a moat protecting a castle. We bumped and swayed across ruts and rocks located between scrub pines, sumac, young poplars, briars, and other such signs of once-productive land that had now reverted to wilderness. Suddenly the main valley opened before us as if a curtain had parted on a pasture in Eden. I'd seen the bowl of Kinsey Valley days without number, but every time I rounded the last curve, the view surprised me all over again. This cloudless spring day was no exception.

The young timber and brush along the road hid an open valley, about a hundred and twenty-five acres of grassy meadow dotted here and there with scrub pine, cedars, rock piles, and huge boulders. Straight ahead lay a ridge of Jones Mountain rising sharp against the sky, its lower slopes misted with the pale green of new leaves. Bear Church loomed at the northeast corner of the tract, sloping down in the eastern flank of Jones Mountain lying between my land and Charles Jenkins's place. A small spring-fed and unnamed run tumbled down the rocky slopes in small falls and pools between the two places. On the west, the Kinsey Run formed a boundary with "the other half of the Kinsey place" for a short distance until a ridge off Bluff Mountain rose to guard the valley.

It was a world to itself. Completely enclosed by forest and mountain ridges, the place had an almost magical atmosphere.

I parked the Jeep beside an overgrown boxwood near a rock pile. Like the stores in Graves Mill, the Kinsey mansion, known to natives as "the old rock house," was in ruins. Even though little remained of the house, the sizable hole that had been the basement indicated it had once been grand. My godfather told me that one of the front rooms of the main house had served as Dr. Kinsey's office when he lived there. As a boy visiting old "Doc" Kinsey with his father, Joe Fray had been fascinated with the jars containing various human organs, and even a fetus preserved in formaldehyde.

"Sure is pretty up here!" Dan remarked, his teeth flashing white against his brown skin. "Nice day, but I reckon we'd best git t'work."

I nodded and we began sorting through the jumble of supplies, filling our tool aprons with nails, clips, and fencing staples. The rough trip up the mountain had tangled fencing bars with wire, nail kegs, and the like, so we set things in order so that we could easily access what we needed.

Dan guided the pickup across the valley to a grassy spot as near the fence as we could come with the truck. This wonderful valley had once sheltered a plantation community. We could see the ruins of what had been the old brew house. Sections of the stone walls stood in a mist of wineberry briars, and from underneath a big black gum tree bubbled a spring, its cold water spilling over into a little brook that had provided the water for distilling and brewing a century earlier. Whenever I stopped there to drink at the spring, I'd find barrel hoops, handmade nails, and staples, as well as the shards and necks of old blue, brown, and green bottles scattered among the stones on what had once been the brew house floor. Dan and I knelt for a quick drink from the spring. There was no time for lingering there today, though. We picked our way through the brush under the cool, sweet shade of the poplars and sycamores.

When we were about three yards from the Kinsey Run, we put down the roll of barbed wire we carried between us. The fence lay between the run and the dusty gravel road that wound its way several miles up the hill to Lost Valley and into wilderness areas belonging to the Virginia Game Commission. Eventually it became an overgrown track in Shenandoah National Park. We crossed the creek, careful not to get water in our work boots, and soon the drumbeats from our hammers added their rhythm to the stream's music.

We were stringing barbed wire, adding a new bottom strand, lower to the ground. Sheep, and especially their lambs, could easily slip under a cattle fence, so it was necessary to secure the wire strands closer together and closer to the ground.

It was slow work, even though this was the best time of year to do it. The undergrowth hadn't leafed out, and the weeds—nettles, dock, thistles, smartweed—wouldn't sprout until later. Still, catbriers and blackberry vines choked areas where we needed to stand, forcing us to spend more time cutting brush than building fence. Dan whistled through his teeth from time to time. To fend off discouragement, I kept envisioning sheep grazing in the mountain pastures. I couldn't spend a lot of time dreaming, though, because the terrain and the toil required my full attention.

We broke for lunch after completing only about fifty yards of the fence, and then it was back to work. Even though it wasn't hot, by two o'clock we were sweating, and I'd lost all sense of anything around me except barbed wire, stakes, and fence clips. I didn't even hear the woodpecker somewhere deep in the woods until Dan mentioned it. We soldiered on for another hour before calling it a day.

Just as Dan and I loaded the roll of barbed wire on a long metal pole to carry it back to the truck, Charles Jenkins's maroon pickup skidded to a halt in the gravel road on the other side of our fence.

"Missy," he yelled, "Missy. I want to talk t'you 'bout somethin'. Meet me down at yer gate." With that, he backed the pickup down the road.

Dan and I looked at each another and he grinned. "Reckon you'd best go talk to Mr. Charlie. I'll load up and head on home."

"Mr. Charlie can just wait until I've helped you carry that roll of barbed wire back to the truck."

We gathered the other supplies and Dan bumped his way out of the valley, back to Luxmont. I walked down the track toward the gate and hopped from stone to stone across the Kinsey Run, arriving out of breath where Charles waited, leaning against his truck and dragging on his pipe. His eyes were serious, and from the way he puffed on that pipe, I knew he had some major project in mind.

"What's up, Charles?" I wanted to know.

He didn't tell me. Instead, he commanded, "Foller me down t' the church. I want t' talk t' you 'bout somethin' down there."

I wanted to yell, "Well, why didn't you say that instead of telling me to meet you at this confounded gate?" But I knew it was not only bad manners, it was a useless exercise.

Muttering under my breath, I picked my way across the Kinsey Run again, hurried to my Jeep, and followed Charles to the old Baptist church. I parked behind his truck on the narrow strip of land beside the building.

Charles was waiting on a little cement stoop at the side door. *What on earth does he have on his mind?* I wondered.

When I reached the stoop, he pulled the pipe out from between his teeth, jabbing the air with it to punctuate the importance of his words. "Missy," he said firmly, "we wants you to git the ol' church open."

"Are you serious, Charles?" I wasn't sure I'd heard him correctly.

"Serious as a heart attack," he replied, but this time there was a twinkle in the blue-gray eyes above his ruddy cheeks. "The ol' deacons' board, what's left of 'em, done talked it over and we wants you to do it."

I stared at him, speechless. Charles always reminded me of the Basque farmers I'd seen in Normandy: square-built, sturdy, shrewd, but wise in the ways of nature and humankind. His coloring indicated that he probably didn't mind a tipple now and again, while the set of his square jaw and the jab of his pipe revealed the choleric temper I knew from experience. I couldn't put the person in front of me together with the words *deacon*, *board*, or *church*.

Charles motioned toward the open door behind him. "C'mon in an' have a look."

I followed him down a dark hallway. The narrow strips of oak flooring were slightly curled at their edges from the damp, and the whole place reeked of mildew.

Charles opened a door a few feet down the hallway and we entered a large room. Feeble rays of light fell through the wooden slats of venetian blinds covering six high windows. I could barely see an elaborate tin ceiling about fifteen feet above me, rows of dusty pews draped with cobwebs, and two hulking kerosene stoves, one on each side of the room. An upright piano stood in the corner beside me.

"Ain't nary a window busted," Charles informed me proudly as he fiddled with the cords on a set of the ancient wooden blinds. Creaking and spilling clouds of dust, the blinds finally surrendered to his efforts. There were wavy patterns in the window's greenish glass. *Those are definitely original.*

With the blinds opened, I could see dark pews, which I judged could seat seventy-five or a hundred people. A row of wide pews filled the center of the church; two rows of narrow ones were arranged under the windows along each of the outside walls. Several dead birds and wisps of hay lay in the dust on the painted brown floorboards.

The pews, probably walnut, were dark with the heavy, blackish varnish in vogue at the turn of the century. The wood grain was probably beautiful if one could only see it! In the aisles between the pews, strips of an old, moth-eaten maroon carpet typical of the period led to two doors presumably opening on the churchyard.

The walls were lined with a beaded wainscoting once painted white but now water- and soot-stained, doubtless from the stoves. The tin ceiling, elaborate and stylish for its time, was also stained here and there. Charles followed my gaze.

"Had some leaks in the roof along back," he said. "Got 'em stopped now, though. Roof's tight, an' that's important."

I nodded but my attention was transfixed by the most interesting art nouveau chandelier I'd ever seen. It appeared to date from the turn of the century, constructed to be fueled with carbide gas. Its four arms, elaborately cast and bronzed, held broken globes. In its day, it must have been the pride of the valley. Four industrial-style round white lampshades hung from chains at the corners of the church. Obviously, when electricity arrived, the congregation abandoned the gaslights but left the chandelier in place.

The two entry doors at the far end of the room matched two facing the rows of pews. We had entered through one of these. Two 1920s-era "preacher's chairs," upholstered in maroon velvet, stood against the wall on the pulpit platform between the doors. A matching maroon settee crouched beside the dusty upright piano in the corner. At the edge of the platform, a skilled woodworker had erected a lectern-style walnut pulpit flanked by chest-high turned posts, probably intended to hold flowers. A massive leather-bound pulpit Bible lay open on the lectern.

"Why two doors at the front?" I asked.

"Women used one door," Charles explained. "Men used t'other, so I heard tell. That was years back. Can't git in the front doors now, not without some troubles. Folks put the key under the mat outside, an' a groun'hog done dug under that mat and *pffft*, that key was *gone*! I got a skeleton key that'll work though."

I nodded. I was unable to find words for the strange feeling of the place: not creepy, not exactly haunted. *Something* . . . I ran my hand along the back of a pew.

"Wood came from right here in the valley," Charles said.

I admired the width of the boards, and then noticed that the racks on the pew backs contained not only hymnbooks but tiny Communion glasses. I lifted one to the light, amazed to find a trace of purple at the bottom.

"Last service here was Communion," Charles said. "That was in April back in '69. Church's been closed since then. We ain't got no church. You could git it open again."

"I don't know . . ." My voice trailed off. *What would that involve?* Something in Charles's voice, something plaintive, yet urgent, kept me from voicing all the reasons why I couldn't possibly help.

I wandered across to the piano, lifted the cover over the cracked and yellowed keys, and struck a chord. To my amazement, even though the instrument was at least a full step below pitch, the strings had loosened harmoniously so that octaves remained octaves, the keys worked, and the thing was actually playable. I picked up one of the hymnals and tested the piano's temperament with a rendition of "The Old Rugged Cross." *Amazing. You might say miraculous!* Yes, this piano could still accompany congregational singing—provided one wasn't fussy about notes matching the tones of a standard tuning fork.

What would it be like to fill this place with singing once again?

"Maybe we could have hymn sings," I said weakly. Charles grinned. He obviously took my comment as an agreement to the proposal.

"You ain't seen it all yet. C'mon."

I followed him back into the hallways, which formed a T. Off the long shaft of it were four darkened rooms, the windows boarded over with plywood. We peered into each of them in turn, but I couldn't see much in the gloom. A door at the far end of the shorter hallway, opposite the sanctuary doors, opened to a set of stairs leading down to a basement. Charles opened that door and stepped aside so I could look down. It was dark down there, but I could see light reflected on the surface of water.

"Guess 't ain't safe t' go down them stairs," Charles muttered. "C'mon this way."

We walked back down the hallway and out into the clean mountain breezes. I took a deep breath, relieved after the mildew and mustiness inside, and followed Charles down a set of cement steps on the side. The landing at the bottom disappeared into an unsavory pond. The basement door was missing, and the spring rains had filled the landing and basement to overflowing.

Charles grunted. "Wait a minute!"

He clumped up to the yard, found a dead branch, and poked the stick into the water, stirring hard and scraping. Finally, there was a gurgle, bubbles popped at the surface of the murky water, and most of it drained out of the stairwell.

"Drains'r clogged," he explained needlessly. He climbed back up the steps to peer through the narrow basement window, cupping his hands around his eyes. Then he stepped back and directed me to look. What appeared to be old theater seats floated in the water along with various unidentifiable objects. *Snakes?*

"Them was fine chairs once't," Charles said. "We got 'em when the ol' theater closed down over in Madison. Right pretty, they was. Red plush. They's ruint now, though."

I agreed, shuddering a little.

"C'mon," Charles ordered. "Have a look at this here graveyard."

I was happy to follow him up the stairs and away from the dank smell of rotting plush. We walked toward the back of the building, where I noticed a privy standing under a huge old maple tree between the church and the cemetery beyond.

"Three-holer," Charles informed me proudly.

"The churchyard is very neat," I said, grasping for something positive to say. I was rather overwhelmed at the moment.

"Yup! I mow it an' keep it that-a-way," he replied. "We don't figure the church is closed, mind you; it's just *in-active*."

I noticed the emphasis on the word and wondered why it was important. I was puzzled but didn't want to risk the time it might take for an explanation.

Charles headed toward the tiny triangle of land he called the cemetery. I stared at the worn gray headstones, but the names rolling off his tongue meant nothing to me. Max Mauck, Collins, Yowell . . . I couldn't follow what he was telling me. I glanced at the slanting sun.

"I think it's time for me to go, Charles," I said, edging toward my Jeep. "Thanks for the tour. I'll be back next week."

"We'll git her open, we will," Charles said, nodding firmly. "We'll put some life back inter this here holler."

I didn't answer him. I started the Jeep and headed back down the valley toward the world I knew, wondering what I should do about Charles's proposal.

Why had the "deacons' board" selected me? I certainly wasn't a preacher. Was it because of my education? I was intrigued, though. There was something about that church . . . *If I accept the challenge, what will that do to my life?* I worried and wondered the entire drive back to Luxmont.

CHAPTER 3

AN UNEXPECTED DEVELOPMENT

His purposes will ripen fast, unfolding every hour; the bud may
have a bitter taste, but sweet will be the flower.

WILLIAM COWPER

BECAUSE HARVEY HAD moved out of Luxmont, it fell to me to clear out the house. Therefore, in addition to managing the farms and keeping the accounts, I was attempting to sort, pack, and dispose of what had been the accoutrements of a common life. The lawyer called to advise me that Harvey intended to move back into the plantation house in the fall, so I had about five months to clean out the three floors.

Like the house, some of the furnishings were antebellum, too massive to keep in any life I could envision for myself, and besides, my husband wanted them sold. Since I had purchased those pieces, I knew their value and provenance. I contacted a gallery in Washington, DC, as well as several others in closer proximity, and because of the quality, the pieces sold promptly. However, there were a number of smaller, older things I'd inherited—tables, chairs, chests, linens—as well as some fine country pieces that I wanted to keep. But what would I do with them? Put them in storage? That was really the only option.

As I had anticipated, it was a week after my tour of the church before I could return to Graves Mill. Dan didn't need the farm truck that day so with Tallis riding beside me, I was driving the old Dodge pickup I'd purchased five or six years before. I'd need to buy another truck soon because the Dodge was staying with the plantation. That was the easiest task on my list of problems to solve. I had two horses—Jay and O'Jay were well-loved friends. Where would I put them? Should they roam the mountain pastures? That didn't seem a good idea because a horse could break a leg if it stepped in a groundhog hole, and there were many on the Kinsey place. *Maybe Dan and I should stop fencing for sheep and build a new, interior fence in an area suitable for Jay and O'Jay.* It never occurred to me to pray for God's direction nor to expect an answer. My mother had taught me to read my Bible every day, and I was faithful in that discipline, but the God who led His people through the wilderness was more idea than person to me at the time.

I reached over and patted Tallis. "Well, old man, how do you think you'll like the mountains?" Dalmatians are hardly mountain stock, and I wondered how well he'd adapt to cold winters and rugged country. And there were the Siamese cats; I was really uneasy about them. "Stop worrying!" I ordered myself. "Cats are survivors. They'll be fine."

I knew I was concentrating on the smaller problems because I didn't want to think about Charles or about the most urgent need of all: where was I going to live? There was no house on the mountain farm. Although there were thirteen springs in the valley, there was no well, and of course, no septic system. But house and well were small matters compared to access. Fording the Kinsey Run with the truck was a simple matter in good weather, but I knew the run became a torrent during heavy rains, and furthermore, even in low-water times a sedan couldn't clear the rocks in the streambed. A bridge would be a necessity, but constructing abutments to withstand the flash floods presented a major engineering project. Once a bridge was in place, the badly rutted, rocky track leading from the road into the center of the farm could be rerouted and transformed into a road.

As I drove, I mentally listed alternatives, attempting to form a plan for my future. One thing was certain though: I must tell Charles today that I could not "git the ol' church open." I had more pressing things to do.

It never occurred to me to look for a house or apartment in neighboring Culpeper or Charlottesville or even in Madison, about fourteen miles from the farm. I was responsible for the mountain. Until I provided for its future, I could not abandon that trust. Besides that, I had twenty chickens, two cats, two horses, and a Dalmatian. Horses and chickens couldn't live in town, and for that matter, the dog and cats were accustomed to open fields. They all needed a place to call home as much as I did; they were all my friends, except for the hens. We were moving to Graves Mill and that settled that.

But I worried as I drove. I knew that building a house would require more time than I had, and maybe even more money. I'd considered bringing a small trailer into the valley temporarily until a house could be built. The trailer would need a septic tank. *I'll need to contact the health department and have the soil tested to see if it perks properly.* Digging a septic system in that rocky territory would be a major undertaking, and though I was sure it could be done, I wasn't sure how complicated the project might be. And there was the matter of a building permit . . . but a bridge and road must come first. It would be next to impossible to pull a trailer into Kinsey Valley without a decent road in place.

My thoughts were so busy with the various alternatives and problems that I scarcely saw the new leaves misting the trees in Graves

Mill or noticed the tractors busy in the fields. At last I reached the farm and crossed the Kinsey Run, and while I bumped my way up to the valley, I pondered the engineering challenges ahead of me, speculating about possible house sites, barn locations, and interior fences. I tried to estimate costs and bring these into line with my budget balance. Whatever else might be true of the life ahead of me, it certainly wasn't likely to be simple.

Finally, we arrived at the garden fence Dan and I had constructed several months earlier. Tallis jumped out of the truck and ran up the road toward the woods. "Go get 'em!" I called after him, knowing he wouldn't rove far.

I stretched and took a deep breath of the spring air, sweet with new grasses, new leaves, and some unfamiliar wildflower in bloom. The gate next to the farm track was sufficiently generous to allow a tractor into the plot. I backed the pickup through it to the garden's edge, unloaded a fork, rakes, shovel, seeds, and some fertilizer, and set to work. I was pleased to see that the little peach and pear trees I'd planted at the back fence were beginning to show new leaves. They'd survived winter. A good sign.

I enjoyed gardening, and as I stood surveying the plot, I envisioned rows of tomatoes, beans, lettuce, and flowers. The fence would keep deer and cattle away from the vegetables, but lettuce was a long shot because rabbits could easily squeeze through the fence and I knew they loved fresh salads. Tallis would be no help either. He didn't hunt. Rabbits could run across his nose and he wouldn't care. Still, I would attempt growing lettuce.

The neat square of woven wire fence seemed oddly civilized and out of place in the otherwise wild valley. Along its northern edge lay a tumbled line of rock that had been the garden fence a hundred years earlier. On the east, the land sloped away into scrub briars, sumac, and thistles, but from the little garden gate we'd placed on that side, a narrow path led to what had been the kitchen spring serving the old

Kinsey place, bubbling up through a pile of boulders. From these, a clear, cold stream flagged with wild irises, cowslips, and buttercups rippled down from the spring to join the Kinsey Run. Every time I came to the spring for a drink, I'd watch the butterflies and think of Moses striking the wilderness rock.

I'd tilled the rich black soil a few weeks before, so it was ready for planting. A neighbor had done the initial plowing the previous autumn, and the winter's freezing and thawing had loosened the sods so the black dirt was easy to work. When the first settlers used this plot, they picked out the stones and used them to build the garden fence so I never hit a rock when I tilled; all I turned up were a few potsherds and an arrowhead. Judging from the quality of the soil, I guessed the old-timers must have used plenty of manure on the patch.

Experts opined that the mountain lands had ceased from cultivation because they were worn out, but local explanations made more sense. The valley farmers pointed out that the mountain farms produced abundantly when mules and horses pulled the plows around the rock outcroppings. When tractors became common, they were expensive and their upkeep demanded wide and extensive acres. The small mountain fields between rocks might be fertile, but they weren't efficient, and eventually small places became pastures or timberlands and the population thinned out. What remained of the local economy became dependent on employment in the outside world. A little warning light flashed in my mind, but I ignored it.

Tallis, satisfied with his inspection, stretched out in the sunshine on the garden's grassy verge. In early times, this had been the Kinsey family's main garden. It was about ten feet from the detached kitchen house, now a pile of rocks just across the track from the hole where the main dwelling had been. When the plantation was a flourishing operation, even the kitchen house had been an imposing building. The lower floor had accommodated kitchen and laundry, and the upper floor had been large enough to serve as a dance floor and community meeting place.

Charles had told me that when Dolly Seekford's father, Buck Hawkins, had rented the place, he and his family, including baby Dolly, lived in the old kitchen house for several years. At that time, electricity was a luxury unavailable in the hills this far up from the world, so Dolly's mother had used flatirons, heated on a wood-burning stove, to smooth the laundry. Somehow, a spark from the fire set the house ablaze, and the kitchen house burned to the ground. At least, that was Charles's story. Others said both the kitchen house and the main dwelling fell to ruins from years of neglect.

I stared at the vine-covered pile of rocks, wishing I could have seen the houses in their heyday. Was there any way to bring life back into these hollows? They held so much history they seemed almost alive even now. Could these hollows ever ring with laughter and singing again? Well, at least one thing was certain: I would not be the one to bring that old church back to life!

The peaceful valley calmed my chaotic thoughts as I worked, planting beans, cilantro, basil, dill, corn, and lettuce. It was too late for peas, but I planted sugar snaps anyway, hoping the pods would mature before the heat of summer descended. At this altitude, the season was about ten days later than down in the piedmont.

I planted flowers, too: cosmos, marigolds, zinnias, and delphiniums. Whether or not I would have a house in which to put bouquets, at least I'd have flowers. And that was something.

Though I could not have admitted it even to myself, the wild loveliness of the valley, folded into the mountain ridges, offered a sheltered, private place, a sanctuary from the busy world. The pending divorce told me I had failed. Divorces did not happen in our family. I was ashamed, and instinctively longed to withdraw like a wounded animal, to nurse my hurts, to heal, and to reorient myself to a changed reality. I didn't miss Harvey very much—we'd lived apart so much of our marriage—but I missed being married and the security it gave. My pride was badly shaken, and the solitude of the mountains seemed to be a refuge from the eyes of the world.

It was nearly noon when I finished planting. I rested on my rake and considered what I needed to do next. *Of course! Find Charles and tell him I can't possibly help him with his project.* What did I know about organizing a church? Nothing! I'd taught catechism and Sunday school. I knew the *Book of Common Prayer* and Luther's Short and Long Catechisms, and I'd studied Greek in undergraduate school, along with courses in the Old Testament. But those were not the skills needed to organize a parish, even if I had the time.

And there was the matter of my pending divorce. That had theological implications too. I knew the Scripture passages very well; I'd read them over and over, often with angry tears blurring my vision. What sort of a life could I have if I weren't married? *And Jesus said . . .* It had seemed so simple that amazing afternoon in St. Peter's Square. All I needed to do was give my life to Jesus. I had no idea then that it is in the valley of humiliation that we find our true worth.

I squared my shoulders and reloaded the pickup. Yes, it would be wonderful to watch a community grow in Graves Mill, but I was not called to be the midwife! I couldn't do it. Charles would be disappointed, but he'd just have to be.

Charles will be home now for the midday meal, so this will be a good time to stop and see him. I don't like telling him, but it must be done.

Tallis jumped into the passenger seat and we were off to settle this church business! As I rounded the bend, I saw Charles pull out of his drive. *I'll have to call him from Luxmont.*

To my surprise, Charles stopped at the church and motioned me to stop. As I pulled into the churchyard I looked up at the weather-beaten sign. Though the paint was peeling, the black Gothic lettering was still clear: Graves Chapel 1885. I took a deep breath and waited for Charles to hoist his portly frame out of his pickup.

"Charles, I've thought it over during this last week and . . ."

"Missy, we got you a parsonage!" he almost shouted. "We done got you a parsonage!"

"You *what?*"

"We done got you a parsonage, that's what. Ol' man Bell, he never would rent that place of his'n. Right there it is, just t'other side of th' votin' house. See there!"

I could see the roof of a low bungalow beyond what had once been the Graves Mill schoolhouse and a tiny white building the locals told me was the votin' house. The bungalow wasn't exactly next to the church, but it was within two hundred yards.

"C'mon," Charles was saying impatiently. "Zeb Bell, he's just come down from Pennsylvania. Mad as fire, he is. Pump done froze over the winter an' he wants t' rent the place. An' it's right by the church, an' you don't got no house up that mountain anyways. So there's yer parsonage. Bell will talk to you t'morrow. He's in Charlottesville today, he said, but he's a-comin' back up t'morrow."

"Who's Zeb Bell?"

"Dr. Zeb Bell owns that place," he explained impatiently. "He lives in Pennsylvania. His dad, Ol' Zeb—this one's Junior—bought the place when Elmo Utz died."

I was completely lost. "Charles, I haven't a clue what you're telling me. Who's Elmo Utz?"

Charles looked at me as if I'd landed from another planet, which was true in many ways. "Elmo Utz ran the store," he said slowly, as if instructing a backward child.

I nodded as if I understood, even though I didn't, and with Tallis at my heels, I followed Charles as he stomped down the road to the "parsonage." I noted a fenced paddock of perhaps half an acre next to the road. Charles unlatched the heavy wire gate hanging across a rutted gravel driveway, and we walked past an ancient two-story frame structure, its vacant windows looking like sad eyes.

"Ol' Acy's blacksmith shop," Charles informed me. I decided not to ask who Acy might have been.

The driveway ran through the paddock to another gate leading into the yard. This one, however, hung open, twisted on hinges nearly rusted away. A row of apple trees, just past full bloom, shielded the house from the road so I didn't get a good view of it until we walked through the second gateway. At first glance, it wasn't impressive.

A covered porch spanned the central section, flanked on either side by what were obviously more recent additions. One of these, next to the apple trees, was an attached garage. A red hand pump stood at the edge of the porch, and in front of the porch, a raised cement slab indicated the pump house for a shallow well. Apparently, the water supply wasn't wholly dependent on that red hand pump! I shuddered a little when I inspected the house more closely. The door frame was painted a hideous dark green, while the sides of the main portion of the house were a patchwork of gray, green, and a bit of white paint.

As if he'd read my mind—which he probably had—Charles said, "Ol' man Bell, he'd drive ten miles to save ten cents. Got paint on sale."

"I see," I replied slowly. "I guess it was a good thing he didn't find a bargain in purple."

Charles guffawed and then turned serious.

"This'd be a good place for you," he said quietly. "You ain't got no business up that mountain by your loneself, no indeedy. An' there ain't no house up there anyways. An' we needs to get that church open. So here's yer parsonage. Dr. Bell should be here 'bout two tomorrow."

My thoughts were as scattered as dandelion seeds blown in the wind. I compared the broad steps and columns of the front porch back at Luxmont with the dismal place in front of me. I thought of Luxmont's immaculate lawns, the neat boxwood hedges, the lovely outbuildings constructed with the beaded siding popular in Williamsburg. Here, the weedy yard extended some distance back toward Store Mountain.

I walked through a double line of peach trees, past an old gnarled plum, and into a wide-open space that had once been a big garden. A strawberry patch had gone wild along one side; last year's asparagus ferns waved near the back fence, and there were blackberry briars in the corner. I was surprised to hear the gurgle of a little spring run tumbling over the rocks, but a fence lay between me and the stream. I could see the grasses and flags waving on the stream's edge, though, and from these the pine-clad flank of Store Mountain rose sharply against the sky. Tallis frolicked happily through the weeds, delighted to inspect new territory. When I turned and looked back toward the church, I caught my breath in surprise at the magnificent view. The little hamlet lay before me, its decaying buildings picturesque under the looming blue peak of Jones Mountain.

Charles pointed to the large building farthest downstream. "That's Elmo Utz's ol' store," he explained.

I nodded, so he continued. "See that little shed in the middle of the field?" He pointed to a tiny two-story building, as weather-beaten as all the others. "Elmo lived there 'fore he got the big house."

"Big house?"

"Yup." Charles pointed to the bungalow. "That's where the big house stood. It caught fire one night—prob'ly bad wirin', so they said—an' burned to the ground. That was after Ol' Zeb Bell bought it."

"So Dr. Bell built this house?"

"No indeedy!" Charles exclaimed. "I done tol' you, that was his pa."

This place seemed to be all names with no faces. It had a history, but the history seemed to have died when the church closed. Or maybe the church closed because the history was all written. *Can anything live up here in the back of beyond?* I didn't know.

My emotions tumbled like cream in a churn. We retraced our steps to the road, and Charles lifted the heavy gate into place and latched the chain before turning to me.

"You be here at two tomorrow, hear?"

I swallowed hard. "Yes, Charles. I'll be here at two o'clock tomorrow."

I saw Dr. Bell's big car when I rounded the curve into Graves Mill the following afternoon. I don't remember now whether it was a Cadillac or a big Buick, but I do remember that it seemed to have the sheen of money. It was parked in front of the bungalow's garage. I bounced my little Jeep through the open gate and up the rutted driveway.

A slender man of medium height was standing on the well-house platform waiting for me. His spectacles glittered in the sunshine, and the spring breezes ruffled his slightly graying hair. He wore neat khaki pants and a sport shirt open at the neck. Even if I hadn't known he was from Pittsburgh, I'd have recognized that he was an outsider by the clothing and the smooth complexion of a businessman.

My palms were sweating from nervousness. *I wish I had brought Tallis with me. He's good at appraising strangers.*

Dr. Bell ambled over, extending his hand. "I'm Zeb Bell," he said, "and I guess you're Mrs. Light?"

"Yes, sir," I replied, relaxing a little. "Charles Jenkins told me you want to rent the cottage here? That the pump froze this winter and . . ."

"That's right," he interjected. "My father built this house after the old Utz house burned. He died before he could finish it, and I'm too far away to take care of it. Come on in."

It was dim inside, and because my eyes needed a few minutes to adjust, my first impression was olfactory. The place was heavy with mold and mildew. In fact, it smelled very much like the church. "Oh, dear!" I muttered under my breath. "I wonder if this is Graves Mill's defining characteristic?"

"It's a little musty in here," Dr. Bell said apologetically. "I think the rug is wet."

We proceeded into the living space, and I spotted a Formica kitchen table with matching chairs and a nondescript hutch beside the brick-faced fireplace. A painted room divider holding plastic greenery separated the kitchen/dining side of a big room from a large brown sofa squatting along the interior wall. A small window at the far side of the room looked out on the voting house, the old schoolhouse, and the church.

"Dad never got around to sealing this floor," Dr. Bell explained. "Moisture works up from the ground, especially in the spring." He crossed the room and squatted under the window to examine the rug.

I followed his example. "Ugh!" I exclaimed. The rug was soaking wet and smelled worse when we lifted the corners.

"I'm afraid this should be trashed," Dr. Bell said. "I guess you'll need to let this floor dry out so it can be sealed before you do anything else." He seemed to assume my tenancy was a settled matter. "Now while I'm here, I'll move the dishes and furniture out. Some of it, anyway. The sofa stays. The beds stay. The wardrobe stays. The sofa is too heavy to move, and I can't store it in the blacksmith shop anyway. Mice, you know. The beds—they came from Dolly's sale. They're in here."

I followed Dr. Bell into a second room, perhaps a little larger than the living area. A walnut Victorian armoire, about six feet tall, stood against the far wall, and a pair of twin four-poster walnut beds sat on a deep-yellow shag carpet.

"Buck Hawkins had those beds made for Dolly's brothers. They forced her to have that sale after her mother died. Dolly was terribly hurt. The boys didn't want the beds, so I bought them at the auction," Dr. Bell said. "They're early Clore. You know about the famous furniture makers down in Madison?"

I nodded, trying to be suitably impressed. The bed frames supported exposed wire springs topped with lumpy mattresses, but the woodwork itself was beautiful. I knew a little about the prices Clore furniture fetched, and these two pieces, being collectors' items, would be worth more than the catalog figures.

"These are wonderful!" I exclaimed. "I've never seen any early Clore pieces except for ladder-back chairs. Those turned posts are beautiful, aren't they?"

Dr. Bell smiled a little at my compliments, but he wasn't finished. "This room is new. Dad built it before he married, but he never had a chance to finish it. Over here, that was to be a shower." He opened what appeared to be a large closet. "The half bath there doesn't have any hot water." He pointed to a cubicle where a cheap French Provincial–style sink cabinet faced me.

I cringed inwardly, but I tried to smile.

"Dad planned to have a little office in the bedroom." Dr. Bell gestured at an open space about six feet square next to the half bath. "He didn't have enough shag rug to cover the concrete, but at least it got sealed. No moisture in here."

The room was lined with a distressed gray fiberboard meant to imitate paneling. The ceiling was acoustic tiles, and the wheat-colored shag was hardly to my taste. My dressing room at the plantation had a lovely Chinese rug, and the bath next to it was fitted with fine porcelain with gold detailing. *This wasn't intended to be a primary residence,* I reminded myself; *it was a cottage for summer weekends in the country.*

"That's the back of the old chimney." Dr. Bell was pointing to the rough rock forming much of the wall beside the door into the living room. "This original chimney was still standing after the fire, and Dad built the house around it. It's really old. Did you notice the pot hook on the living room side? That's original."

He ran his finger over the mortar between some of the stones, and a small shower of sand and dust fell to the rug.

"That's from the fire. I guess it needs a little tuck-pointing," he said apologetically.

"Now, you can't change anything here. Dad died so soon after he married my stepmother that he didn't have a proper will, only a holographic document and his talks with my brother and me. My stepmother has lifetime rights to come here to stay if she wants. She's never wanted to come up here, but if she wants to come, she can."

We moved back into the main living area, and I noticed that the blue paint from the sixties on the kitchen walls didn't match the blue figures in the curtains. Linoleum covered the only countertop, and the brownish walls on the living room end made the place seem darker than it really was.

We continued our tour. Adjoining the kitchen was a small bathroom and a bedroom just large enough for a double bed and a couple of chairs. There was a small closet with no door. Both rooms were carpeted with a greenish indoor-outdoor material. The bedroom and the bathroom each had a dark square of window looking out into the garage.

"Dad intended to build a laundry room out there," Dr. Bell explained. "He never had time to frame the doors where those windows are now."

I took a deep breath, thinking to myself, *I'll only be here until I can build something on the mountain.*

"C'mon. Let's have a look at the yard." Dr. Bell headed out the front door.

On our way across the porch, I noticed a door between the garage and the main house, its frame painted the same green as the frame around the main door. It opened easily, but there wasn't much to see beyond it. The threshold stood at least three feet above the dirt floor in the garage.

. "That's where the laundry was supposed to be," Dr. Bell explained. "Dad thought it would be a good idea to be able to reach the bathroom from outside without going through the kitchen, but he never put in the walls or the flooring."

Aside from some cobwebs and a dusty yellow riding mower, the space was empty. Well, it had a good roof, and it would shelter my Jeep and some of my world-scrapings, particularly an Indonesian carriage my husband had brought from Jakarta. I had no idea what I could do with the thing, but it was one of the items on the "dispose of" list which hadn't sold.

"Now those apple trees," Dr. Bell said proudly, pointing to the row beside the garage, "those are the result of my dad's grafting a couple of old-fashioned varieties on the same tree. In the front, those are Grimes Goldens and some Granny Smiths. In the middle there, he's got Sheep's Nose and Red Delicious, and at the back are Black Twig. You don't find some of those varieties anymore, but they're the best."

I knew gardening; I didn't know much about orchards, but I figured I could learn.

"I have horses and chickens . . ." I said a little apologetically. "Two horses and about twenty hens."

Dr. Bell's blue eyes widened slightly. "I see . . . Well, you can put the horses in that lot there between the road and the yard gate. Charles has a few steers in the field around Acy's blacksmith shop and the old stores, but when he takes 'em out this fall, you could put the horses in there for the winter. If you can wait until then, you'd have about ten acres' pasture, with the spring run behind your garden there for water. The open sheds on both sides of the blacksmith shop would give 'em some shelter in the winter. As for the chickens . . . well, if you clean out Elmo Utz's old house, I reckon you could put the hens there. I warn you, though. The place is full to the rafters. Elmo never threw anything away. Never! All the old catalogs and stuff from the store, he just stuck in there. And I think the skunks have been nesting in it too."

"I know I'm not supposed to change anything, but could I build a little run for the chickens?"

"Sure. It's only the house and yard I'm worried about. *She* won't care about Elmo Utz's old shack or the stores." I understood that *she* was the stepmother.

"How much rent are you asking?"

"There's a lot of cleanup for you to do," he replied slowly. "Especially that living room floor. I think seventy-five dollars a month is fair. That includes the house, garden, pastures, and your future chicken house. It's cheap, but since you're going to be opening the old church, that's my contribution."

I almost choked at that assumption but managed to ask, "Do you think your stepmother would mind if I put linoleum on the floor in the living area?"

"I'm sure that would be fine. Well, when do you want to start?"

I took a deep breath. There really wasn't anywhere else to go in Graves Mill except this "parsonage." I pulled out my checkbook.

"I'll send you a lease as soon as I get back to Pittsburgh," Dr. Bell assured me. "Meanwhile, your check will serve as a receipt."

CHAPTER 4

SAVED BY A DIAPER

As long as the most important thing in your life is to keep
finding your way, you're going to live in mortal terror of losing it.
Once you're willing to be lost, though, you'll be home free.

ROBERT FARRAR CAPON

DR. BELL KEPT HIS WORD. Before returning to Pittsburgh, he cleared the cottage of dishes and all the furniture except the pieces he told me had to remain. He left the keys with Charles, so later in the week I collected them and went to see my new quarters.

As I looked around, my first question was, "Where will I put my furniture?" I answered it by spending the afternoon measuring walls to see where my desk, chests, harpsichord, and piano would fit. There wasn't room for many pieces, but I refused to be discouraged. I made lists of supplies and contractors that I would need to make the "parsonage" livable. At the top of the list was "flooring company."

Fortunately, one of my friends owned a carpet and flooring company in Charlottesville, so my next expedition was to his store, where I was delighted to find a remnant of linoleum designed to imitate blue-and-white Moorish tile. It was tasteful and sophisticated, and because it was a remnant, I got it for half price. When I mentioned the problem about the leaky floor to my friend, he assured me that his craftsmen could seal it and install the linoleum a day or so later.

As I drove back to Luxmont, I was encouraged. *Perhaps the cottage can be made beautiful after all. And if that's possible, there might even be hope for Graves Mill.*

The next week, the floor was completed. There was even enough linoleum to cover the "office space" adjoining the bedroom. I moved the big Victorian armoire that Dr. Bell left behind into the space, facing it opposite an eighteenth-century armoire I brought from Luxmont. The two pieces were ill matched, but I needed the storage in both armoires for the suits, skirts, and gowns I had moved from the plantation.

The lovely dresses breathed New York and London, and I couldn't bring myself to part with them. Whether I would ever wear them again or not, I was certain that I'd never again visit the little boutiques where I'd purchased those elegant dresses. I carefully adjusted silk, satin, and chiffon in the armoires, remembering evenings at London's Royal Opera and events at Washington's Kennedy Center with my husband. I caressed the lush fabrics. In Graves Mill that world seemed very far away, but the dresses brought pleasant memories.

"Well," I said to myself, "if you ever need an elegant frock, you'll have one! These are timeless classics."

Pruning vines takes time. The spiritual pruning Jesus promised takes even longer. It had not occurred to me that the Lord was doing some vineyard work in me, so rather than accepting the shearing, I was hoarding the trimmings. I was no St. Francis. I had no intention of leaving my finery behind.

One morning when the boxes were still piled high in the cottage, Tallis began to bark. Someone—or something—was in the yard. At first, I paid no attention because Tallis had been a nuisance all morning. This was not his home, and he was uneasy. He'd poke his nose between me and whatever I was doing and whine to be let outside. Once outside, he barked to come in. However, this time Tallis rushed to the door in watchdog mode, growling warning and defiance.

I peered out the kitchen window and recognized Dolly Seekford climbing the porch steps. The year before, on one of my trips to inspect the mountain farm, I'd paid a neighborly visit to Dolly and she had shown me through her place that day.

An interesting example of local architecture, it was really two houses joined together by a long porch in the center. The back section consisted of a big cheerful country kitchen on the first floor and what had probably been the quarters for "hired help" upstairs. Dolly had chosen one of these rooms above the kitchen for her bedroom, and in fact, she elected to live mostly in this section of the house because it was cheaper to heat and much cozier than the front half. The front section was formal, consisting on the lower floor of a living room that could have easily accommodated twenty people, a parlor of equal size, and a hallway from which a grand staircase led to spacious bedrooms on the second floor.

"Quiet, Tallis!" I commanded, grabbing his collar before opening the door. Tallis subsided and Dolly made her way gingerly past him. Every time I had seen her she was neatly dressed, and this morning was no exception. Every single strand of her short dark hair, slightly touched with silver, was curled as if she'd just visited the hairdresser in Madison. She wore crisply creased slacks and a blouse that flattered her trim figure.

She found the single empty chair at the kitchen table, and I introduced Tallis. Dolly stroked his head and Tallis promptly nuzzled her thigh, leaving slobber marks on the slacks. Dolly didn't seem to mind. She was clearly fond of dogs and accustomed to having them about. I dimly recalled the beautiful gray-and-white dog guarding her lane when I drove past. *What was its name? Oh, yes—Weegie, for Norwegian, because it was a Norwegian elkhound.*

"Would you like some coffee?"

I was being polite, but my mind skittered about like a rat in the attic, trying to remember where I'd put the percolator and coffee. Finally, I located both and in a few minutes had brewed the strong black stuff she told me she preferred. Then with coffee, cigarette, and ashtray at hand, Dolly settled back and began reciting several chapters of her life story. Though I knew it wasn't polite, I returned to my unpacking, pouting inwardly that she didn't offer to help. She couldn't have been very useful, of course, but my spoiled little soul expected everyone to be sympathetic.

She was divorced, she said, and she'd had the responsibility of tending her aged mother and raising her two children alone. She had worked as postmistress at the little Graves Mill post office to augment their income. It hadn't been easy.

"I was always rippin' an' runnin', tryin' to get it all done, and you'd better believe it was *cold* in the winter back then, an' I had them children to raise. I'd have to trudge down from the house in snowdrifts up to my knees, an' my fingers would be so stiff I could hardly light that stove in the post office!"

Suddenly the narrative shifted from past to present, and she was telling me about a man she cared about, someone to whom she'd been very kind. From her description of him, though, I came to the conclusion that he was selfish and engrossed in his own problems.

"He'll never marry me," she said flatly. "He's got his own life, an' it's a nice one. He just likes to sit in my warm kitchen when he comes here, an' he really loves my cookin'!"

The pathos in her voice finally penetrated my self-absorption, and I turned from the sink full of soapy dishwater. Her dark eyes met mine, and there was so much hurt, so much anger, and so much loneliness in their depths that my heart ached for her. As if I had put on spectacles, I saw the lines in her face, the gray flecks in her dark hair, and the yearning for intimacy, for joy. I understood, at least a little. I was learning what it meant to be divorced and alone, and for a few moments, we were sisters in that sorrow.

I did not know what to say, and I had hardly learned to pray, but silently, and as best I could, my heart cried, "Lord, give her something lovely, please! Grant that something good may come, some joy here in these hills! I can't see how that can be, but please, Lord, help her!"

Dolly's eyes dropped to her coffee cup. I refilled it, and perhaps weary of her own story, she turned to the valley's history and the story of the final days of the Graves Mill congregation.

"It was the women," she said. "They couldn't get along. We'd just finished buildin' the parish hall, an' when it came time to paint, every woman wanted a different color on the walls. They stopped speakin' to each other, and then they stopped comin' to church. They came close to hair-pullin'."

"Why did the congregation build the parish hall?" From what I had gleaned of local history, Graves Mill had turned into a ghost town in the thirties when the Shenandoah Park moved the mountain families out of their hollows. The parish hall must have been built in the fifties. "Why did you need the space twenty years after most of the people had left Graves Mill?"

"We built the Sunday school addition in 1955. You wouldn't believe . . . we really had a Sunday school in them days! All the folks came from Graves Mill to Wolftown an' over on Middle River. We only had preachin' once a month or so—maybe every six weeks—but we had a Sunday school every week. C. K. Rhodes was the Sunday school superintendent, an' we had the Ladies' Missionary Society. Charles Jenkins's mother had the meetin's in her parlor, an' we sat on that horsehair furniture."

"Scratchy, I guess?" I was beginning to understand that the church had been a social center, probably the glue that held the community together. No wonder Charles was so anxious to see its doors open again.

"You better believe it! And the revivals—they always came in August, an' the church would be full those days. You should have seen it then! We got them Sunday school rooms built because folks donated lumber, the women saved from their egg money, an' the farmers gave what they got from God's acre."

"God's acre?"

"That was land they set aside for the Lord."

I nodded, but suddenly I felt very small. I'd never in my life set anything aside for the Lord. Well, I had put money in the church's collection plates, but somehow, reserving a section of land for the Lord God was more intentional and reverent than anything I'd ever imagined doing.

I had just opened my mouth to ask more questions when Charles's pickup skidded to a halt at the gate. He climbed out, bounced up onto the porch, and stuck his head in the doorway. When he saw Dolly, he came inside, and after shoving boxes and crumpled paper from a chair seat, he plopped down opposite her.

"Missy, when you fixin' t' git that church open?" he wanted to know.

"Charles, you ought to know better than that!" Dolly nearly shouted. "Gettin' these people here to work together—that's impossible an' you know it. Remember what happened when you an' Hume and C. K. tried to farm together? Nobody got along, an' folks haven't forgotten it neither. What's the matter with your head?"

Charles grunted and dragged on his pipe.

"Worth a try, seems t' me," he finally growled.

Dolly jumped to her feet. "Well, I *never*! Charles Jenkins, you don't have the sense God gave a goose! You remember our last preacher? He worked his heart out—even said he'd come up here for nothin'—an' it didn't help."

Charles merely nodded. Dolly thanked me for the coffee and stormed out of the cottage.

Charles looked thoughtfully at the piles of boxes crowding the little cottage.

"You ain't got no place for all that stuff," he observed. "Seein's how yer a-goin' t' be our preacher, an' we can't pay, mebbe you could put some o' that in them Sunday school rooms up yonder. Let's have a look."

"But what about the community, Charles? If Dolly's right . . ."

"Don't pay her no mind, Missy. She's jus' fussin' this mornin', that's all. Dolly owns the post office building an' rents it to the Postal Service. Ruth Lillard keeps a record of expenses an' Dolly has to pay. Those women are just alike; both o' them'll squeeze a quarter till th' eagle screams."

That "reassurance" wasn't reassuring. It was obvious from what Charles had just said of the relationship between Ruth and Dolly that all was not always as peaceful as the scenery in Graves Mill. I was uneasy. But Charles was already out the door and there seemed no alternative to the proposed inspection. We walked up to the old church, with Tallis frisking around us.

The whole Sunday school addition was dark, of course, but Charles had retrieved his flashlight from his pickup, and by its light, I saw that all the rooms were empty. I chose a large space at the back, smelling of mold and mildew, doubtless because of the water in the basement below, but it would indeed provide temporary storage space. I could keep boxes of china and crystal there, things I'd never need in Graves Mill. I'd have to be careful about books—the mildew might damage them—but perhaps a few boxes might be stored in the church. At least it would be storage close at hand until I moved up to the mountain farm.

When I shook Charles's hand and agreed to the arrangement, I wasn't thinking of books or even the mountain farm. I was thinking of Dolly. Did God care about a lonely woman in a little, lost place like Graves Mill? And if He didn't care about Dolly, would He care about me?

Charles walked back to the cottage with me, then headed over to the post office in his truck, hurrying to arrive before it closed. *That reminds me*, I thought. *I need to rent a box at the post office for my mail.*

I made sure the electric coffeepot was disconnected and the cottage secure. With Tallis at my heels, I walked the thirty yards from the cottage to the fork in the road, and crossed the bridge across Kinsey Run just above its confluence with the Rapidan. There, nestled at the edge of the wilderness, stood the tiny representative of the US Postal Service. Though invisible from the cottage, the post office sat directly across from the entrance to my new driveway. Willows, sycamores, and brush sprouted verdantly along the banks of Kinsey Run, forming a screen between the cottage and the activities across the run.

As was true of many rural communities, the post office was the valley's social center and general meeting place. It was open only in the mornings, so farmers stopped by on their way to town or the fields. Women gathered to tell stories and discuss gardens, family, local scandals, and the lack of rain. Men came to tell stories and to discuss ball games, local or national, they'd seen that week. They exchanged remedies for cattle ailments and the latest advance in electric fencing and fertilizer, and of course, they worried over the lack of rain, too. At least, that was a concern that summer.

Ruth Lillard had succeeded Dolly as the postmistress. She was a substantial, motherly figure and the quintessential farmwife. She grew a big garden, preserved fruits and vegetables, and made sure her children got their 4-H projects done well and on time. She worked half a day, and since the post office was about a mile from her front door and the Lillard fields lay just across the Rapidan, she was within hailing distance of her children and husband. She could be back in the farm kitchen at lunchtime. It was the perfect job for a farm-wife. She had a warm smile, but her sharp eyes under a heavy shock of short-cropped black hair warned me that she didn't miss many nuances in the events around her.

Ruth was sorting mail when I stepped into the tiny, dim building. It wasn't much larger than twelve by twelve feet, with a third of the space partitioned off. Rows of ancient mailboxes just inside the door formed part of this divider, with a picket fence and gate that stretched from the mailboxes to the back wall completing the rest. Ruth passed stamps and mail through a small barred opening between the mailboxes. There was no electricity. Light came through a single window behind Ruth's desk, supplemented by the open doorway on sunny days. When the door was closed against inclement weather, light filtered through the glass panes in the top half. The walls and floor were constructed from the same unpainted tongue-and-groove pine boards, and a small brown oil stove squatted under mounted deer antlers in the center of the back wall. A lineup of well-worn ladder-back chairs sat stiffly across from the mailboxes.

I explained who I was and where I was living, and Ruth handed me some advertising circulars—my mail for the day. Of course, my explanations were purely perfunctory because the onlookers knew every detail of my arrival, thanks to the local grapevine operating through the telephone, CBs (most of the farm families owned and operated citizens band radios for communication across the fields and mountains), or the morning gossip at the post office.

"We don't charge for the boxes," Ruth explained. "All the mail is general delivery, so if you want your mail, you have to come to the post office before noon and pick it up." At noon, Ruth locked up and left for the day.

A young woman sat in one of the ladder-back chairs facing the postboxes and gate. When I came in, she was talking to Charles while two children played at her feet. She looked up when Ruth introduced her and her children to me. "That's Pam Quemiere and Tilah and Travis." Tilah was a lovely little blonde child about a year old; her brother, Travis, busy with his toys, was three or four. Pam's long blonde hair fell across her shoulders; her nose was dusted with freckles, and she smiled brightly. I noticed her Birkenstock sandals and her healthy, eat-and-live-right complexion.

Pam and her husband, Richard, lived in one of the houses perched on the bank of the Rapidan River, opposite the road and Elmo Utz's store.

Charles turned from his conversation with Pam to look sternly at me.

"Blackberries're ripe up the mountain," he said. "You want a fine batch of 'em, you better get up there a-fore the birds eat 'em all."

"Thanks, Charles," I replied. "I'll see about it."

Then, thinking it would be a good idea to make friends with my neighbors, I turned to Pam. "Would you like to go with me tomorrow?" I asked. "We could keep each other company."

Pam's face lit up. "I'll meet you here at the post office about 8:30," she replied enthusiastically.

The next morning I packed several buckets into the Jeep and met Pam and her two children, who were waiting on the front steps of the post office. Pam and Tilah sat in the front seat next to me and Travis sat in the back. Pam had never seen the little valley before, and I was looking forward to her reaction. I wasn't disappointed. When we emerged from the scrub woods into the clearing, she cried out in delight.

"What a wonderful place! From the road, no one would dream this valley was back here." I stopped the Jeep and we sat silently for a few moments, taking in the view.

"It is a treasure," I replied as I took my foot off the brake. "I really love this peaceful valley. Now, as I recall, the blackberry vines will be around those rocks in the middle of the field and along the banks of the run over there on the west side."

We set out for the rocks with the children in tow. Pam managed them amazingly well as we tramped through the wild valley picking the lush fruit from clumps of briars growing around the big rock outcroppings, some eight or ten feet high. Travis dashed about looking for treasures and was thrilled to find dry milkweed pods and small pebbles sparkling with fool's gold. Pam carried Tilah between clumps of blackberry vines and when she stopped to pick, spread out a small blanket close beside her. Tilah played happily there with the pebbles and pods Travis deposited on it. Neither of us thought of the bears, snakes, and other hazards often hidden in the vines. Fortunately, all went well.

Pam chatted comfortably while we picked. Her husband, Rich, had a Pentecostal background, but they did not go to church now. Rich was trained as a physical education instructor, but he and Pam had decided that the "good life" meant going back to the land. In fact, they were part of the "back to the good earth" movement of the time. I would meet other families later.

"Rich wants to have draft horses someday," she confided as she dropped a handful of berries into her bucket. "We've got goats now. I sell the milk and make cheese. It does bring in a little money. I don't know about horses, though. They're *big*, I know that, and I bet they eat a lot."

"Draft horses!" I exclaimed in amazement. "How would you make a living using horses? Could you even find the equipment to use with them—things like plows and harrows and hay rakes, not to mention harnesses—in this day and age?" I had stopped picking, but Pam's small, work-roughened hands continued their efficient business among the blackberry briars.

"The Amish use horses and Rich says they do well enough, and we could too. This is good land here, and we could raise vegetables and fruits. Of course, the Amish have the necessary tools and we could get some from the settlements in Pennsylvania, but Rich would like to find old things nobody's using. That way, we might not need to pay very much." She sighed. "We don't have much cash money. It's not easy to make ends meet as it is, never mind buying tools and horses. By the way, there's a food cooperative in the county. Ever hear of it?"

Needless to say, I had not. In fact, I disdained buying from the local market, preferring to drive thirty miles to Charlottesville or eighty to northern Virginia. But perhaps it was time to change my epicurean habits. "Could you tell me more about it?" I asked cautiously.

"A group of us buy food in bulk, things like cheese, rice, beans, and flour," she said. "We take turns picking up the stuff at the warehouse in Charlottesville, and when it's your turn to pick up, you weigh out the portions for all the people who've ordered. My turn only comes around about twice a year. I bring the orders home with me, and then folks pick them up at my house. There are co-ops in several counties around here. There's one in Orange, one in Greene, a couple in Charlottesville. Buying in bulk saves a lot of money and time, especially if you make your own bread the way I do. You get a whole month's supply in one trip. You should join. We could work together."

I had no idea how to shop through a co-op and was dismayed at the thought of endless beans and rice, but the wistful note in Pam's voice tugged at my heartstrings. "I'd love to work with you, Pam. You'll have to show me what to do, though."

God, do You really care about a little lost place like this? I believe You care about Pam and her children, but what does that look like in their daily lives? And are You asking me to do anything besides pick blackberries with them?

By eleven o'clock, the children were ready for their naps, so we loaded our buckets of berries into the back of the Jeep and climbed in for the journey home. I had driven only a few yards down the mountain track when steam billowed from under the hood.

My heart sank. We were at least two miles from Graves Mill. The surrounding mountain ridges prevented sound from carrying down to the farms and post office, so yelling for help would be useless. I lifted the hood and gingerly unscrewed the radiator cap, but no scalding steam erupted. The radiator was empty, and the hose was loose. I reconnected the hose as best I could.

"We need water in the radiator," I reported needlessly. "Do you have a clean diaper? I'd noticed that Pam used cloth diapers. Cheaper than Pampers, they didn't require disposal, a feature important to "good earth" people. "We can put a bucket of blackberries in the diaper and I'll use the empty bucket to get some water from the spring."

Pam shuffled through her diaper bag and triumphantly produced exactly what I needed. I emptied the blackberries from a half-full bucket into the ample diaper and trudged down to the kitchen house spring behind my garden. The water I managed to carry back didn't fill the radiator, but I figured it was enough. I closed the hood and started the Jeep, but we bounced only about twenty yards farther when a cloud of steam rose again. Now I was sweating, and it wasn't from the heat of the day. I felt responsible for Pam and her children. *I must find a way to get us back to Graves Mill, and soon!* I looked under the hood. The hose had blown off the radiator—again.

It was almost noon and the children were hungry as well as tired.

Tilah was whining; Travis was wailing. I grabbed the bucket and made three more trips to the spring to fill the radiator, hoping that would get us to the hamlet. We rumbled and bounced a few more yards before the steam billowed forth. Once more I popped the hood and saw the radiator hose had disconnected for the third time.

I glanced at my watch. *Maybe I should leave Pam and the children and run for help. Most of the men will be home for their midday meals. It would be relatively easy to find someone with a tractor to get the Jeep off the mountain. I don't want to leave Pam here alone, but what else can I do?*

It finally occurred to me to pray. "Lord, there must be some way! I've tried everything I know. Please help me to get Pam and the children off this mountain!"

And then it came to me clearly, as if the word had been spoken in my ear.

"Pam, do you have another diaper?" I asked.

"No, I don't," she said. "Tilah's wearing the only dry one I have left."

"Could I have it?"

"Are you kidding?" She stared at me for a minute. "No, I guess you're not." She unfastened the diaper pins and handed it to me, leaving Tilah's bottom naked in her lap.

"Thanks." I reattached the hose using the diaper as a clamp. By the time I finished, the children's decibel level had increased—Tilah was crying and Travis was howling. As quickly as I could, I made several trips to the spring, praying I wouldn't scoop up any sand, and when I judged there was enough water in the radiator, I gave the diaper a parting yank and climbed behind the steering wheel.

The Jeep rumbled to life. Holding my breath, I coasted down the track, easing the Jeep over the rocks until, after what seemed hours, we reached the farm gate.

Meantime, Pam was crooning in a low voice, "Tilah, you will stay dry. Tilah, you *will* stay dry. Mama will give you a nice, clean diaper in just a few minutes."

The makeshift repair lasted until we reached Charles's drive. Tilah didn't leak and neither did the radiator hose. For days afterward, Charles relished warning everyone to beware of Graves Mill's new resident because "that woman'll even steal the diaper off a baby!"

A garage towed the Jeep into Madison, where the mechanics diagnosed a crack in the engine block. The blackberry adventure was its last trip to the valley. I acquired a secondhand four-wheel-drive pickup suitable for rocky terrain and a little gas-efficient Chevette for long-distance trips. Because of the blackberry adventure, I was appropriately equipped for my new world. More important, I was beginning to understand that I must rely on God's providence and guidance to sustain me up there on that beautiful mountain.

CHAPTER 5

"THEY DONE *LIED* T'ME!"

*A face I cannot see, a voice that by faith alone I think I can
recognize, says, "Come," says speak my true and lively word, says
bring the good news into whatever bad news your feet may find.*

FREDERICK BUECHNER

SUMMER ALREADY lay upon the land. The cornstalks had tasseled, and
the second hay-cutting was not far off. Only a few weeks remained
before I had to be out of the plantation house. I continued to pack
feverishly, consigning books to boxes and china to crates, and though
I had little time for the farm accounts, I did not dare neglect them.
I knew they must be in perfect order when I turned them over to
Harvey. I conferred with Dan but only occasionally went out to the
fields with him. Though my heart ached for both of us, I knew that
the foundations of our common life had been smashed forever and
my focus must shift to a new community.

My last days and hours at Luxmont were a blur of pain and hard
work. I knew from my measurements that the Graves Mill cottage could not contain all my furniture, and even with the extra
storage in the church, I had more baggage than accommodations.

I arranged for a reputable moving company to transport most of the fine antiques to storage in Fredericksburg until I could build on the mountain. I made many trips back and forth between Graves Mill and Luxmont, depositing boxes of books and china in the parish hall, linens and simple tableware in the cottage. When the big antebellum house was nearly bare of rugs and furniture, the old pine floorboards creaked and groaned with changes in temperature and humidity. The echoes seemed a suitably gloomy accompaniment to the final chapter of my life in that world. I was too numb to pray, too disheartened and wounded to cry out to God.

Although I don't recall my last day at Luxmont, my recollection of my first days—and nights—as a full-time resident in Graves Mill are as vivid as if they were yesterday's adventures.

The early summer of 1977 was hot and dry. I was grateful that Dr. Bell had left a window air-conditioning unit in the Graves Mill cottage. However, it was noisy and blocked the light from the bedroom window. Fortunately, the temperatures were a little cooler in the mountains than in the flatlands, so I used the air conditioner as seldom as possible, reminding myself to give thanks when it roared and rasped. At least it was there and it worked.

I was in a new and strange world, scared and depressed. During the day, I rinsed china and pots, cleaned shelves in the kitchen, washed windows, and swept out cobwebs. And missed Mary Helen. Back at Luxmont, we had worked together at such tasks or she did them for me. Now I had to adjust to scrubbing, cleaning, and organizing alone. I fervently disliked ironing, so Mary Helen had always done that, and without her cheerful assistance, I had a choice: I could either press curtains myself or hang them replete with wrinkles. I ironed them.

"Get used to it!" I'd scold myself. "This is the way life is going to be from now on. You've done these things in the past. Other women do them. So can you. Just be grateful that your husband was generous during those years and was willing to pay a housekeeper!"

With all the adjustments and activities, I didn't have much time or energy to feel sorry for myself during the day. At night, though, I had no defense against grief, and I could not bear the thought of sleeping in the cottage. I had struggled and strained, pulling new ticking over the lumpy mattresses on Dolly Seekford's beds, but when I sat on the edge of one, the metal springs creaked and squawked. That settled it. When dusk fell, I crawled into my sleeping bag on the porch.

From my bed on the cement slab I could see the stars far more clearly than had been possible in the flatlands, where electric lights competed with the celestial lanterns. Across the road, Kinsey Run splashed along its rocky bed and the Rapidan River whispered on its way to join the Rappahannock. Occasionally, one of my horses neighed in its new paddock. Tallis, the Siamese cats, and the chickens were still at the plantation farm, and though I missed the dog's companionship, the cats' purring, and the rooster's crows, the water music and the proximity of my horse-friends brought comfort and quiet. As I lay on the porch, life seemed possible in this strange new place.

Occasionally rebellious thoughts crept into a corner of my mind—that perhaps God didn't exist or wasn't good or didn't really care about me—but I dismissed them instantly. Two things kept me from quarreling with God. For one, I had tasted His presence in St. Peter's Square, and I could not doubt either His reality or His love. Second, I had agreed to open that old church up the road and maybe even share the Scriptures with residents in this mountain hollow. To do that, I knew I must hold fast to the truth that He is good, that He loves us, and that He is our help in time of need.

I continued to sleep outside on the porch for several nights. The last night of my bivouac, I awakened just before dawn when something brushed across my arm. I opened my eyes and stared at a skunk's snout pointed curiously at mine. I lay very, very still. "Lord,"

I pleaded, "please send it away! Please!" Finally, after what seemed hours, the little fellow waddled off toward Store Mountain.

"Thanks be to God Tallis isn't here!" I exclaimed. "That would have been a disaster!"

After the skunk's visit, I moved my sleeping quarters indoors, determined not to mind the creaking bedsprings.

When I finished unpacking most of the boxes and the cottage was somewhat organized, I brought the cats and Tallis to Graves Mill. The cats, accustomed to roaming the farm at Luxmont, disappeared after several days. They were never seen thereafter, and Charles told me that very likely a fox had dispatched them. I was shocked and grieved. It was indeed a different world up in the hollows. I was disoriented, and so was Tallis. He moped for a week. A trip to the mountains was one thing; staying there was another. Sometimes he rubbed his head against my knee, whining softly. Sometimes he stood at the door, as if to say, "Come on, it's time to go home." And I would say through my tears, "Tallis, old man, it's okay. We live here. This is home now."

The chickens were the last of my menagerie to be moved. The house was almost settled before I could focus my attention and time on the prospective "chicken coop." It presented significant problems. As Dr. Bell had warned me, the little shed, formerly Elmo Utz's home, was full—if not to the rafters, at least halfway up the ladder to the sleeping loft.

I guessed that the Graves Mill storekeeper had saved every piece of string and wire because it "might come in handy sometime." Sorting through piles of old gun catalogs and discarded merchandise from the 1890s—including ladies' high-top button shoes, skirt hoops, and ruffled blouses—was hard work, but as I loaded half a century of discarded merchandise into the pickup, I felt as if I knew the store and its owner much as an archaeologist knows a culture when he studies its artifacts. In fact, the piles of goods and papers taught me as much about the village history as Charles's stories, and in working through the detritus, I began to enter that history, even accept that I would be part of it.

Each time I piled another armload of rotting dry goods or catalogs into the pickup, I looked over at the sagging tin-roofed building, boarded up and silent, huddled under a gnarled apple tree about twenty yards from my prospective chicken coop. I could almost see the horses and wagons lined up at the hitching rail in front of the Graves Mill general store.

There would have been women wearing those buttoned shoes and men buying bullets and children running here and there, begging for penny candy. I grieved as I discarded so many interesting pieces of history along with mountains of newsprint and a feather bed leaking clouds of goose down, but Dr. Bell had been correct about the skunks, too. It was useless to attempt rescue and renovation of the goods. After several days and many trips to the county landfill, the truck reeked of skunk and mildew.

At last I cleared the lower floor, and Dan came to Graves Mill to help me build box nests, a chicken roost, and a small fenced run for the birds. I borrowed a chicken crate from Joe Fray, and soon the white leghorns were scratching in their new yard and clucking comfortably in their nests. They didn't seem to mind the lingering smell of skunk, a scent which eventually disappeared, displaced by odors of dust and poultry.

My godparents, Joe and Mary Temple, were glad I had my chickens, but my relocation to Graves Mill was difficult for them. They had loved the big plantation house and had been proud of my position in the county. Now they were worried about my safety and highly uncertain future. I knew they wondered by what miracle I'd be able to adapt to this new life, so different from the world to which I had become accustomed. I was wondering the same thing. They were nothing if not loyal, though, and I was grateful for their encouragement and support. Of course, I told them about my agreement with Charles to reopen the church.

One evening Tallis announced Joe's arrival, dashing out to welcome his friend, with tail wagging so hard I could barely see it. The dog was wary of strangers, but Joe was family and Tallis was clearly glad to see him.

"Good dog, good boy. Now go sit," Joe said, as I hurried to greet him.

A faint breeze stirred wisps of his thin gray hair. The setting sun reflected in his glasses so I couldn't see his eyes, but I *could* see that he was beaming. He carried a sheaf of papers and was obviously pleased with himself.

I could barely restrain myself from asking Joe what this visit was about, but I knew it would not be good manners to inquire before I invited him inside for iced tea or coffee and a crumpet. *Do I have any tea on hand?* I wasn't sure.

Fortunately, Joe asked for water and a cookie. He was probably as anxious to explain his errand as I was to know about it, but he dutifully investigated the cottage's three rooms before we sat down at the long pine table in the main living area. He made some comments about the dry weather while nibbling a cookie, but I knew his mind was on the papers he had laid beside his plate. Finally, the preliminary niceties completed, he cleared his throat.

"This is an application for the Lutheran seminary in Roanoke," he explained. "If you're going to be a preacher up here in the hills, you'd better get into Roanoke this fall. Go and talk with Pastor Hall about it."

Why hadn't I thought of that? I had been feeling trapped and helpless, but this seemed to be an open door. The seminary made perfect sense.

Joe left shortly afterward, but not before giving me a fatherly lecture. Graves Mill was a wonderful place, he said, *for summer visits.*

"Now you go see Pastor Hall," he insisted as he climbed into his Buick.

Bill Hall was the pastor of Hebron Lutheran Church, where I'd been baptized and where I attended every Sunday. I called him the next morning and told him about Joe's visit and suggestion.

"Are you free to stop by the parsonage this afternoon so we can talk about this?" Bill asked. A few hours later I found myself facing him across his desk.

Bill, his wife, Helen, and I were good friends, but on official occasions, he usually sat behind his desk. This was obviously an official occasion—a *very* official occasion, judging by his expression. His round face was not smiling as Joe's had been the previous evening.

"First," he said, clearing his throat, resting his elbows on the desk and touching his fingers together at the tips, "you must apply for postulancy."

"What's that? I don't want to enter a convent, Bill! They've asked me to open a church that's been closed for eight years. I must do something about it and do it soon!"

He ignored my outburst. "Postulancy," he explained patiently, "is the process of study and spiritual formation leading to ordination. You must be accepted as a postulant before you can begin to study for the ministry. There are psychological and physical examinations, as well as academic requirements. Now, you can get a master's in religion without becoming a postulant, but that will not prepare you for the ministry."

"I see," I replied, though I didn't really see at all. "And how long will this application for postulancy take?"

"Probably about a year," he replied.

"A year!" I exploded. "I need to do something *now*!"

"If you're called to the ministry, a year shouldn't be a problem," he said. "You will be required to give up any plans to open that church. You can't be pastor—even a mission pastor—of a church while you're studying to become a minister."

I thanked him for all the information and started home, tears of frustration on my cheeks. I wasn't angry with Bill. He had been kind and gracious when he explained the Lutheran process to me. But what was I to do now? I was already moved into the Graves Mill cottage. Charles and a growing number of people in the valley expected me to open Graves Chapel, but how could I do that with no training or experience?

"Lord Jesus, what do *You* want me to do?" I cried. "Why am I in Graves Mill? Help!"

When I got back to the cottage, I went to my harpsichord. I played for quite a long time, hoping the music would settle my mind and emotions, as it often did. Because my mother was a violinist, music had always been part of my life, and even as a child, I had known that melodies can deliver a troubled mind from turmoil. That afternoon, Bach and Handel turned my complaints to praise, and as I played, I was grateful to have had the means to purchase the German instrument. Finally, I rose from the music bench to pace back and forth.

Maybe this visit with Pastor Hall was a sign. Dolly had said this project was impossible. Pastor Hall's information seemed to confirm that judgment. I continued to pace while I considered my options.

"I can tell the community I can't help them open the church. Perhaps it can be done, but *I* cannot do it.

"I could try another denomination. Perhaps the Episcopal church would allow me to go to seminary immediately." I dismissed that option. I vaguely remembered hearing somewhere that their ministry process was similar to that of the Lutherans.

"I could try ministry with no training and no plan."

Even as I considered the alternatives, I knew that none of these options would satisfactorily resolve the problem.

I stared out the window at the shabby old church. I couldn't possibly rehabilitate the structure, plan services, and evangelize to build up a congregation. "What else *can* I do, God, but admit defeat?"

It is when we come to the end of our wisdom and wits and we know we're helpless that God sends an answer. As I struggled with defeat and despair, suddenly I knew what to do. It was a completely unexpected answer. I could start a Bible study.

Where? In the cottage, of course.

When? In a couple of weeks, maybe three, to give myself time to prepare.

Feeling as if I'd been given the secret for something as fundamental as the law of gravity, I rushed to the phone to call Charles.

"I've been thinking," I said, "that before we try opening Graves Chapel, it would be a good idea for us to spend some time studying the Bible, so we know what we believe." (*What I believe too*, my heart added.)

There was a brief pause. "Yup," Charles replied. "Reckon you got that right. How you plannin' t'do this?"

"Well," I said slowly, "I've been thinking we could meet here at the cottage. Does that seem like a good idea to you?"

"Reckon so," he said. "When you goin' to start?"

"I was thinking about beginning in a couple of weeks."

"Well, th' corn's ready fer silage choppin' right now, an' folks're workin' late. Make it three. An' Pam Quemiere says she needs your help with feedin' the menfolks their dinner. Might call her in the mornin'."

At last I had a plan! "Thank you, Lord, that I've kept my books in Graves Mill," I exclaimed as I hurried to the chapel with a flashlight and hunted through boxes until I located some commentaries.

I decided I'd begin with the Gospel of Luke because, of the four Gospel writers, Luke was a Gentile and his account of Jesus' life reads more like a history than the other three. Luke's account offers more details and background than Mark. Matthew places more emphasis on the Old Testament prophecies, and John's wonderful book soars to great spiritual heights, but I thought it might be better to consider that later. I began studying, jotting down facts and consulting alternate readings referenced in the commentaries. I sketched a brief outline of Roman history at the time when Jesus lived on earth. In short, I was preparing for the Bible study exactly as I would have prepared for a college lecture. It was all I knew to do. However, God is generous. He'll take what we have to offer Him and use it according to His plans.

When I called Pam the next morning, I was already so excited about the possibilities of a Bible study I almost forgot to ask how I could help with "feedin' the menfolks." She was happy about the upcoming Bible study, but it was clear her mind was focused on the dinners she was expected to provide in the coming week.

"Could you please fix the meat for me?" she begged. "I really don't want that smell in my house." I remembered that when we were picking blackberries, Pam had told me that she and her family were vegetarians.

"What do you want me to cook? And how many will be coming for dinner?" Dinner was the midday meal, served about one o'clock.

"Well, you could make pot roast, or chicken, or ham. Maybe all of those before we finish. Chopping the corn and packing it in the silos takes a few days. The men help each other, and the women do the same, so I don't have to do everything. The Lillards, Marietta and Ruth, will be helping me while the men are up this way, and I'll help them when Rich goes down to help Scootie. There'll be five or six men, maybe a couple of women."

I almost dropped the telephone receiver in astonishment. What Pam was describing was altogether different from Dolly Seekford's insistence that families didn't get along here in the valley. Perhaps people did work together after all! I began to feel a glimmer of optimism about future possibilities.

"Scootie?" I asked.

"That's Ruth's husband, Randall Lillard."

"Oh! Do we start tomorrow?"

"Yes. If you could cook the meat there and bring it over about noon, I'd be so grateful."

I agreed to the plan, hoping I had a big pot roast in the freezer that my godfather's twin sons, John and Jack Fray, had installed for me in the kitchen area.

Later, when I reflected on the conversation with Pam, I realized I had been provisionally accepted into the community. That is, I had been accepted as much as anyone whose grandfather wasn't born in Graves Mill would ever be accepted.

Fortunately, there was a pot roast in the freezer, and the next day, just as I finished cooking it, the phone rang. It was Dr. Bell.

"*She's* coming to Virginia," he said. I knew he meant his stepmother. "She may want the house. She has a place in Williamsburg and she may choose to go there. But if she comes to Graves Mill . . ."

"I see," I replied, my heart in my shoes. "I'll be sure the house is clean and ready for her in case she does arrive."

The call ended after a few pleasantries.

I hope Mama-san doesn't have guests. Tallis and I might need a place to stay.

With the warm pot roast nestled in a basket, I was late arriving at the house across the river, and the men were already washing up when Pam ushered me into the house. We put the pot roast on a big platter, sliced it, and added it to the dishes already steaming on the table. By the time we had it in place, the men arrived, sat down, and began to eat There wasn't much conversation because they were hungry and were intent on getting back to the fields.

"There isn't room at the table for all of us," Pam explained, "and the men need to get back to the field. We women will eat later."

"I'm sorry I can't stay," I replied. "Dr. Bell called to say Mrs. Bell may be coming. She has the right to the house if she wants it, so I'll need to be there just in case. That's why I'm late."

I was sorry to miss being with the other women, though it may have been a mercy. I would have been ill at ease among the farmwives, for as yet I had no defined role among them. Finally, Dr. Bell called to assure me that his stepmother had decided to stay in Williamsburg for the week. By that time, the cottage was spotless, and I was exhausted from the uncertainty. Mrs. Bell never did come to Graves Mill, and in fact, that was the only time there was any threat of a visit.

Meantime, Charles spread the word that when the silage chopping was finished we'd be starting a "Bible meetin'" at the cottage. The phone lines hummed up and down the valley for the next couple of weeks. What I didn't learn until much later was that the valley people decided that if Art Mollé came, they'd know God sent me to open the church.

Art Mollé was an émigré from northern Virginia, an outsider. He was divorced and was rumored to have "strange women" in his house. Because he owned the old place just above and within a hundred yards of the post office, it was easy for the whole community to keep an eye on his behavior. The general consensus was that his behavior wasn't quite respectable. Out of all the local residents, he was the least likely to join the Bible study.

On the Thursday evening of the first Bible study, a very tall, heavy man arrived at the cottage door several minutes before the hour. His bald head loomed over a large, fleshy nose, and the expression in his eyes was not reassuring. Tallis barked furiously, picking up on my sense of unease. I held Tallis's collar, petting and quieting him.

"That dog okay?" the man boomed. "Won't bite, will he?"

I shook my head.

"This the Bible study?"

I jumped. "Yes," I said timidly. "I think everyone is coming at seven."

He squinted at his watch and I stared at his big hands. "I'm Art Mollé," he announced. "I know who *you* are." Tallis continued to growl softly.

Without waiting for me to respond or invite him in, he lumbered past the room divider Dr. Bell had left in the cottage to separate the kitchen and living room areas. I had painted the shelves and moved the divider to form a barrier between the outside door and the kitchen area. It held books, jars of beans and rice, my prayer plant, an amaryllis, and a pot of ivy. It made a cozy corner for my ancient Boston rocker, too.

Not knowing quite what to do, I edged over to it and started picking dry leaves from the ivy, praying someone else would arrive soon. I am ashamed to admit that I had not prepared for this meeting with hours of prayer. I had not sought the Lord's guidance, nor had I prayed for His Spirit to overshadow the proceedings. However, Mr. Mollé's presence gave me impetus to correct that immediately. I prayed desperately that someone else would appear.

That prayer was heard. Tallis barked again and I heard voices on the porch.

A gray-haired lady of perhaps fifty years entered, followed by a portly man with white hair and a mustache, bearing a decided resemblance to Colonel Sanders of Kentucky Fried Chicken fame. Two teenage girls trailed behind them. It was Kathleen and C. K. Rhodes with their daughters, Diane and Suzy. I'd met the family at various Lutheran festivals and functions down in Madison.

"Honey, I'm so glad you're doing this!" Kathleen exclaimed in a lilting southern drawl. "We've just been needing something durin' the week. And your house is so nice . . . Would you look at those rugs? And that corner cupboard! Don't you just love old things? Now isn't this cozy! And Art Mollé! Why, it's *sooo* good to see you here."

I could feel the muscles in my shoulders relaxing. Now that Kathleen had arrived, I didn't need to worry about trying to talk to Mr. Mollé. I could stop worrying about Tallis, too, because he had stopped growling. He nuzzled Kathleen's hand and finally settled down at her feet.

I turned to C. K., extending a hand.

"Evenin'," he said. I guessed from the tone that he had a fine singing voice. "Nice day, wasn't it?"

"We do need rain," I replied, knowing that the men were beginning to haul water to the cattle.

He squinted at me from under his bushy white eyebrows, seemingly surprised that I would have noticed.

"Yup. Been needin' rain for some time now." C. K. turned to Art Mollé and said with special emphasis, "*Good evenin'*, Art. Glad to see you!"

"Please have a seat," I said, waving toward the leather settee and chairs arranged in a semicircle before the fireplace.

I heard more feet scraping across the porch, and Charles marched into the room carrying a battered leather Bible under his arm. *Oh no, Mr. Mollé doesn't have a Bible! I wonder if I have enough extra Bibles in the house.*

Next to Mr. Mollé, Charles looked quite small. Charles was actually just a little shorter than I was, but his forceful personality made him seem larger than he really was.

"Evenin'," he said, removing his pipe from between his teeth.

He spotted a clothes rack I'd mounted on the wall in my improvised entryway. Someone had cut out a cat shape with a jigsaw and had mounted pegs on the board. Charles studied it for a minute, chuckling. "Don't have enough critters, so's you got to put one on the wall." With an elaborate, sweeping gesture he hung his cap on one of the pegs, then shuffled to the kitchen area and plopped down at the head of the long drop-leaf pine table I'd placed in the center. "Well, if it isn't Mollé!" he said. "You gettin' religion in yer old age?"

"I reckoned I better come tonight or I wouldn't know what's happenin' 'round here," Mr. Mollé replied as he sat down next to Charles. The two began catching up on whatever had interested them since their visit at the post office that morning.

I kept myself busy serving coffee and lemonade, all the while praying silently, "Lord, *help*!"

The screen door scraped open, and Ralph McDanolds came in. I'd met him briefly at Pam's home when I had helped with the dinners. Everyone called him Skip, for reasons lost in his history.

"Hello, Skip," I said. "How was your day?"

"Oh, tolerable," he replied. "Thought I'd come and check out this Bible study. Hello, Suzy. Hi, Diane. Evenin', C. K., Kathleen . . . and if it ain't Art Mollé! Evenin', *Art*," he said with a mocking bow. I noticed the peculiar emphasis on Art's name but decided everyone was as surprised as I that he'd come.

Skip sat down between Diane and Suzy on the settee. I paused for a moment to study the trio. I estimated Skip to be somewhere between twenty-five and thirty-five. He had dark hair and eyes, in sharp contrast to Suzy's red hair, china-blue eyes, and fair complexion. Diane was fair too. Her shoulder-length hair was a light brown with golden highlights. Taller than her sister, she was quite statuesque. No wonder Skip took a seat between them.

More scraping and thumping on the porch announced Rich and Pam Quemiere and their two little ones. Pam quickly commandeered the old Boston rocker at the end of the kitchen area, holding Tilah, who shyly surveyed the scene from the safety of her mother's lap.

Travis took command of the toy box in my little study. And Rich took a chair at the kitchen table next to Charles.

"Well, Art Mollé!" he drawled. "Great to see you here. We were all wondering if you'd come."

"Wouldn't miss it," Mr. Mollé assured him, which elicited general applause.

I noticed that like Mr. Mollé, Rich didn't have a Bible. I hurriedly found two paperback copies in my study and passed them to the men. *I'll need to have more Bibles on hand next week. Who knows how many will forget to bring a copy?*

I was about to find a seat and begin when Dolly arrived. "Hello, everybody," she called. "What a week! I've been rippin' an' runnin' the whole time. You wouldn't *be-lieve!*"

Her voice was a little high and penetrating. All eyes turned to Dolly.

"Isn't this great?" she asked the room full of people, and without waiting for a reply, hurried to where I stood beside the coffeepot. "Oh, you have coffee! Wonderful! Black, please. Remember, I like it black."

I started to say, "I'm so glad you could come," but before I could get the words out of my mouth, she had turned back to the company.

"Great to see you, C. K., Kathleen! Rich, Skip, Charles, Pam . . . and *Art!*"

She found a chair at the kitchen table. I eyed the harpsichord stool. I could easily position it beside the harpsichord at the top of the room where I'd be able to see everyone and everyone could see me.

"Is that a piano?" Dolly asked. "It's so *little* . . ."

"It's a harpsichord," I replied.

"What's that? A harp-what?" Charles jabbed his pipe in the direction of the instrument.

I started to explain, but Kathleen rose to the occasion and gave a quick lesson on the differences between a harpsichord and a piano.

She'd studied music before she married C. K. and was an accomplished pianist. As I refilled coffee cups, I tried to gather my scattered wits.

"Lord," I whispered to myself, "I can't do this. I don't really know why they all came tonight, but You do. Please help!"

I thought the excitement and anticipation—and indeed the turnout—was because we were holding our first meeting. I did not guess that as far as the community was concerned, something far more interesting than a Bible study happened when Art Mollé walked through the parsonage door—his presence was an indisputable confirmation that God had brought me to open that old church in Graves Mill. The Good Shepherd brings in the sheep in all sorts of curious ways.

It was time to begin. I took my place beside the harpsichord and asked C. K. to offer an opening prayer. He bowed his head and prayed briefly. I opened my Bible.

"I thought we'd begin with the Gospel of Luke," I said, trying to sound as if I knew what I was doing. "Luke was a Gentile, like us. We're Gentiles."

"Well, we sure ain't Jews," Mr. Mollé bellowed.

I looked at him sternly. "Jews are the chosen people, Mr. Mollé. They're God's special nation. We're grafted into the tree because of Jesus."

"What do you mean, grafted?" Skip wanted to know.

This is not going well.

"We'll come to that in a while," I said, "but briefly, because Jesus died on the cross and paid the price of our sins, anyone who believes in Him becomes one of the chosen people. We're grafted in to that tree. You can read about it in Romans 11. Now, would you please read the first verses, say verses one through twenty-five?" Skip found the passage in his Bible.

Skip had a good reading voice, and everyone was quiet while he read the story of the birth of John the Baptist. I explained that Luke's Gospel was written for a man named Theophilus and that we knew the book of Acts was the second part of it, since it is also addressed to Theophilus. This information seemed to be new to some in the room, so feeling more confident, I began to discuss the historical context of Luke's writings. I had only mentioned a couple of the Herods when Charles interrupted.

"When do we get to them three kings? What's their names? Casper an' Mel-chi-or . . . an' . . ."

"That's in Matthew, Charles. And we can't be sure that there were three kings. We don't know how many there were. The story grew up that there were three because they brought three gifts: gold, frankincense, and myrrh."

"There's three kings!" he exploded. "The preacher done told us there was three kings."

"Well, let's look at Matthew," I said, abandoning my lesson plan for the moment. "Turn left past the book of Mark and keep going back until you get to Matthew, chapter 2." I waited as pages rustled.

Finally, Charles found the place in his King James Bible. He read slowly, "Now when Jesus was born in Bethlehem of Judaea in the days of Herod the king, behold, there came wise men from the east to Jerusalem, saying, Where is he that is born King of the Jews? for we have seen his star in the east, and are come to worship him." His voice trailed off, and he mumbled as he read on. Suddenly he exploded.

"They done *lied* t'me!" he shouted. "They done lied. There ain't nothin' in that there book 'bout three kings, and them wise men, they ain't got no names. They done *lied*!"

"I don't think the teachers exactly lied, Charles," I said.

"Missy, they done lied an' there ain't no two ways about it. I reckon we done right when we picked you to git that ol' church open. An' right now, we's gonna learn the truth outta this ol' book!"

What was happening? I wasn't sure. What if God really had called me to live and work among these people? What if I never moved on up to the mountain? What then?

Later, after everyone departed and I had put the cottage back in order, I sat down in the same seat Charles had occupied at the head of the pine table. I was tired, but because of the excitement, still very wide awake. The Bible I'd loaned to Mr. Mollé lay in front of me, so I opened it, thinking I would read until I could sleep.

I glanced down—Mark chapter 15, the account of Jesus' crucifixion. I hadn't planned to read that tonight. But my eyes seemed to follow the words on their own. "And the soldiers led him away into the hall, . . . and they clothed him with purple, and platted a crown of thorns, and put it about his head. . . . And they smote him on the head with a reed, and did spit upon him."

I stared unseeing at the page. They smote and spit on Him, the Lord Jesus Christ. Tears began to flow down my face. The apostle Paul's words from Romans 8:32 came to my mind. "He who did not spare His own Son, but delivered Him up for us all, how shall He not with Him also freely give us all things?" I could see Jesus twisting in agony on the cross. Delivered up for us all.

"If You want me to love these people because You did, if You want me to be Your missionary here," I whispered through my tears, "how can I say no?"

CHAPTER 6

DINNER WITH MAMA-SAN

I think that as long as we can feel things we walk by feeling,
as long as we can see things we walk by sight; but when we
can't feel and can't see, then we really do walk by faith, and
that is the real following of Christ.

FATHER ANDREW

"HONEY, HOW ARE YOU getting on up there in the wilderness? I worry about you, you know."

I knew my friend Frances Lee Lull's voice immediately. Fondly known as Mama-san among her close friends, children, and grandchildren, she was definitely "Old Virginia." A descendant of Robert E. Lee's family, her Southern pedigree was impeccable, though she wore the distinction lightly. Her lineage gave her entrée to the Daughters of the American Revolution as well as the Daughters of the Confederacy, and access to all the "right people." She owned a small farm in neighboring Orange County, part of an old plantation called Springhill.

Though she moved in elite circles, Frances Lee was not wealthy compared with most of her friends. Her father had been a missionary bishop in China during the glory days of the China Inland Mission.

At fourteen, Frances Lee came to the United States as a precocious college student. As I recall, she studied at Smith, and to pay for her education she cleaned stables as well as grooming and exercising horses. She was a superb horsewoman, and the work allowed her to ride. Though it may have been legend, I was told that she rode in the Paris Olympics.

It was because of horses that we became close friends. I met her at a party in Orange County during the early years at Luxmont, and when I told her that though a novice, I liked to ride, she invited me to try the trails at Springhill on one of her horses. I bought my own mount shortly afterward, but whenever I had any problems, I asked her advice. It always amazed me that she "adopted" me because she was one of those people who are truly legendary in their own time.

We shared a love for classical music as well as horses. After graduating from college, Frances Lee consented to an arranged marriage to a biology professor and began studying at Westminster Choir College in Princeton, New Jersey. Her husband died unexpectedly in his thirties, leaving her with a small daughter and no money. Realizing that she needed a more practical education, she enrolled in Duke's engineering program, and after graduation, became a buyer for the fashion industry. Because she spoke fluent Mandarin, after World War II the US State Department sent her to Asia to develop cottage industries there. New York and Paris yearned for Chinese and Indian silks but could not use them because the colors weren't standardized; a second bolt of rose silk would not match the first. Frances Lee thought about the problem and realized that the one thing common to all households from India to Japan was the American Coke bottle and cap. Those were everywhere! So she worked with the Indian and other Asian households to establish a recipe for each color: so many Coke bottles of water to a set number of bottle caps of dye. It worked, and the cottage industries prospered because New York and Paris bought silks and even cottons in great quantities.

Somewhere in her travels Francis Lee met Admiral Lull, the scion of another pedigreed Virginia family, and after tours in Asia and Morocco (she built a hospital in Morocco!), they moved to Washington, DC, where Frances Lee directed thirteen choirs for needy and disadvantaged children, some disabled, some from orphanages. I never knew the Admiral and we did not talk about him. He abandoned Frances Lee when the doctors told them she was dying of cancer.

"Fathers John and Richard are coming down for the weekend," she was saying to me now. "You remember them, of course? I want you to come on Friday. No excuses, now. We love you and we miss you. Come!"

I smiled to myself. I could almost see her nodding her head of curly, short-cropped black hair, blue eyes sparkling. "Of course I'll be there," I replied. I remembered the two Roman Catholic priests as pleasant men in their early forties whom she'd known because of her work with the children in DC. Now that Frances Lee lived in the country, the priests would come to visit whenever they could in order to enjoy the Virginia countryside.

"We'll be informal this time," she continued. "I think we'll dine on the patio since the weather is fine, so we won't dress."

Won't dress? It took me several seconds to digest what she was saying. In Graves Mill, I sat down to dinner whenever I could get to it and generally "dressed" for the occasion in old jeans and a work shirt. In Frances Lee's world, when people dined with friends, the men wore suits and ties and the women donned understated but expensive frocks. When Frances Lee said I need not "dress," that meant I could wear either silk slacks or a skirt with a linen blouse and pumps. The men would wear dress shirts, open at the collar, but without ties. The rules were never stated, but of course, those who were admitted to these social occasions understood the requirements. Frances Lee had taught me the code, and I was always grateful for her guidance.

"Now, darling, tell me how you're getting on up there?"

I described our first Bible study.

"What an adventure you're having, dear!" she said, laughing heartily. "How are you progressing with that sheep ranch?"

"I'm afraid I haven't made any progress at all. I've been too busy teaching and helping neighbors with meals while the silage chopping was underway . . ."

"Oh, my dear! Now you shouldn't be doing *that*! For goodness' sake, what are you thinking?"

"It's all right," I replied soothingly. "I think my role is a bit like a volunteer in the Peace Corps."

"Well," she said a bit abruptly, "I'll look forward to seeing you on Friday, and we'll have a good chat. Come about five-thirty, hear?"

On Friday afternoon I took Tallis for a long walk, hoping that would keep him contented in my absence. While I dressed, Tallis watched me mournfully, whining softly as he usually did when he saw me putting on "city clothes." I patted his head and scratched his ears, and he slumped off to stretch out on the hearth rug. "Guard the house, now!" I said gently, and he thumped his tail before putting his head down on his paws with a resigned sigh.

I got into my Chevette and headed south toward Wolftown, looking forward to returning to my familiar Old Virginia world, if only for an evening. Frances Lee's farm, Springhill, lay about three miles beyond the village of Rapidan, nestled in the lovely piedmont countryside. The distance between us was only about thirty-five miles, but the two cultures were a thousand miles apart, as even the changing scenery indicated. The Graves Mill Road curved its way past modest houses and small fields to Wolftown, following the Rapidan River, but beyond Wolftown, the terrain changed from ridges and rocky hills to rich open lands leading into Orange County, where broad pastures and hay fields lined the road. Occasionally I glimpsed the porticoes or chimneys of a big country house peeping through stands of ancient oaks. Sometimes there was a wrought-iron gate, through which I could see a paved, tree-lined drive vanishing into the distance. I remembered visits to some of the magnificent antebellum houses at the ends of those drives, homes nestled among magnolias, boxwood hedges, and formal gardens. Horses grazed peacefully in meadows enclosed with white board fences—fences I knew cost thousands of dollars to paint and maintain.

The route I chose that day brought me to the village of Rapidan. Graves Mill was at the headwaters of the river; Rapidan was on the same stream, and Emmanuel Church, where Francis Lee was a member, perched on its banks. I almost waved as I passed the white Gothic building. I had attended services there with Mama-san, so I knew many of the people: Clarence Chambers, Admiral Jackson, Sarah Smith, Father Barton.

I felt a stab of nostalgia as I passed the elaborate gates guarding the drive to a particularly fine house. The year before, the owners had invited Mama-san and me there for afternoon tea. We'd pulled up to the neoclassical facade and walked between Corinthian pillars, and when we rang the bell, a little maid in a black dress and white apron appeared to usher us into a small mahogany-paneled room furnished with eighteenth-century antiques. We had a delightful afternoon, nibbling watercress sandwiches and eating superb pound cake with the fragrant tea our elderly little hostess poured from a heavy silver pot into delicate china cups. We dabbed our mouths and fingers with gossamer lace-edged tea napkins. Our host and hostess had just returned from New York, where they'd spent a month or so, and before that, they'd been in Europe.

Mama-san brought the couple up to date on news of the church and community, but we avoided discussions of religion, politics, and current events. There were strong opinions on both sides of the political and religious divides, so it was understood that these subjects were not appropriate for genteel tea party conversation on a pleasant afternoon in the country. Instead, the ladies discussed the latest fashions, and the gentleman told us news of his grandchildren and horses, both being dear to his heart. The portly old man lacked the experience and the physique to become a rider in the county hunt, but he did keep a few pedigreed horses, and that was sufficient for participation in the Hunt Club's breakfasts even though he couldn't wear the "pink" coat.

I enjoyed the perfect taste and arrangement of rich rugs, polished walnut woodwork, damask wallpapers, and gleaming silver. The hosts were not native Virginians, but the husband had made a fortune in the North and purchased a piece of American heritage, renovated it, and by virtue of house and fortune, entered the best of the local society. If you lacked a pedigree, money and good manners went a long way toward opening the right doors in that world.

Several months after our lovely afternoon tea, our hosts invited the local gentry for an evening's entertainment. I was unable to attend, but Mama-san told me of it, as did several others. One of the guests, a friend of mine, had married a lovely girl from the Caribbean. Her wealthy parents had sent her to London's best finishing schools, and she prided herself on her aristocratic lineage. In Old Virginia, however, what mattered were hair, eyes, and the color of your skin. Her black hair, luxuriant and straight, and her skin, the color of wild honey, suggested Indian and African heritage. When the couple arrived at the party, the butler solemnly announced only her husband when he threw open the door into the drawing room. The butler himself was black, but even for him, integration was one thing; mixed marriage was another!

The young couple had no warning, and so there they stood in front of the company, frozen in fury and embarrassment. No one knew exactly what to do, so there was an awkward silence for perhaps three seconds before everyone began to chatter, saying anything that came to mind to cover the social chasm opening at their feet.

Our gracious host and hostess hurried to the pair to welcome them to the party, trying desperately to erase the awkward situation. The young people circulated among the guests for perhaps ten minutes before their quiet departure.

The neoclassical architecture and verdant fields cradled a lovely world, certainly, but I knew its rules were rigid and its teeth could bite. But then, wasn't that true of most of our social worlds? Jesus told us to love one another, and that's fine when we all agree on the unspoken parameters. But when we don't? In the mountains I already knew that there were clan divisions and economic divisions, and Graves Mill's little congregation had collapsed over an argument about paint colors. The rules were different, but the underlying problem was the same.

It had been about six months since I'd visited Springhill. I parked next to the priests' car, thinking, *It's so good to be home! This is my world; these are my people. I've been an alien in a strange land . . .*

The original house had burned years before, but the kitchen, though damaged, had survived mostly intact. Its cavernous eighteenth-century fireplace became the focal point of a big, dark-beamed room where I spent many hours sipping strong coffee and discussing everything from the Old Testament to herbal remedies. When Frances Lee was diagnosed with cancer more than twelve years earlier, the specialists tried radiation and surgery but finally sent her home to die. The Admiral had abandoned her in the midst of her treatments, but her friend Bill Norton refused to accept the death sentence. He had served in the military in Japan (it was he who began to call Frances Lee Mama-san, and the Japanese nickname stuck), where he learned alternative herbal treatments, saunas, and massage. Bill's own marriage had fallen apart some time before, so he took the initiative and found the ruins at Springhill. At first, Frances Lee slept on the ground until Bill could repair part of the house, but with his treatments, Frances Lee recovered completely. They had been together ever since.

Their relationship was undefined; we simply didn't discuss such things in polite circles, though everyone speculated privately. Bill was an atheist; Frances Lee attended Rapidan Episcopal Church. While Frances Lee was the epitome of Old Virginia, Bill was a Wild West cowboy, born in Wyoming, in love with horses, riding, wilderness, and open country. So far as I knew, he'd had little formal education beyond high school, but he knew carpentry, plumbing, horticulture, and of course, Oriental medicine. They were an odd pair, but they did complement each other well.

I opened the front door just as the setting sun over the Blue Ridge Mountains behind me cast a golden glow on Springhill's brick and frame facade. "Is that you, dear?" Mama-san called from the kitchen. "You're on time! Good girl. Come help me here, but first give me a big hug."

I hurried across the Oriental rug in the slate-floored entryway and into the kitchen where Mama-san's curly black head was bent over a pile of lettuce. At the sound of my footsteps, she straightened up, giving me a long, searching look as she reached out for the hug. She seemed reassured that I was well, and we set to work. She asked me to arrange parsley around a platter of sliced Virginia ham.

Mama-san could not afford the household staff her more wealthy neighbors employed, though she did have a faithful cleaning woman who came to help with laundry, silver polishing, dusting, and other such maintenance work. For really formal occasions, she employed a temporary maid to serve her guests, but for intimate gatherings such as this one, we ladies would be the servers.

While Francis Lee and I were putting the finishing touches on the dinner entrees, Bill had been proudly showing Father Richard and Father John the grape arbors he tended near the patio. At Mama-san's direction, I carried a platter to the serving table outside and called the men to dinner. I knew both priests from previous visits, and I was delighted to see them again. After greetings, hugs, and compliments to Bill on his grape husbandry (I could see the heavy clusters of red and green grapes from the patio), I hurried back to the kitchen to help Mama-san carry the rest of the meal outside.

Though we dined on the patio, we gathered around a table spread with a crisp linen cloth and napkins. Needless to say, there were no hamburgers or hot dogs. Rather, there was superb chicken salad, fresh sliced tomatoes, the aforementioned Virginia ham, a delicate lettuce salad, hot rolls, a French potato salad, and other delicacies. The priests ate with gusto, clearly delighted with the meal. The conversational menu was as varied as the food; at Mama-san's, politics, religion, and controversial topics were encouraged, with one exception that I was aware of—bell-bottom pants and jeans, quite fashionable at the time, were a forbidden subject.

We covered everything from the recent death of Elvis Presley and his impact on the culture (Frances Lee lamented the changes), to President Jimmy Carter's pardon of Vietnam War draft dodgers, to Pope Paul VI and the proposed Vatican II reforms. When Father John commented about the current state of the church, Bill snorted. "Doesn't amount to a hill of potatoes! Religion is all smoke and mirrors. Nobody has ever seen God. We know there isn't any heaven up there in that blue yonder. And you can't prove God. When we die, that's it! And nobody's ever come back to tell us otherwise."

"Yes," I said, surprising myself. "Yes, Somebody did come back."

The priests stared at me for a second, then they took the cue, and for a few minutes, tried to argue with Bill. As usual, arguing with Bill was futile, and Frances Lee turned the conversation to current events in the Episcopal church, particularly plans for a new prayer book. Churches had been ordered to try the experimental versions. Unfortunately, the first time I encountered one of the experimental prayer books, the preacher for the day (our regular pastor probably didn't want to face the congregation's reactions) told us that the church needed to take lessons from Madison Avenue and get itself up to date. I was appalled! Madison Avenue, indeed! Weren't we supposed to be "in the world but not *of* it"?

"That trial liturgy limped," I exclaimed, "and not just because it was unfamiliar! After all, there are three masterpieces that have set the standards of excellence for the English language: Shakespeare, the King James Bible, and the *Book of Common Prayer*." It was a bold speech and the other four were staring at me, but I plunged ahead. "I was so distressed with that lackluster book that I tore it in half, put it in the offering plate when it came around, and walked out. I'll never know where I got the strength, but it was an appropriate gesture." I could feel that my face was flushed, but everyone was laughing.

"I don't know how you were able to do that," Father Richard remarked, looking at me with sudden interest. "I've seen those books, and they are at least a quarter of an inch thick. Was it the theology that troubled you?"

"No," I replied. "I didn't appreciate the plebeian English." Suddenly it hit me. *The Graves Mill Bible study. Good grammar? Nonexistent. Beautiful liturgy? No indeed!* The stammering prayers the participants offered were eloquent to my ears, and their profundity deep, owing nothing to rhetoric. *What was happening to me?*

Frances Lee smiled at me and said, "Well, dear, at least you won't need to worry about silly prayer books up in those mountains!"

"Yes, I know Jeannie is living in the mountains now, but what does that have to do with prayer books?" Father John wanted to know.

"My little girl is teaching those mountain people the Bible," Frances Lee answered. "Now, darling, you must tell the boys about your adventures in the wilderness."

All eyes were focused on me, but I hardly knew what to say. How could I describe Charles, or Dolly, or the Bible study on Thursday evenings? It was a different universe than theirs. Finally I found my voice and tried to describe the valley, the mountain farm, and the empty church. I told them that the remnants of the Baptist congregation expected me to restore worship there. "The trouble is," I concluded, "I don't really know how to lead worship, let alone manage a parish."

Father Richard frowned and looked at Father John, who nodded and spoke. "This is very interesting. We'd like to visit you. May we come tomorrow afternoon?"

I think my mouth dropped open. "W-w-well, uh, of course. That would be delightful," I lied. In reality, my heart had sunk down into the pit of my stomach.

Father Richard was a small, dark-haired man with sensitive, fine-drawn features and kindly eyes. I knew he sensed my dismay. "We'd really like to come," he said gently. "We've never been in the Virginia mountains, you know, and I'm sure the country up there is truly beautiful. I know we're imposing, but we really would enjoy a tour."

His tone soothed my apprehensions enough that I was able to say heartily, "Oh, it won't be an imposition at all! Please come! I know seeing those hills will be a treat for you."

We agreed on two thirty the following afternoon. I gave them careful directions and drew a map for them before Frances Lee and I carried the dinner dishes to the kitchen. I looked forward to rejoining everyone in the living room, where I'd spent many happy hours listening to Frances Lee play the big grand piano, the focal point of the room. As I crossed the expanse of off-white carpet to take a seat in one of the damask-covered armchairs, I stared at the pale wool, thinking, *What luxury! A white carpet! This wouldn't stay pristine through one evening in Graves Mill!*

As she usually did after a dinner party, Mama-san seated herself at her grand piano, and the music of Beethoven and Chopin flowed from her nimble fingers. I always considered this the best part of any evening at Springhill, but that night I was tired, and before a second selection, I rose, made my apologies, and said good night.

The moon was high and there were only a few thin wisps of cloud in the velvety star-spangled sky. The moonlight turned the pavement into a silver ribbon as I drove slowly toward Graves Mill, thinking about the evening at Springhill. It had been a pleasant interlude, but I had not felt as comfortable and at home as I had expected. I had an uneasy suspicion that I was learning something about what is really important for this life and the life to come.

The next afternoon, I nervously prepared a tea tray for my guests. I didn't have any fancy tea biscuits, decorative mints, or special imported tea. All I had was plain supermarket tea and whole wheat crackers, plus some Wisconsin cheddar from our food co-op. *This will have to do.* At least I could use my Chinese porcelain tea service and little linen napkins with lace edges. I knew attempting to offer Luxmont hospitality in Graves Mill was rather pretentious, but despite the fact that I was less than cheerful at the thought of ironing those tea napkins, I continued my careful preparations. I ordered Tallis to be on his best behavior. "You are forbidden to shed any more of your white Dalmatian hairs after I vacuum these rugs! Remember, now, Mary Helen isn't here to do any last-minute cleanup."

If I had doubts about my afternoon tea, at least the late summer weather was ideal for the priests' visit.

"What a magnificent day!" Father John exclaimed as he extended his hand. "Your directions were perfect. This is certainly a quaint corner of the universe, isn't it?"

"You mean it's a ghost town," I replied with a grin. "In the glory days when the logging railroad came through here, there was a thriving population. We still have a post office, and there are a few souls scattered through the hollows. Do come in, won't you? Would you like to see the mountain farm before tea?"

Though they knew very little about the mountain farm, they did want to see more of the country, so after a two-minute tour of the cottage, I brought the pickup around. One glance at the knife-edge creases in the priests' trousers and their low shoes told me that hiking was out of the question. Tallis loved any excursion in the truck and needed no encouragement to jump into the back of the pickup, and we were off.

At the gate, Father Richard climbed out to open it for me, but after he struggled ineffectually with the lock for several minutes, I hurried to help.

"There's a trick to it," I said, hoping to cover his embarrassment.

We bumped up the rough track, the two men desperately holding on to the dash.

"Are there any bears up here? Or wolves?" Father John wanted to know.

"No wolves," I replied, steering hard to avoid a particularly deep pothole. "There are bears. We might see one, and if we do, just stand very still and wait until it moves on. We have had reports of a cougar roaming these hills, but we won't see it in the daytime."

"Oh!" was all Father John said, as I made a sharp turn around an old black gum tree and the truck lurched over a rock.

We took that final turn, and suddenly the mountain basin appeared before us.

"What a place!" exclaimed Father Richard. "From the road, you'd never know this was here."

The two men climbed out of the truck. Tallis was already on the ground, running here and there, sniffing and yipping in delight. I led them on a brief tour of my garden plot, the Kinsey house ruins, and the old kitchen spring. Both priests looked as if they'd seen an angel.

"This is about as close to heaven as I can imagine being," Father Richard said reverently, sitting on one of the big rocks beside the spring, watching the crystal-clear water bubble up from beneath the largest of a circle of boulders. "This would be a wonderful place for a retreat!" Apparently he'd forgotten all about the bears. I was tempted to mention rattlesnakes, but I held my tongue.

We climbed back in the truck, and after a swing around the big meadow, we turned back to Graves Mill, stopping at the old church.

Neither man had much to say as we walked through the building. *It must be the musty odors and the dim corridors. I am sure they think opening a church up here in the hollows is an impossible project.* We spent a few minutes in the sanctuary. The afternoon sun filtered feebly through the dusty blinds. Father John studied the ornate chandelier but said nothing. Father Richard mounted the steps to the pulpit and turned a few pages in the big pulpit Bible on the lectern. During an earlier visit I had swept the floor and carpet clean of hay, dead birds, mice, and droppings, so the room wasn't as dirty as when I first saw it. As I turned to lead the way out, I had that odd sense of a Presence again. *Were the saints who once worshiped here watching?* I could almost hear the rustle of petticoats and silk bustles.

Back at the cottage, I poured tea and passed the cheese and crackers. Father John nibbled at a cracker, took a sip of tea, and carefully replaced the cup in its saucer. He leaned forward, looking intently at me. "Now tell us exactly what you're doing."

"Well," I began hesitantly, insecure and apologetic before their theological expertise, "I'm teaching from the Gospel of Luke. As you've heard, the old-timers wanted me to 'git the ol' church open,' so it seemed best to start with Scripture."

Both men nodded thoughtfully, and feeling encouraged, I continued with descriptions of Charles, C. K., Dolly, and the other members of the group. My guests were so quiet and so focused on what I was saying, it seemed as if time had stopped. Now I believe that both were praying at that moment, but I was too inexperienced to understand that then. Though I could not have put it into words, I could almost feel Something with us in the quiet room.

"Why aren't you in seminary?" Father John's question startled me so much that I merely stared at him.

"We've seen the church," Father Richard added, "and we can see that you're doing the right things, but you need training. Why aren't you in seminary?"

"*You're* asking *me* why I'm not in seminary? You're Roman Catholic priests. The Catholic church doesn't believe women should be ordained to the priesthood!"

"You're not Catholic," Father John replied quietly, "and we don't know what God will do with you here. But why aren't you in seminary?"

I described my visit with Pastor Hall and the postulancy process. Father Richard rubbed his ear; he looked at Father John, then me, and said quietly, "You could attend the Consortium."

"What on earth is *that?*"

"The Consortium is an association of seminaries in the Washington area, including Wesley Theological Seminary, the Episcopal seminary, Catholic University, and the Lutheran school in Gettysburg," Father Richard replied. "A student can take courses from any of these seminaries and the credits will transfer to any of the other schools. Why don't you call and see if you can begin training through one of their programs? We'll telephone you Monday with the references and numbers you will need."

I'm sure my mouth had dropped open. "You're saying it's possible to go to seminary? That there's a way through all those closed doors?"

The two men smiled in answer.

"Thank you for a delightful afternoon," Father John said. "What a pleasant change from our city streets!"

"It's been a lovely retreat," Father Richard added. "We really appreciate your hospitality." Before rising, he folded his tea napkin and placed it neatly in his saucer. "We must be going now. It's a long drive back to DC."

"I will call you Monday morning with those numbers," Father John assured me.

From the porch I watched as their car disappeared around the curve. I never saw them again. It was as if two angels had arrived to give me direction for the way ahead, and having delivered their message, vanished into the mists of time and eternity.

CHAPTER 7

OFF TO SEMINARY

Don't worry about what you ought to do. Worry about
loving. Don't interrogate heaven repeatedly and uselessly
saying, "What course of action should I pursue?"
Concentrate on loving instead.

CARLO CARRETTO

ABOUT EIGHT O'CLOCK Monday morning, the phone rang. I knew it
was Father John even before I picked up the receiver.

"This is what you need," he said. "Call the administrative offices
for the Consortium after nine. Tell them your story and they'll direct
you to the right seminary and department. May the Lord bless you
and give you good success!"

Hanging up the phone, I stared out the kitchen window through
my tears. "Thank You, Lord," I whispered. "I don't know what You
want me to do. I don't think I'm called to be a preacher, but at least
there's a way forward. Thank You!"

I paced the kitchen floor and the porch for an hour. Tallis whined,
sensing my tension. Finally, the old grandfather clock struck the hour
and I dialed the number on the wall phone, my fingers trembling like

my anxious heart. *What if the person who answers tells me there isn't a place for me? What will I do?*

After several rings, a man's gravelly voice was on the line. "You've reached the Consortium. How can I help you?"

"I was referred to the Consortium," I said as calmly as I could manage, "because I have a growing mission in the Blue Ridge Mountains. The community wants me to reopen an old church, formerly a Baptist church. I'm not a minister, and I really don't have any background except college courses in Old Testament, some Greek studies, and some reading in theology."

There was a momentary pause before I heard, "I think you belong at Wesley, under their rural missions department. Call this number . . . And best of luck."

I took a deep breath. At least the voice hadn't said, "Don't bother me!"

I dialed the number he gave me. This time the voice at the other end of the line was fatherly. I explained my situation again, but with more confidence than the first time.

When I finished, he said, "That's very interesting. Can we meet at Wesley next Monday at eleven? We can discuss a course of study."

"Thank you so much!" I couldn't contain my excitement. "I'll be there."

My next call was to Pastor Bill Hall at Hebron Lutheran Church. I explained what I'd done and asked if he'd give me a recommendation.

"I'll be glad to do that," Bill replied. "I'll have it ready for you to pick up a week from Wednesday."

"I'm supposed to be at Wesley at eleven on Monday morning," I said, a little fearful that he'd change his mind.

"No problem. You can stop by here on your way to DC. I think it will take about two to two and a half hours to get to Wesley."

When I hung up the phone, I nearly danced a jig, but I needed to find my résumé, college transcripts, and various other materials in the boxes stored in the church. I grabbed a flashlight, and within minutes was at the church's side door and making my way down the dark hallway. The boxes were huddled along the back wall. "My whole life has come down to just a jumble of cardboard boxes." Even as I whispered the words, I knew it wasn't true. There was the mountain farm, and perhaps a whole new chapter awaited me on Monday.

Fortunately, I'd labeled everything, so I didn't have to search long. Doubts still played through my mind as I retraced my steps to the side door. "What makes you think you can do this?" I asked myself. "This place is a disaster. How on earth are you going to refurbish this wreck?" I stepped outside. "Well, you absolutely *can't* do it" I whispered, "but maybe God can. Well, of course He can, if He chooses." I resolved to leave the long-range planning to God's providence, though keeping that resolution would never be easy for me.

Back at the cottage, I began to pack my briefcase. "Lord, thank You for providing everything I need for the immediate future, including this interview. Please help me to leave the long-range planning to You. Help me to know that You will provide what I need in Your perfect timing. You do not forget a single sparrow, and even the hairs on my head are numbered. Help me to remember!"

The remainder of the week seemed to pass at the speed of a tortoise. I didn't dare tell the Bible study about the interview on Monday, in part because I knew how gossip raced up and down the valley and I could imagine additions and distortions to the story. I did have the sense to call Ada Casazza, an old friend who lived in northern Virginia, to ask the shortest route to Wesley. I knew she'd know a back way that would help me avoid running into traffic, and indeed, she gave me exact directions.

I fussed over every possible detail, including what I was going to wear. After trying on half a dozen possibilities, I finally selected a tailored blue wool suit with a short-cropped jacket. On Sunday, I went to church as usual. When I shook hands with Pastor Hall afterward, he nodded and said, "See you tomorrow!" Caring for horses, chickens, a dog, and the house provided enough exercise that weariness trumped anxiety. I slept soundly until the alarm went off at four-thirty on Monday morning.

I fed the horses and chickens by starlight. The horses didn't need much care because there was still plenty of grass. They nuzzled my hands while I gave them a little molasses feed, and I hugged O'Jay's neck. "I'm sorry we'll miss our morning ride today." The chickens were still roosting and clucked sleepily as my flashlight darted here and there as I checked the nests for eggs and made certain there was plenty of feed in the troughs and that the water tank was full and clean. Yes, there was plenty of straw on the floor. *This might be the first of many predawn mornings.*

I'm sure I ate breakfast, though I don't recall it. I showered and dressed, promising Tallis I would be back as soon as possible, and was off to Pastor Hall's parsonage in Madison before 8:00 a.m.

He greeted me warmly at the door before we walked to his office together. It was a familiar place, for I'd spent hours there working on the parish newsletter I'd edited for a couple of years. His big desk was in the center of the room. A wave of sorrow and nostalgia washed over me while I ran my fingers along one edge of the desk, knowing that in some way I couldn't quite name, I was saying good-bye.

"Here's your letter," Bill said with a broad smile, handing me an envelope. "Best of luck up there in Washington. Drive carefully now!" His wife, Helen, appeared from the kitchen and gave me a hug, and they both walked with me to my car. Bill shook my hand heartily, still smiling.

Thanks to Ada's directions, I arrived at Wesley Theological Seminary with no problems. I checked into the reception area and was directed to the chairman's office in the department of rural ministry. I breathed a sigh of relief. I was on time.

The chairman was an older man, quiet, graced with gray hair and a wry sense of humor. He motioned me to a seat and asked me to tell him my story once more. When I finished, I pulled out my files and Pastor Hall's letter. He glanced at the letter and waved the rest away.

"I don't really need those," he said gently. "Report to my class on Monday morning. Now, go down and register for Statistics and Rural Parish."

So much for my careful preparations.

I didn't know that in the Methodist church it was fairly common to send aspiring clergy out into the parishes while they worked toward ordination because out in the field, their call to ministry is tested through the work. Had I been a member of a Methodist congregation, my way forward would have been much easier. I wasn't a Methodist, but the chairman was obviously intrigued with my story and advised me to become a special student under his direction. Then he made it clear that there would be limitations.

"You will not have any academic or ecclesial credits when you finish this program," he warned. "You will be equipped with the tools you need to work in a mission parish, although you cannot be ordained as a pastor."

I was relieved that he didn't ask whether I'd discerned a call to the ministry and so grateful for the opportunity to learn that I accepted at once. But I had one request. I had noticed a course titled Church and Community listed in the catalog. "Would it be possible to enroll in that course too?" I asked.

He placed a call to the professor, and to my delight there was still an open space and I was accepted. I could scarcely believe I was awake and all this was actually happening!

There was quite a long line waiting to register and pay the fees, and as I chatted with the young men standing near me, I learned some were Episcopal, some Roman Catholic, and some Lutheran, with most of the rest being Methodist. Because the seminaries all belonged to the Consortium and students could take courses at any of them for full credit, I would encounter many different perspectives through casual conversations as well as class discussions. I shouldn't have been surprised to encounter so many people from different denominational affiliations taking classes because specialized courses like rural parish studies were offered on only one campus.

There may have been a few women in the line, but none stood near me. A young man behind me, probably ten years my junior, was anxious to tell me his story. "I knew the Lord had called me to the ministry a year ago, but I fought Him. You know how it is."

I nodded, though I had no idea what he meant.

"God is very patient," he continued. "He kept telling me I should come here. My minister said so too. Finally, I gave in and here I am. What brought you to Wesley?"

I thought for a minute. *I hadn't really heard a word from God. Why was I here?* Did I love Him enough to drive two hundred miles every week in order to serve Him and the flock He'd placed under my care, at least temporarily? I finally replied, "God kicked me."

He threw back his head, laughing. "I know exactly what you mean! I've got some boot prints back there myself."

Classes started the following week. Fortunately, the three I signed up for all met on Wednesday: Rural Parish, Statistics, and Church and Community. There were only a few students enrolled in rural parish studies and only four or five in statistics. Obviously these were not popular courses. However, when I arrived early for Church and Community, the classroom was full. There was a clerical collar among those gathering, and when I introduced myself, I learned that he was an Episcopalian from the seminary in Alexandria. I was impressed.

As the students gathered, a tall blonde woman sat next to me, introducing herself as Olga Fairfax, seminarian. Blue eyes shining, her smile warm and happy, she fairly exuded enthusiasm. She had the low, penetrating voice of a preacher or a teacher. I could easily imagine her calling a roomful of inattentive students to order, and it was already clear that Olga never knew a stranger.

She was married to Carl, she told me, had gone to finishing school, had taught art in high schools, and now was planning to be a Methodist minister. She was in her second year at Wesley. I liked her immediately.

"Now tell me about yourself," she commanded.

How could I possibly explain Graves Mill? Or Luxmont? "Well," I said slowly, "I have a mountain farm down in the hollows of Virginia . . ."

"How *wonderful!*" Olga boomed. Heads turned. I lowered my voice, hoping she'd do the same.

I told her that I was living in an edge-of-the-mountains community, next to an old, empty Baptist church and that the locals wanted me to get it open. "I figured I'd better find out what to do before I go any further," I added wryly.

"What about the farm?"

"Well, I plan to raise sheep up there," I replied. "The last family that lived there raised sheep. I talked with the ag experts and other sheep ranchers, so I know what needs to be done."

"That is *fascinating!* You're going to be a real shepherdess. Wonderful!"

After the lecture, Olga turned to me. "Do you know the way to the dining hall?"

Of course I didn't. "No, but I brought my lunch."

"So do a lot of students, but we all eat together in the dining hall.

Come on and join us! And just for future reference, the food here is really very good."

I followed Olga to the cafeteria feeling rather awkward, but when I saw the large table-filled room and the crowd of diners, I was more comfortable. I opened my brown bag, pulled out the peanut butter sandwiches and an apple I'd packed that morning, and shuffled through my purse for my pocketknife. I quartered the apple as I'd learned to do in the mountains. Suddenly I had that uncanny sense that I was being watched and looked up to see everyone at the surrounding tables staring at me.

Olga was laughing so hard she was holding her sides. When she finally caught her breath, she introduced me to the others as the little mountain girl–shepherdess. Everyone was smiling, and suddenly at ease, I began telling stories about the mountains. Because Graves Mill was so different from their worlds, the students were fascinated with descriptions of the mountains, the people, and farming.

When I drove back south with my new textbooks, I smiled all the way, giving thanks for Olga. I knew somehow that this was the beginning of a lifelong friendship.

In the weeks that followed, both my classes and my fellow students introduced me to theologians, scholars, and biblical discourse I had never even dreamed existed. I had acquired one of Rudolf Bultmann's books several years earlier simply because I'd read that he was important. I didn't have anyone to discuss the book with—theology was not a topic of common conversation in the country—which probably was a good thing because I got so angry with his ideas that I threw it on the floor and discarded it.

The propositions were those Bultmann published in *New Testament and Mythology*, thinking he would make the gospel "believable." The message of the New Testament is mythological, he said, and in order for those who hear it to develop faith, the Word must be "demythologized." Furthermore, he contended that the New Testament writers believed that God and other supernatural forces intervene in our world, but we know better now. I didn't have any theological background, but what he proclaimed disturbed me deeply. I believed that the New Testament was true and that God did answer prayer. Frightened that a theologian could even think such thoughts, I never read any more of his work, and because I was not on a path to ordination, I was able to avoid his writings for many years afterward.

I had also read Jürgen Moltmann's *Theology of Hope* when I lived at Luxmont. His theological perspectives seemed more traditional than Bultmann's. Although I wasn't sure of the political and social implications of what Moltmann said, at least he believed in hope and said that God wasn't finished with the world. I appreciated his observation that if we believe in the "end times," we should fight against poverty and oppression.

Although I personally found such theological discourse intellectually stimulating or depressing (depending on what I was reading), it wasn't something I could expound upon with the people of Graves Mill. Everything was simpler for them. *Hope comes by faith, through prayer, and if God doesn't answer with miracles, there's not much hope. Yes, Jesus is coming again. He might come tomorrow.* In the meantime, what people need is a God who is real, a God who loves each one— now, today! I was beginning to understand that my work would be to share the news that God does care about His creation, about His people, and about the economics of small communities.

At seminary I was no longer limited to my own perspectives. There were both conservative Christians and progressive liberals taking classes through the Consortium, so discussions were often lively. I recall one third-year student who was finishing his degree while pastoring several small rural churches. He was a small man, but he had a commanding presence and his deep-set eyes flashed when he talked about Jesus. "This is called a seminary," he said one day, "but it should be called a cemetery. It's a place where many come to believe in their head knowledge, and in the process they forget the living God."

And I thought that seminary was a place where everyone loved the God of Abraham, Isaac, and Jacob, and His Son, our Lord Jesus Christ! It was a surprise to realize that we were at different stages in our journey and that some of the pilgrims were just beginning the road to the One who loves us. In later years, I would learn that many of the students I thought to be superficial and merely intellectual then would grow in faith to become the most stalwart disciples.

Those were new perspectives, but the most significant discovery for me was becoming acquainted with the very early Christian martyrs and writers. I didn't learn much about them in my classes, but I heard their names in the cafeteria. I found books about them in the bookstore.

I learned of Ignatius of Antioch, martyred about AD 107, and of the seven letters he wrote to the churches on his way to death in Rome. Everything he said centered on the mystery and wonder of Jesus Christ, and that mystery was his very life. I discovered that Justin Martyr, who died about AD 165, left a record of early liturgy, and I was amazed to see how closely it tracked with the *Lutheran Book of Worship* and the Anglican *Book of Common Prayer*. Just thinking of the centuries of worshipers since those early Christians, I found myself reveling in the continuity of faith and practice with hope for the future. The Lord God of the Scriptures had been with His church for two thousand years; surely He had not left us at the end of the twentieth century!

There were many other discoveries. Seminary presented me with a veritable treasure chest of witnesses. There were Irenaeus of Lyons, John Chrysostom, and Basil of Caesarea, and from later centuries,

John of the Cross, St. Teresa of Avila, and of course, St. Francis of Assisi. They were men and women so full of love for Christ Jesus that their legacies were important not just for their time, but for Graves Mill in 1977, and indeed for all time.

Finally, I found the courage to read Dietrich Bonhoeffer's *The Cost of Discipleship*. I had always been afraid of it. Cost? It was one thing to read about Ignatius and his death as a martyr in the second century because he refused to deny the faith; it was another to realize martyrdom might still be required. When I finished Bonhoeffer's book, I shuddered at the thought that God might ask me to walk such a steep and difficult road of faith, but I was also more certain that the God of the Testaments is real, that He so loved the world that He gave His Son, and that because He cared that much, I could trust Him.

The Lord knows what we need. If I had not discovered the great men and women of the early church and their testimonies of hope and faith, I doubt I would have had the courage to continue either my studies or the work in Graves Mill.

If my faith and hope found new strength through those discoveries, my rural parish course and the course in church and community showed me that to open a church in Graves Mill was to swim against the current. These studies proclaimed that the modern church must close small, inefficient rural churches such as Graves Chapel. Most of the residents, said the textbooks, travel outside their localities to find work in the cities, so the economic bonds that once held people together no longer exist, and it is difficult to maintain a community or a congregation. In most cases, children from old families move away to pursue their careers. Newcomers populate the small towns and hamlets, and without roots in the country, they won't help to form a parish. Therefore, the church should centralize, pay its minister well from a larger congregational offering, and expect people in the surrounding hamlets to drive "into town" for services.

That described Graves Chapel's history, of course. It was closed because it could no longer pay its way, and without pastoral care, the people scattered. But there was a problem with the theory. Some of the local people didn't fit in the town churches and wanted a community. They remembered the days when people stayed on their home places, when families joined together to plant and harvest, when cider making was a festival time. A big church may have small home groups or house churches as part of their structure, but they are not like the original interdependent community. They are not attached to the soil and trees and rivers. They do not fill that longing to belong somewhere, to some people, to some place where everyone knows your name and even your father's name.

I was beginning to understand what it means to be a people of God and why Graves Mill wanted its old church doors open even though the economic and cultural forces against it were formidable. I thought of the people who had been coming to the Bible study. The Lillards had moved their membership to Fairview Christian across the ridge. Dolly worshiped in Wolftown, as did some of the summer people. C. K. and Kathleen Rhodes were members of the Lutheran church in Rochelle. If Graves Chapel opened its doors, how long could it realistically survive on nostalgia?

One day I sat on a rock beside the kitchen spring listening to the mountain run rippling over the rocks while Tallis frisked along the track above the garden. The Kinsey place had been a busy farm once; it was empty now except for Charles's cattle. So were the little home places up beyond Lost Valley. "Lord, do You really want Graves Chapel's doors open again?" I whispered.

Tallis came running back and nuzzled my knee. I patted his head, got up, and started walking back toward the gate. There seemed to be no answer, so I headed home to begin my next class assignment. But as I mounted the cottage steps, I knew somewhere deep inside that men like Ignatius had stayed true to their Lord and that men like Karl Barth and Bonhoeffer had challenged Bultmann and others who argued against the truth of Scripture. If my Lord wanted that old church open, I'd keep on working.

"Lord, do You really want Graves Chapel's doors open again?" I asked again. I still didn't know if and when it would happen. In the meantime, I would keep preparing.

CHAPTER 8

A DEATH IN THE FAMILY

Real answers are answers to real questions. Death is a
real question. If faith is a real answer, it must face that
real question; it must stand face to face with death.

PETER J. KREEFT

TUESDAY, OCTOBER 18, 1977, was just an ordinary autumn day in
Graves Mill. The farmers were mending fences, finishing the fall
plowing, or feeding the cattle. The silage was long since stored away
for winter, and the corn had been picked. In some valley fields, the
broken stalks of corn stubble shone pale yellow in the autumn light,
but other fields that in July had been a forest of tall green corn were
now plowed into neat brown furrows.

My mind was busy deciphering the mysteries of parish statistics
for my Wednesday class, but I could hear Rich Quemiere's tractor in
the field across the river, pulling a low, wooden flat sledge we called
a stoneboat across the furrows. Every few minutes, the motor would
idle as Rich stopped and climbed down to pick the larger rocks out
of the newly turned soil. He'd pile them on the stoneboat, move the
tractor a bit farther down the field, and repeat the task. Because it was

on the edge of the mountains, this was stony land and stone picking was necessary for all the farmers almost every year.

Actually, it wasn't a completely ordinary day. The Dodgers and the Yankees were playing the sixth game of the World Series, and every man who could slip away from the fields was watching the unfolding drama in New York on TV. The Yankees had tied the score in the second inning when Chris Chambliss hit a two-run homer after Reggie Jackson walked on four pitches. The world outside Graves Mill remembers this October day as the day Reggie Jackson, "Mr. October," hit three home runs in Yankee Stadium to lead his team to an 8–4 victory. We would remember a different history.

I didn't notice when Rich's tractor stopped humming, but I did hear the Rescue Squad's wailing siren, so I laid aside my studies to pray for whoever needed emergency transport to the hospital. Then I went back to work. As W. H. Auden wrote,

> *About suffering they were never wrong,*
> *The Old Masters: how well they understood*
> *Its human position; how it takes place*
> *While someone else is eating or opening a window*
> *or just walking dully along.*

Suddenly the telephone rang. Perhaps it is only in retrospect that I thought the ring had an ominous sound, but I think I did sense trouble coming. It was Pam Quemiere, sobbing and hysterical.

"Please come! Please come now!"

"Come where, dear heart? Where are you?"

There were a couple of heavy sobs, and I could hear her catching her breath. "Th–th–the University Hospital. Travis . . ." She broke off in a wail. I waited, trying to pray.

"What's happened, Pam?" I hoped my voice was calm and comforting.

There were a few more sobs before she could speak again. Then, "Rich was picking stones . . . Travis fell off the tractor. Rich ran over him . . ."

I felt a cold shudder of horror climb my spine. The stone boat. Travis was with Rich. The Rescue Squad. That's why the siren had split the October quiet.

I never did learn whether Rich didn't see his son fall or whether he couldn't stop before either the stoneboat or the tractor tire ran over Travis's head. At the moment, those details didn't really matter. *Travis, that little bundle of energy? This can't be happening, God!* I was seeing the little body crushed under one of the huge tractor tires. I stared at the Moorish linoleum patterns, trying to dispel the sense of unreality.

"Please come!" Pam begged. "Please pray! You're the only pastor we've got."

"I'll be there as soon as I can," I promised, suddenly galvanized to action.

Even before I hung up the phone, I was making a mental list. First, I must let Tallis out, then call my Rural Parish professor at Wesley. I was due to be in class the next day, but who knew how long I'd be in Charlottesville at the hospital? I dialed the number, praying he would be in his office. He was.

I told him what little I knew, again studying the Moorish pattern in the linoleum to keep my thoughts from cycling into panic.

"Of course you must go to the hospital," he said gently. "Be with the family. They will need you. And don't be afraid. I'll be praying for you." And then he hung up.

I stared at the receiver for several seconds. *Praying for me? He would be praying for me?* Somehow, his words cut through the sense of unreality. This was no dream.

I changed my jeans for a skirt, patted Tallis, and mechanically turned the little Chevette toward Charlottesville and the University Hospital.

I remember the ribbon of highway stretching ahead of me toward the city. The distance seemed interminable. A child was hovering somewhere between life and death, and I had been called to serve as Christ's representative, His disciple. *Graves Mill isn't a retreat. It isn't an adventure in rural living. This is a call on my life. This is a serious responsibility.* "Lord," I whispered, "I don't know what to do or what to say, but You promised to be sufficient for us. I've only been in seminary a few weeks. I'm not trained for this. Please help! Please be with me. Please give me the right words for Pam and Rich!"

When I arrived at the hospital, a nurse directed me toward the waiting room outside the IC unit. Travis was, she said, in very critical condition. I made my way through a labyrinth of halls. The floors seemed strangely shiny and cold. That was the first of many trips through those impersonal clinical spaces, and ever after I always had the same impression of a place where all who entered were numbers, statistics, and case histories. Nevertheless, each time I was sure God was there, walking those hallways with me.

Finally, I found the waiting room, but I hesitated. What would I say? What could I possibly do to help? I had no idea. "You promised to give us the words!" I whispered again. "Help!" I made my way into the room, my heart pounding.

Rich and Pam were crouched in chairs under the window. Pam was white, her face drawn tight like a mask. Rich's eyes were wide, his face slightly contorted in guilt and fear.

He looked up at me and said in a hoarse whisper, "Pray! Pray he won't die!"

"Yes," I said, surprised that my voice was calm and quiet, and perhaps the tone more than the brief prayer lightened the atmosphere. We sat and talked about nothings the way people do when the obvious subject is too big and terrifying to mention. The minutes seemed to be hours, but by clock time we didn't wait long. A physician appeared, his expression very serious.

He cleared his throat, and I sensed that he didn't like being the messenger. Finally he said softly, "Your son is in very critical condition. We don't think he can survive his injuries."

"You're telling me he's going to die," Rich said flatly.

"I believe he'll live through the day," the doctor replied gently. "It would be wise for you to go home now and get some rest. There's nothing you can do here. The boy isn't conscious, you know. If you wish, you can come back this evening. Would you like to see him?"

Pam and Rich hesitated. Suddenly I knew as clearly as if God had spoken the words aloud in my ear that we must go to the IC unit. I stood up. "Come on," I said quietly. "Come."

We followed the doctor into Travis's unit. The small body was covered with a sheet and there were tubes everywhere, so for a second the cubicle seemed to be a sterile white wilderness. And then we saw it—a scene I will never forget. The surgeons had cut away part of the skull so that the injured brain had space to swell, and it had mushroomed outside the little head. The face was hardly visible. Pam and Rich stared, shocked and silent before the reality of their son's condition.

We left the room quietly and reverently, as if we'd visited a holy place. I think we all knew we were saying good-bye.

I didn't have the maturity or the faith to process the questions that came leaping into my mind. *How can we call You good, God? Why didn't You take care of this little life? Where were You? Where are You? Can we trust You? Why don't You hear our hearts' cries?* Those questions would haunt all of us later.

Meantime, the parents needed my full attention. In the seasons ahead, I was to learn that in a crisis, those called to serve must put aside grief and personal questions in order to be fully present to those in need. My own grief and struggles were for afterward. That day, though, I acted purely by grace and God's good guidance.

By then it was mid-afternoon, and I led the way out of the hospital. When we reached the parking lot, I urged Rich and Pam to join me at a restaurant to get something to eat. To my surprise, they agreed. In retrospect, I think they didn't want to go home, back to a house empty of Travis's shouts and thumps. I led the way to one of the local steak houses. Still docile, the couple followed me into the dim pseudo-British-pub dining room, and when the waiter brought water and our menus, they actually looked at them.

Though it felt surreal to be doing these simple things, some color came back into Pam's face and Rich's brow smoothed so that it no longer resembled a washboard. Their voices were almost normal when they gave the waiter their orders. The food arrived quickly, and to my relief, Pam and Rich actually ate some of their portions.

The drive back to Graves Mill seemed to take years, and the clock hands dragged through the evening hours. I slept fitfully. Early the next morning, Pam called to tell me Travis was gone.

"I'm so glad you made us see him," she sobbed. "If we hadn't seen him . . . well, we know it was best . . . he wouldn't ever have been normal again . . ." her voice trailed off. The anguish was so intense over the phone I could almost see the tears falling down her cheeks. I didn't ask if she and Rich had gone back to the hospital, or if they were there when Travis died. Those details didn't really matter before the immensity of her anguish.

The whole community felt the shock and grief, and everyone gathered around the parents to support and comfort them. The women brought food to the bereaved family, and there was a steady procession of friends visiting and caring as best they could. Because I was merely the Bible study teacher, and because we had no functioning church in Graves Mill, my role faded into support from the sidelines. I was content to have it so; I knew I'd done what I was called to do for the time being.

Both Lillard families belonged to Fairview Christian Church in Hood, so as neighbors and landlords, they helped Rich and Pam make the arrangements for the funeral in the little country church on the other side of the ridge from Graves Mill. It was probably three miles in a direct line from us, but because of the ridge, to reach it we drove to Wolftown and then turned back up into the hills. Hood may have been a thriving community at one time, but now there was a post office at one side of a small general store and gas station, an emporium the Hood family owned and operated. The only other building signifying a village was the little white church building and its cemetery resting at the foot of the mountains. That day, however, traffic in Hood rivaled a city's noon-hour crush.

I don't recall much of the service in the church. I remember that the room was packed with mourners that breezy fall day. Most of the residents of Wolftown and Graves Mill turned out, and I sat amid dozens of people I didn't recognize. I couldn't even see Rich and Pam from my place in the crowd. I didn't know the pastor, and his words made no impression. Finally, we processed outside for the interment in the cemetery beside the church.

I stood on the grassy slope among the tombstones, watching the crowd and feeling oddly detached. By then, the little country road bordering the cemetery was quiet, and beyond the church's steep roof, I could see the mountain ridges stretched upward against a blue sky. The autumn wind rattled a few dry leaves, and all around me gray tombstones dotted the field, anonymous despite the names and dates etched in their faces. "'God is our refuge and strength,'" I whispered. "'Therefore we will not fear . . . though the mountains be carried into the midst of the sea'—and Lord, those hills aren't moving!"

Words from Job 14 seemed to float on the autumn wind. "Man

born of woman is of few days and full of trouble. He springs up like a flower and withers away; like a fleeting shadow, he does not endure." Those were not exactly comforting words, but the verses seemed to echo among the tombstones. Travis had been a "fleeting shadow," yes, but surely he'd been more than a shadow, hadn't he? Hadn't he left a mark on all of us in his passing, perhaps a mark etched more deeply because he passed from us so quickly? Was that the answer to the questions echoing in my heart's chambers? Or was it that he was forever etched in the heart of God?

At last the service was over and we all went back to our houses and our work, leaving the little body in his grave under the shadow of the hills.

In the following weeks, Rich and Pam came to Bible study, though not as regularly as before. They carried their grief deeply, haunted by guilt, anger, and sorrow. I offered what sympathy I could, but I knew it would never be enough to salve the wound, so I recommended "professional" help. They took that advice and began attending grief management meetings in Culpeper. We all prayed for their healing, knowing that only God is big enough to fill the void caused by such a great loss.

Thanksgiving was fast approaching, and up and down the valley people were saying, "This Thanksgiving will be so hard for Rich and Pam! Poor folks. Poor Tilah. Even that little thing will feel it, don't you know!"

I'd had a fleeting thought that perhaps I should invite the Quemieres to the cottage to mark the holiday with me. But I hadn't followed through. At a November Bible study, everyone arrived early before the Quemieres. Charles sat at the table with his pipe and Mr. Mollé was beside him, offering various observations on the day's news in his booming voice. Skip cleared his throat, and sensing something important, everyone quieted down.

"Thanksgiving is coming," Skip said, "and I don't think Rich and Pam should be alone. Why don't we have a community Thanksgiving, all of us together?"

"You are exactly *right!*" Kathleen exclaimed. "Just think what it would be like with Travis's empty chair at the table!"

No one said anything. I think we were all envisioning that empty chair. Finally, C. K. Rhodes nodded. All eyes were on him. "I think you're right, Skip. We used to do things like that in Graves Mill."

And then a surprising voice piped up.

"Y'all could come up to my house," Dolly Seekford said in a slightly strained voice. "I haven't had a big party since the sale, but I guess I could open up the front of the house. We can put up tables." "The sale" had been the auction to divide the property between Dolly and her brothers after her mother died.

Dolly never opens the front rooms. This is an extraordinarily generous gesture on her part. Almost a miracle.

I looked around the room. As I glanced at each person, it suddenly hit me. *They're hungry. Not for food, but for community.* These people had known community at one time, had known what it meant to work together, struggle together, and yes, fight with one another. At least when people quarrel, they're not indifferent toward one another. It's the indifference that condemns us to a lonely, solitary world. The little gathering now had a purpose and a plan to care for some of their own and a rising glimmer of hope for a shared future.

I don't recall what I decided to cook for the event. It really didn't matter because all of the ladies up- and downriver prepared favorite recipes. I did visit Dolly a number of times beforehand, acting as a consultant, an encourager, and a sounding board for her complaints about how all of this was going to result in a huge heating bill. That was Dolly. If she hadn't worried about expenses, we'd have wondered if it really was Dolly hosting the neighborhood event. Yet despite the fretting, and probably because of it, we all knew she was happily anticipating Thanksgiving. The big house would be alive once more with laughter and conversation. Rich and Pam wouldn't be alone, but neither would Charles or Mr. Mollé or Dolly. I looked forward to giving thanks for the harvests with my neighbors. Somehow, it really did feel like a new beginning.

Sometimes because our hearts are dull, it takes a tragedy to open our spirits to God's abundant possibilities.

At the next Church and Community class, Olga sat beside me as usual. We exchanged greetings and I said, "You'll never guess what's happening in Graves Mill this year! My neighbor Dolly is opening her house, and the whole valley will gather there for Thanksgiving dinner. Of course we're doing this because the little boy died in that tragic farm accident, but just think! Isn't this what the church is supposed to do and be in the community? Isn't this what we're learning here? Would you like to come?"

To my amazement, Olga replied, "Oh, I'd *love* to do that! What fun! What time should I come?"

"I think we're planning dinner about five-thirty," I replied. "It will be too late for you to drive back home, but you're welcome to stay with me at the cottage." Olga was never one to turn down an adventure.

It was only after I'd issued the invitation that it hit me. I wasn't living at Luxmont, where I'd had at least three spare bedrooms and as many baths. I lived in a three-room cottage with only one bathroom. Where would Olga sleep?

Back home, I spent a few minutes studying the twin four-posters in the bedroom, but when I thought about the creaking springs and thin mattresses, I decided it wouldn't do to put her in one of them. Besides, Tallis liked to curl up on his blanket in the back corner. Who knew how he'd react to a stranger in his space?

The main room had a leather love seat, two Queen Anne side chairs, the pine table and assorted chairs, piano, harpsichord, and rocking chair. The only available place to sleep was the floor! I surveyed the little study beside the kitchen and next to the bathroom. I'd covered most of the brilliant green indoor-outdoor carpeting with a Polish rug from Luxmont and had placed my antique Chippendale desk under one high window, from which I could see the sky while I studied.

Lovely walnut bookcases sat on the inside wall, holding my special books and some reference materials. Opposite these and under the dark square of window looking out on the garage sat the ugly brown hide-a-bed sofa which had been in the living area when I arrived. Dr. Bell had insisted the sofa stay in the cottage because if he put it out in the blacksmith shop, the mice would ruin it. I had disliked the thing since the moment I saw it, but suddenly I realized, *I have a spare bed. I can do this!*

To my amazement then and now, the thought of big bedrooms, gracious appointments, or private baths for each guest vanished. I wasn't interested in what I couldn't provide, at least not at the moment. There were so many people to love; what more could I ask? As I rummaged through the trunks stored in the old church, looking for sheets to launder, I found myself singing.

Thanksgiving dawned dark and rainy. The raw wind whipped through the valley, and I shivered in the rain while I laid out hay for the horses and grain for chickens. I hurried through my tasks and went back to warm up the cottage.

"I don't think Dolly will have very many people at her party," I muttered to Tallis while I poked damp logs, hoping to encourage the sputtering fire. "Surely Olga won't come all the way from Silver Spring!"

I waited all day for the telephone call from Olga I was sure would come, saying she decided to stay home in such miserable weather.

I underestimated Olga. She arrived about five o'clock with her eightysomething mother! *Now what am I to do? I've only planned for one person! Oh, dear! They'll have to sleep together. Why didn't I make up the beds in the bedroom?*

There was no time to change my plans. I invited the ladies into the cottage, offering them tea or coffee.

"Oh, no!" Olga replied. "Let's go to Dolly's, please. And you'll never guess what mother and I are planning! We're going to China! We want to stand on the Great Wall."

Before I could reply, she was moving toward the door. I grabbed my jacket off its peg and my contribution to the feast, backed the car out of the garage, and helped Olga and her mother into the Chevette. It was too dreary and wet to walk even the quarter mile to Dolly's door.

It was a good thing that we arrived early, but we weren't the first to get there. Dozens of people crowded into Dolly's front rooms, people I'd never met before from up and down the valley. Olga was in her element; she and her mother promptly disappeared into the crowd. I circulated as best I could, feeling oddly displaced and useless. I think C. K. blessed the food and the gathering, and from a distance I could see Rich and Pam surrounded by friends and neighbors. Pam was smiling for the first time in days, and Rich looked relaxed and almost happy. *Mission accomplished.*

After dinner, there was no room for me in the kitchen, where half a dozen women were washing dishes and packing up leftover food. I moved from one group to another, shook Rich's hand, gave Pam a hug, and wondered what I was supposed to be doing. I was learning something I had also sensed at the funeral. I would find that I'd be deeply engaged in people's lives at times, as I had been with Rich and Pam at the hospital. I would share precious moments, deep griefs, terrible fears. I would be called to bring the Word, to pray, to be

Christ for those in need. But when those moments passed, people went on with their lives and I returned to being one of the crowd.

I was beginning to understand what it meant to be a disciple of Christ. I was called to be a servant, but service would never be about me.

It was late when Olga, her mother, and I got back to the cottage. Tallis was delighted to see us. I held the door open for him, and he was off like a shot, though he came circling back three or four times. When Tallis finally signaled that he was ready to come inside, I wiped his feet on an old towel, then turned my attention to my guests. I showed them into the study, still chastising myself for not preparing the big bedroom with the twin beds. The thin double mattress on the hide-a-bed would have to make do for the two ladies.

As I laid out towels, Olga asked if she could put their orange juice and milk in my tiny refrigerator. I stared at her in disbelief.

"Did you think you might starve down here?" I asked, incredulous. "I know we're primitive, but we're not *that* far from civilization!"

Olga blushed. "Oh, of course. We just didn't want to cause you any trouble."

It wasn't the last time I had visitors who thought they needed to bring supplies when they ventured into the mountains!

That Thanksgiving dinner began a tradition in the valley. Every year most of the Graves Mill residents gathered to celebrate the harvests and to offer thanks to God for His provisions. Every year, Olga came down from Silver Spring, Maryland, to be part of the event. The following year, her husband, Carl, came too, and when baby Grace came into their lives, the three always spent the holiday with us. There was only one difference from that first Thanksgiving. Olga never spent another night in Graves Mill—she and her family would come down in the morning and drive home in the evening! So much for that spare bed!

Thanksgiving showed me that the Graves Mill community had the seeds to begin a church, but I knew it would take long seasons and many struggles to grow the tree. Would I have the skills and resources to tend and nurture it? I didn't know.

Nor did I know the answers to the bigger questions: Is God good? Why didn't He save Travis? Why did Travis die? Now, after years of study and many deathbeds and funerals, I know the theological answer: We live in a broken world. God could "fix it," but He gave us the freedom to make choices, and those choices can and do bring tragedies, divisions in families, and great sorrows, as well as times of great rejoicing. I believe that, but knowing the answer isn't always comforting to the ones going through difficulties.

I do, however, know Him. I know He forgives my failures. I know He sent His Son to die on the cross. I know Jesus rose again. I've seen God's care and providence through season after season. In the end, His Word, His presence, and His love are enough for all of us.

CHAPTER 9

"HE WILL CARRY THE LAMBS"

At its heart most theology, like most fiction, is essentially autobiography.

FREDERICK BUECHNER

HIS WORD, HIS PRESENCE, and His love *are* enough.

That's true, but it is not easy to remember on a cold winter's day when Thanksgiving's glow is only a pale memory. *Keep your eyes fixed on Jesus,* I told myself. *This woman needs encouragement and so does her child.* Despite the blast from the hot kitchen range, I shivered, chilled by the desolation of the weedy yard outside and the dilapidated porch I'd just crossed. Did God really want me to spend the rest of my life visiting broken children and broken-down cabins?

I followed the mother's bent shoulders as she walked across the worn linoleum and through the tiny hallway. How had my great-grandfather survived visits like this? He had been a circuit-riding preacher and missionary to the Indians in Michigan when the territory was frontier, and I grew up hearing stories about his good works and adventures. I admired him very much and treasured a little canvas-covered diary and appointment book he'd carried in his saddlebags when he was visiting various corners of his charge. Although I had great respect for him and the ministry he did, I never wanted to follow his example. Missionary work was too hard. Country preachers didn't make any money. Why would anyone want to take such a rough road? But here I was, and within seconds, I would see the girl I'd come to visit.

"Listen," the caseworker from social services had said. "I know this isn't exactly your thing, but this child has a bad neck fracture—at least, I think that's what it is—and she's in a cast. She can't attend school, so I've been sending volunteers to help her keep up with her classes. Could you go down there this morning?"

What else was it the caseworker had said? "The girl is depressed and moody"—that was it. Oh, yes, and her best friend was killed in the auto accident. I prayed silently but desperately, "Lord God, help me to find the right words. Help! Help!"

Two doors opened off the tiny hallway leading from the kitchen/living space, and the mother motioned me to enter the second. I found myself staring into a pair of hostile blue eyes. The girl on the hospital bed was perhaps fourteen years old. Her limp blonde hair framed a plump face above the white cast encasing her neck and probably her shoulders. The rumpled sheets and blankets were drawn up almost to her chin, so I could only guess how extensive it was. While the mother explained my errand, I stood awkwardly beside the bed until she fetched an ancient ladder-back chair with a broken rush seat. She set the rickety perch at the foot of the bed where her daughter could see me, then left us to ourselves. I lowered myself carefully, clutching my notepad and the textbooks I'd picked up from the bedside stand.

"You can't move at all?" I asked as sympathetically as possible.

"No."

"Are you in pain?"

"No."

"Shall we try a lesson now?"

I expected another no, but there was no answer.

I leafed through the schoolbooks, praying desperately for guidance. Fortunately, a sheet detailing assignments for the week had been inserted in the grammar book. I turned to the appropriate pages and tried a question.

"What is a compound sentence?"

No answer.

"Have you studied this section at all?"

The girl stared straight ahead.

"I'm trying to help you keep up with your schoolwork," I said as gently as I could.

Silence.

I shuffled the books on my lap, careful not to shift my weight too much, a move that could prove fatal to the chair beneath me.

Ah, there was a literature text! Thanks be to God! I looked at the assignment sheet again and opened the book to a short story. I read for the next half hour. Whenever I glanced at the girl, her gaze was still fixed straight ahead, although I thought I saw a slight change in her expression. She seemed mildly interested, though I suspected she would have preferred a torrid romance novel instead of a Mark Twain tale. Finally, I finished the story and closed the book.

I thought about asking a few questions to see if she comprehended anything I'd read but decided against it.

Suddenly, the girl spoke. "It was awful," she said in a high-pitched voice. "Just awful. And she's dead—my best friend's dead!"

What should I say? In seminary, I was learning that a counselor is to be sympathetic. "Listening is important," the professor had said repeatedly.

"I'm so sorry," I replied. "Of *course* it was terrible."

"You don't understand a thing about it!" the child almost shouted.

"Not you! You're the new preacher up Graves Mill way, ain't you?" She practically choked out the last words.

I didn't move. "I'm not a preacher. And I may not understand, but I can try," I replied as quietly as I could.

"Never mind." Her lips tightened in a straight line.

I slowly stood up and put the books on the nightstand. "May I pray for you?"

Her stare was withering and hateful. "No! I don't want your prayers. Go away!"

Praying silently, I beat a hasty retreat from the room, said good-bye to the mother, got in my truck, and headed back to Graves Mill.

This isn't the way ministry is supposed to happen! My textbooks and professors presented an entirely different scenario in which the visiting minister would listen sympathetically until the troubled parishioner laid out all the soul's burdens. Then there would be prayer and the sufferer would smile with relief. Afterward, the lady of the house would serve tea or coffee and everyone would celebrate, confident that the Lord would provide for all needs, heal all wounds, and transform all the suffering to comfort and good health.

I was learning one rule for these hills: it wasn't wise to expect niceties here! This family's home scarcely had a living room. I sighed, trying to look on the bright side. *At least these folks aren't hypocrites.*

While the truck bounced from one bump to the next, I kept thinking about a hot cup of tea ahead beside my fireplace. I didn't want to think about my failed mission. I knew if I did, I'd weep.

"Lord, where were You?" I whispered.

When I opened the cottage door, Tallis dashed outside, ran ecstatically in circles, and then shot past me to stand panting beside the fireplace, his tongue hanging out one corner of his mouth. This was his usual welcome-home routine, and as usual, I laughed, patted his head, and felt immeasurably better.

A hot cup of tea would set the world right. In fact, lunch wouldn't hurt either. My stomach was rumbling; no wonder—it was already past one o'clock.

The kettle had only begun to steam when I heard a roar down at the gate and Tallis began to bark. Only Charles Jenkins's old maroon pickup made that kind of racket. "He must have discovered a break in one of the fences," I muttered under my breath. *Just what I wanted. Spending the afternoon out in the cold, stretching wire and chasing cows all over the mountain.*

Charles brought the truck to a screeching halt just short of the extension of the porch stoop that covered the shallow well and pump. The familiar short, round figure stomped up the steps and burst into the room, his cap askew, his pipe firmly clenched in his teeth. He removed it to shout, "Missy, Missy, you git that gun o' yourn! Now! We's got 'em! We's got 'em, an' ain't airy a body about 'ceptin' you, so's you'll just have t' do. C'mon, shake a leg there! Ain't no time t' waste!"

I wasn't anxious to "git that gun," and I had no idea who we had "got" nor where.

"Slow down, Charles," I begged. "What's this all about?"

Charles's face turned red. "Rustlers, that's what. An' I got 'em this time. Now git that gun! Move, I tell you!"

The seminary professors said we were to encourage community. I didn't exactly understand how rustlers might fit into the paradigms I was studying, but this seemed to be a community concern.

I vaguely recalled hearing that because beef prices had climbed, cattle theft was on the rise in the area. The rustlers came at night with a refrigerated truck, killed and butchered the animals, and after burying the hides and hooves, they would transport the sides of meat a hundred miles north to Washington, DC, or head south to Richmond, Virginia. In these metropolitan markets, fresh high-grade beef commanded a tidy sum. Charles had lost several market-ready steers earlier that week.

"How do you know you've got the rustlers, Charles? And where?"

If his color was an accurate indicator, Charles's blood pressure was rising. He stabbed the air with his cold pipe for emphasis. "Up at th' Fray place, next t' yourn, o' course. I done drawed a line in th' dirt front o' th' gate. That-a-way, any truck goin' through would leave tracks, an' I'd know if they's only one set, I got th' rascals. They's only one set. Now git that gun an' *move* a-fore they come out."

Obediently, I went to the bedroom and quickly changed into my jeans and flannel shirt. After pulling on heavy hiking boots and a warm jacket, I reluctantly strapped on my gun belt. I'd never worn the .44 Magnum pistol before, and I was much more worried about the gun going off accidentally than about using it on rustlers. I checked again to make sure the safety lock was on.

I'd purchased the .44 as protection against bears and rattlesnakes. I'd practiced shooting against the rocky cliff in the backyard, but I still wasn't comfortable with the big weapon. And I certainly wasn't comfortable with the idea of chasing real, live people with gun in hand. That looked good in the movies, but this was no motion picture.

Tallis frisked around my legs, anxious to go with us.

"You ain't takin' that dog!" Charles yelped. "Ain't no good huntin' anything. Too *gen-teel*, he is!" Charles barked a short laugh, clearly proud of using the word.

"I suspect I'm about as useful as Tallis," I replied.

Charles shifted his feet. "Ain't got nobody else," he repeated. "Quit flapping yer jaw an' c'mon."

I climbed into Charles's truck, pushing aside fencing tools, cattle ID tags, and some old rags. We spun out on the gravel as Charles roared the truck up the winding road toward Thoroughfare Mountain. We passed the entrance to my mountain farm, and a quarter mile farther up skidded to a halt before a metal gate leading into the Frays' tract. Charles rented a few acres of pasture beside the road from them, and I'd heard it was from this isolated place that the alleged rustlers had taken his cattle.

I spotted the padlock on the gate and Charles handed me the key. It was the passenger's responsibility to jump out and open gates.

As I struggled with the rusty padlock, I could easily guess what Charles was muttering as he watched, but at last the thing sprang open. I draped the chain over the top of the gate and pulled the creaking metal barrier aside so that Charles could drive through. When he cleared the opening, he stopped, climbed out of the truck, and began studying a narrow strip of dust ahead of his pickup.

"They's still in here!" Charles muttered triumphantly. "Only one set o' tracks. We's got 'em."

Clenching his pipe firmly between his teeth, he turned the lock on the truck's wheels to put it in four-wheel drive, then hoisted himself back into the cab. I secured the gate and hurriedly followed him.

The old truck groaned and rattled as we hurtled up the rutted logging track leading into the forested mountain. I grabbed whatever handles I could to keep from smacking my head against the truck's roof, all the while continuing to pray that my gun wouldn't discharge. The ridge above Kinsey Hollow rose to almost three thousand feet, but at about fifteen hundred the terrain became much too steep for a road. *We can't possibly travel much farther.*

In fact, Charles was forced to stop several hundred feet short of my desperation point.

"Can't go no farther," he muttered. "Git out. We walk from here."

"There's a truck there," I gasped, pointing to a shiny pickup parked just ahead of us, partially hidden behind a rhododendron bush.

"Yup!" Charles replied. "Git that license number in your haid now an' don't fergit it!"

I memorized the license plate number and studied the truck. It was beautiful, complete with a new bed liner. I knew the bed liner alone cost plenty because I'd coveted one for my old Chevy. Whoever was in the rustling business was apparently making a good living from it.

"C'mon," Charles whispered. "An' don't make no noise."

I knew Charles was taking this expedition seriously because he'd left his pipe in the pickup's ashtray.

The foot trail was very clear. Half-dead weeds and old leaves had been trampled down to form a clear path leading off into the forested cliffs. Charles led the way, and I followed, trying to be as quiet as possible. The big gun's holster bumped against my hip.

"Lord Jesus," I whispered, "please get us safely off this mountain. Somehow! Please! You promised to give Your angels charge over us, to keep us in all our ways. Lord, help . . ."

I must have prayed aloud. Charles turned his head and glared at me.

"Be quiet!" he commanded in a loud whisper. "We don't want them fellers t'know we're a-comin'."

I nodded and concentrated on avoiding patches of dry leaves that might rustle and twigs that would snap if I accidentally stepped on them. It was a bone-chilling day and I shivered as the wind cut through my layers of clothes. The patches of sky visible through the bare tree limbs were foreboding. Was this expedition really part of my job description as Graves Mill's representative of the church?

Charles continued to forge ahead, stopping every hundred yards or so to listen and study the tracks. Nothing seemed to be stirring on the mountain, at least nothing I could hear, but Charles was an experienced woodsman. As nearly as I could judge, we were alone. Except for whoever had parked that truck below us. That was not a good omen. *Snap!* The inevitable happened.

"Be quiet!" Charles whispered. "I told you not to make no noise. Say, you got that gun loaded?"

"Yes, Charles," I whispered back.

Charles wasn't satisfied. "What you got it loaded with?"

"Snake shot," I replied.

"SNAKE SHOT! YOU GOT IT LOADED WITH SNAKE SHOT? ARE YOU CRAZY? WHAT IN THE WORLD ARE YOU THINKIN'?"

His shout echoed back from Bear Hunt Ridge. He continued verbalizing his opinion of me and my behavior in words I'd never heard before. The air was almost blue with the string of expletives, and any rustler anywhere on the ridge was probably well on his way the other side of Jones Mountain.

When he finally stopped to catch his breath, Charles glared at me. "An' why do you got that thing loaded with snake shot?" he gasped.

"I didn't want to hurt anybody, Charles," I replied.

I heard a few more new words and expressions focusing on my inadequacies and inept intentions. I had never been called such names in my life.

Finally, "Woman, don't you know that in these here mountains, they'll kill you first an' ask questions later? Folks disappear in these hills an' ain't never heard from no more."

"I thought I'd just shoot at their feet," I replied. "That would stop anyone, wouldn't it?"

I was afraid Charles might have a stroke on the spot, but he collected himself sufficiently to explain, as if I were a three-year-old, "No! They'd shoot th' both o' us—an' *they'd* shoot t' kill."

"Well," I replied evenly, "whoever's up here knows that we're on the mountain now, Charles."

He swallowed hard. I could see the veins in his neck as he struggled to restrain himself, but he didn't answer. Instead, he pulled a mean-looking revolver from his pocket and continued following the track. I stumbled along behind, no longer attempting to be quiet, and praying desperately that we wouldn't come face to face with anything or anyone. I didn't understand why Charles continued to push his way up the ridge when obviously the driver of that truck below us knew we were coming.

Charles stopped abruptly at a turn in the track. We had come upon a small clearing, and there in the middle of it was a pile of fermented mash. I could smell the alcohol in the cold air. "What . . . ?" I sputtered.

"Sour mash," Charles grunted. "They been baitin' bear out o' th' mountain, out o' th' park. Them furriners up there in Washington, they pays big money fer bear galls. I see! Rustlin' is jus' a side business."

I studied the pale yellow mash, a mound of soaked, cracked corn. The grain might have been used to make bootleg whiskey and kept for this purpose rather than discarded, but more likely it was cattle or hog feed, soaked and fermented to lure the black bears within easy shooting range.

I opened my mouth to ask Charles if my deductions were right but realized he wouldn't tell me anything. It seemed as if almost every man in Madison County had his own particular distiller and I knew the secrets were well guarded, so if it did happen to be a bootlegger's by-product, I wouldn't be given that information.

Charles finished his inspection, turned without a word, and started back the way we'd come. There were no more admonitions to "be quiet," and nothing more was said about my gun. When we reached the trucks, Charles once again ordered me to memorize the intruders' license plate number.

"They's makin' plenty, sellin' them galls," Charles muttered.

"Thousands, I should think," I replied, "if that truck is any indication. But why do they want bear galls?"

"Some sort o' love potion, so's I hear. We got 'em, though!" Charles replied with satisfaction. "We'll call th' game warden an' Deputy Hume Lillard th' minute we gits home. I knows who 'tis, anyways."

Charles's gnarled fingers turned the key in the ignition, the truck shuddered to life, and we rattled our way down the mountain to the gate. As I started to jump out to open it, a thought occurred to me.

"Charles, this gate has a padlock. How did those men get through? And why don't you just put a new lock on the gate? Sure, they could take a hacksaw and get through, but at least that would make it breaking and entering, not just a trespassing complaint. Right now, someone just unlocks the gate and helps himself."

"I done asked the Frays 'bout that," Charles replied. "They tells me that the hunt club folks has keys an' we can't jus' put on a new lock."

"Hunt club?"

"In Wolftown. Folks as belongs to th' club gits rights t' hunt on places. They hunts on my land. They's okay. But maybe somebody outside got a key."

"So that means there are a lot of keys floating around?"

"Yup."

"Listen, Charles. I'll talk to the Frays. I think if they understand what's happening, they'll be glad to change the lock here. In fact, I suspect they'll put a much heavier chain on the gate too."

Charles studied me in silence for a few minutes. "Maybe you ain't so useless after all." I knew that was as close to a compliment as I was likely to hear.

Back at the cottage, Tallis repeated his welcome performance yet one more time. I gingerly unbuckled the heavy gun belt, unloaded the bullets, and with a fervent prayer of thanksgiving, put the holstered weapon back on my bedpost.

I turned on the kettle for tea and got out a jar of peanut butter. It was almost five o'clock, and I was starving. A peanut butter sandwich would taste like heaven's banquet.

I checked the telephone answering machine for messages. There was one from social services.

"I don't know what you did," the caseworker said, "but whatever it was, the mother is very grateful. I called this afternoon and she said her daughter's mood was much improved. Thank you."

I stared at the machine, then played the message over again. There was no mistake. "Lord, You know I didn't do anything in particular," I whispered. "I don't understand at all, but thank You! And thank You for getting Charles and me off that mountain!"

The next morning when I entered the post office, I knew something was wrong. Charles was inside, sitting silently, not even arguing with Mr. Mollé, who was leafing through a catalog.

"What's up, Charles?" I asked.

He didn't answer for a minute. Then he straightened his back a bit and growled, "Hume Lillard says the law can't do nothin'."

"*What?* Why not?" I couldn't believe my ears.

"Seems we's got to catch them varmits shootin' 'cross the bait. Otherwise, ain't no law broken an' they can't arrest nobody."

"So the crooks will just keep on doing what they've been doing?"

"You got that right, Missy. Now you watch yerself up there on that Kinsey place, hear me? You watch yerself."

CHAPTER 10

"A *WOMAN* CAN'T . . ."

God's gifts and his call can never be withdrawn.

ROMANS 11:29, NLT

OFTEN GOD'S PROVIDENTIAL direction becomes clear only in retrospect. As the weather turned colder, other than seeing people at the Bible study, I wasn't intimately involved in my neighbors' lives. It's curious what that does to a person. When I was focused on others, I didn't miss the luxuries of my former life, but when I was left to myself, I complained to God at least thirty times a day. "O Lord, have mercy on me! Why have You made the way so hard?" Yet I began to be more diligent about simple spiritual disciplines—praying continually and reading Scripture daily. I began to look forward to the morning and evening prayers from the *Book of Common Prayer*. My Father in heaven knew I needed discipline to draw me closer to Himself. Of course, as the letter to the Hebrews says, "No discipline is enjoyable while it is happening—it's painful!"

I was having a difficult time transitioning to the austere living conditions. My accommodations were luxurious compared to some houses in the valley (I had a bathroom and running water), but at first I didn't see it that way. I mourned not having a "real" full-size refrigerator. When I arrived, the cottage lacked that amenity, and realistically there was no space for one. Thankfully, small, four-foot, dorm-size fridges were the "in" thing for college students, so I found one easily and put it in the kitchen. It required defrosting once a week, and I hated the work, but at least it was something.

The cottage lacked the necessary plumbing and electrical hookups for a washer and dryer, and a trip into town to a Laundromat took the better part of a day. So for convenience, during the warm months I would fill two big galvanized washtubs with water from the spigot at the end of the porch and leave them sitting in the sun until the water temperature was at least lukewarm. Then I would take an old-fashioned scrub board and go to work. I tried using modern detergents, but it was difficult to get all the soap out of the fabrics. I resorted to Fels-Naptha, an old-fashioned bar soap that worked very well. Of course, everything was line dried, and eventually I began to cherish the smell of sun-dried laundry so much that when possible, I continue the practice to this day.

In the cold months, however, there was no choice but the thirty- or forty-minute trip to a Laundromat. The best one was in Orange, not far from Frances Lee's home, but I dreaded going there. I feared meeting people I knew from my former life while carrying a basket of dirty clothes. I tried to be philosophical about it and not dwell on the beautiful washing machine I'd had at Luxmont. It was even harder not to think of Mary Helen and her faithful assistance. Her friendship, laughter, and love had made tasks such as laundry and cleaning a pleasure. One winter day as I pulled sheets from a commercial dryer, my eyes flooded with tears. "I'm so lonely," I whispered to myself.

The laundry was only one challenge. The fireplace required

constant vigilance during the winter months. If there was snow, I had a long driveway to shovel, as well as paths to the chicken house and the horses. And since I was no longer living on a working farm, it was necessary to buy and haul hay for Jay and O'Jay. Their saddles and all the tack required regular upkeep with saddle soap. In cold weather they needed special attention, and of course all the animals had to be wormed. Learning to live with all these tasks and to perform them well and cheerfully provided ample opportunity for spiritual formation.

The Scriptures say, "Whatever you do, do all to the glory of God." I did have a vague sense that caring for the things God had given me—even horses and harnesses—could be a sign of Christ's presence. To prove that point, all I needed to do was listen to Charles or Rich talk about the "shiffless" character of those who did not care for their herds, their houses, or their fields. So I polished the house, tended the fireplace, and used the currycomb on the horses until their coats gleamed.

In Romans 5:3-4 the apostle Paul says that suffering produces endurance and endurance produces character and character produces hope. I knew in my head that was true, but my struggles were so intense and immediate that I could not draw comfort from that. I couldn't see God's redeeming work, His sanctifying grace operating on my behalf for my good. God was pruning me just as Jesus says in John 15:1-2, "I am the true vine, and My Father is the vinedresser. . . . Every branch that bears fruit He prunes, that it may bear more fruit." Would I survive the painful process?

Early in the spring, Charles and I set out to repair a patch of fence together. Some of his calves had pushed against the wire along the roadside, breaking a couple of strands. Neither of us could easily string the new wire alone, so I loaded a roll of barbed wire into my pickup along with the tools and other things we would need. I also threw in my sickle, pruning shears, and a scythe because the wild grapevines had been climbing the poplar trees along the Kinsey Run's banks and we needed to clear out the underbrush to get to the fence.

When we arrived, I went to work with my pruning shears, cutting my way through the tangle of vines. When I'd cleared a space, I stepped back to judge where to go next. To my amazement, I saw a stream of clear sap gushing from the raw, freshly cut end of the vine's trunk. The sap had been surging up toward the leaves and tendrils, preparing for the plant's resurrection. I watched in awe until Charles called me back to the task at hand.

Somehow I sensed that God was showing me a real-life parable, though at the moment I didn't make the connection. My pride in my former house, in my social position, in my education—all of it needed pruning. I knew that God wasn't slicing away my life at its trunk, although sometimes it felt that way. Until I was willing to let God cut the excess branches from my heart, His life would not be able to flow abundantly through me—for my sake and the good of His Kingdom. I had given my life to Christ, and I knew that He was my only anchor, provider, and guide toward a future I couldn't really envision. I had clung to Him through the long, cold winter nights and endured, hoping against hope. Yes, I was still hoping, though for what I wasn't quite sure. Sometimes I hoped for that sheep farm on the mountain. Sometimes I just hoped for spring.

It wasn't long after Charles and I finished mending fences that the first bloodroot pierced the rich forest loam in Canterbury Hollow halfway up the mountain. The breezes were mild again, and I was encouraged because my seminary work had gone well. Since I was not taking the courses for credit, the professors were not required to grade my papers and tests, but they had all given me A's on every submission. Back in Graves Mill, the Bible study began to grow until most of the valley people were attending, including Ruth and Scootie Lillard. The cottage could barely accommodate the twelve or fifteen people crowding into the living area.

We had tried moving from house to house, but someone would inevitably forget who was hosting the group that evening. Sometimes the scheduled host would call at the last moment to say the corn picking was running late and the men were still in the field so it wouldn't be convenient to have the meeting that night. Or perhaps the host would cancel the meeting because the wheat harvest wasn't finished or the spring plowing required the whole family's attention. Although changing locations was an ideal way to share our lives and labors, it didn't work. We finally decided to go back to meeting at my cottage, cramped as it was.

I was overjoyed at the turnout. We were finally showing signs of a revival, or so I thought. I had been reading about examples of past revivals in my church and community class, how God sometimes raised up churches in unlikely places, empowering them mightily with the Holy Spirit. *Maybe that could happen in Graves Mill!* As I read and learned, I was becoming ambitious for a spiritual awakening in the valley. I thought I could actually bring it to pass. How little I knew!

If I had been completely honest, I was probably more interested in my own image as a missionary than in the eternal future of the people. I was too inexperienced to understand that revival seldom comes without considerable prayer and evangelizing groundwork. Although most of the people attending our weekly Bible study had at least some knowledge and acceptance of the gospel, they needed training in discipleship, something I was only beginning to learn myself. But as it happened, God had a different training program planned for me. Those God calls He also equips, one way or another.

One late spring evening the cottage was packed full of people; every seat was taken and the younger folk were sitting on the floor. We had just begun when a bearded stranger strode into the house, picked his way through the crowd, stopped in front of me, and shook his finger under my nose.

"You're sendin' 'em straight to hell!" he thundered. "You don't really believe the Bible. If you did, you'd know that you, a woman, *cannot* teach Scripture—and you certainly can't teach men! A woman can't do it!"

He continued his tirade, but I didn't hear him. I was transfixed by the fury on his face. Stunned, I didn't know how to answer him. Everyone else sat in shocked silence too. I knew what the Scriptures said—that women must be silent in the church. I had a dim sense that there was more to be said, but I was at a loss to defend myself with a theological response. As quickly as he came, my accuser turned on his heel and marched out of the cottage.

There was an awkward pause. Then one by one, the members of the Bible study made their excuses and left, like a flock of chickens scurrying for cover when a hawk flies overhead. I was left to pick up the empty coffee cups, cry, and pace the floor.

I didn't sleep much that night. Instead I spent hours crying out to God for help and direction.

The next morning, Charles called.

"That wuz some meetin' last night," he began.

"Yes, it certainly was."

"You doin' okay? What you aimin' t' do 'bout all th' fuss? Y'ain't quittin' now, are you?"

"Charles, tell me what folks are saying today. What is Graves Mill thinking this morning?"

There was a long pause. I sensed that Charles didn't want to answer my question. "Some's sayin' one thing, some 'nother."

"What are they saying, Charles?" Although I couldn't hear it, I was pretty certain that he was shuffling his feet, anxious about my reaction to what he was about to report.

"Well, Missy, some's sayin' that wimmin can't teach men. Some's sayin' that wimmin's 'posed t' shut up in meetin's, an' of course Kathleen's sayin' that wimmin's got sense an' God didn't put no gag order on 'em—that wuz Paul, so she says."

"I see." I swallowed hard. "So the valley is divided, isn't it?"

Another pause. "Yup. I reckon so. Course our *friend* there, he thinks all wimmin ought t' be barefoot an' pregnant. Keeps 'em in line that-a-way."

Finally, the words came out. "Charles, I think I'd better resign. I don't want to be the cause of division here. You don't need that!"

Silence. I knew this time that Charles really didn't know what to say. All his hopes of seeing the old church alive once more were vanishing over Jones Mountain like smoke on a windy day. Finally he said, "The Book does say wimmin shouldn't be a-preachin'."

"Yes, Charles. It does say that. I don't understand it because there are women teaching Sunday school and mothers who train up their sons in the Word at home. Even the Baptists have women missionaries. But the real point is that I'll just cause trouble here. So I need to resign."

Tears flooded my eyes when I hung up the phone. I was angry and frustrated. *Why am I here, God? Why did You open the door for me to go to seminary? What is the point?*

"Lord," I said aloud, "I never did really want to do this. I don't belong here. Why didn't You send a man, at least six feet tall and a crack shot with a rifle? They'd respect someone like that! I've had enough."

I sat down and looked at my bank statements. *This Graves Chapel project is going nowhere. I'm not getting anything done on the mountain farm. I don't have the money to survive indefinitely without any income. It's time to go back to the civilized world.* What didn't occur to me was how soon after thinking I had seen the signs of revival I was now ready to quit at the first sign of trouble.

I slipped into a light jacket and Tallis pricked up his ears. "Yup, old man, I'm going up the mountain. Want to come?"

He wagged his tail and whined, anxious to be on our way. "This is not going to be simple," I said, looking into his mismatched eyes. "There's Jay and O'Jay. There are those chickens. Wherever I go, you'll just have to come with me somehow. I don't see how, but we'll figure that out later."

We walked briskly up the road, crossed the Kinsey Run, and finally reached the valley pasture. I leaned on the garden gate, staring at the jumble of weeds in the Kinsey garden plot. This second spring, I'd tilled the old garden at the Graves Mill cottage, planting the vegetables close to the kitchen. It made more sense than trying to tend a garden so far away from the house. Tallis ran up and down the valley, circling back to me for an occasional reassuring pat.

I looked at the mountain ridge above the valley. "Lord, I want to go to northern Virginia," I prayed. "I have friends there. I can study at Wesley or American University. I can live a normal life. If that's okay with You, Lord, then please help me with all the logistics."

After a brisk hike up the mountainside, I still had no plan, but I did feel better when Tallis and I headed back to the cottage. Leaving Graves Mill wasn't going to be easy, but as I paced the floor and prayed, I had a growing confidence that the Lord was going to show me the way.

While I was thinking and praying, the phone rang. It was my old friend, Ada Casazza, calling from Manassas in northern Virginia. I had often stopped to see her on my way home from my seminary classes, but since the semester had ended we had not seen one another. I told her what had happened, and she promptly invited me to come and stay with her and her family until I could figure out what to do next. She and her husband, Larry, had three children. I knew they didn't have any spare bedrooms, so I told Ada I would be happy to curl up in my sleeping bag in their breezeway. I thanked her profusely and thanked God for providing housing for my transition.

I had a place to stay, but that didn't solve the problem of accommodations for two horses, twenty chickens, and Tallis. I had thought that Tallis would stay with me, but I couldn't impose any further on the Casazzas. Suddenly a Graves Mill neighbor came to mind, a man who lived down the road. *He might be willing to help.* He was considered a bit peculiar by a lot of people, and most of the women were somewhat afraid of him, but I wasn't. I decided to go and talk to him. When I told him what I wanted, he seemed glad to have the chores and some extra cash.

I showed him how to care for the horses and chickens and suggested that he start before I left in case he had any questions or difficulties. He did the chores efficiently and the horses seemed to like him, so I was satisfied the livestock would do well under his care. After all, animals often seem to be better judges of character than people.

But what to do with Tallis? *Of course, Dan and Mary Helen!* They loved Tallis almost as much as I did. I called Mary Helen, and as I suspected, she and Dan readily agreed to keep their old friend at Luxmont, at least for the time being.

Because I didn't know what the future held, I decided I'd continue to rent the cottage and pasture at least until September. I could travel back to Graves Mill once a week to mow the yard, pick vegetables from the garden, and pay my neighbor for doing the chores. By September I thought I would have some idea about where I would live and what should be done with the horses, chickens, and mountain farm.

As I contacted more of my friends about my decision, Mama-san, Pastor Hall, the Frays, and even my seminary friends all agreed that I should leave Graves Mill and the chapel project behind.

Joe and Mary Temple were especially glad to hear of my plan. "It's about time you got out of there!" Mary Temple said.

"We don't like to see you go so far away," Joe added, "but Graves Mill is no place for you."

I stayed with the Casazzas for a couple of weeks until Anne Carson, a seminary friend, called to tell me that one of the American University professors needed a house sitter for a couple of months in Chevy Chase, Maryland. I told Anne I'd be delighted to do it, and she made the arrangements. Even though I had tried to be useful and as unobtrusive as possible at the Casazzas', I knew it was still an imposition, so I gratefully packed my gear and moved to Chevy Chase.

The house was large. I noticed immediately that whoever was responsible for the cleaning had done a superficial job at best, especially in the kitchen, which was trendy for the time, complete with a brick floor. *It would look much better if I strip all the old wax off.* Cobwebs and grease had accumulated on the wrought iron pot rack that dangled over the counter. I cleaned the kitchen and then moved through the rest of the house until everything was shining, top to bottom. When I wasn't working, I would go for long walks in the neighborhood, attend daily services at Washington National Cathedral, and visit with friends when they were in town.

Anne Carson was part of a liturgical dance group at American University, and I enjoyed meeting with them and watching their practices. Once a week I drove to Graves Mill to pick up my mail, mow the yard, buy supplies for the chickens and horses, and pay my neighbor for his services. He was the only person besides Ruth

Lillard I saw. I carefully avoided running into any other people from Graves Mill.

My weekly errand made it impossible to go to church on Sunday, but I was spending a lot of time in area churches during the week. I was a regular at the National Cathedral for morning prayer, and sometimes I returned for vespers. There were midweek services at Church of the Apostles, and sometimes I attended Mass at a nearby Roman Catholic church. I was enjoying discovering a variety of worship styles, including liturgical dance and guitars instead of organ accompaniment. All of this was new to me, even though it was quite common in the 1970s. There was one church, though, that I wanted to visit as soon as possible.

When I was in the mountains, I had occasionally attended Emmanuel Episcopal Church in Rapidan. The Sunday before I moved from Graves Mill to Manassas, I told the rector, Mr. Barton, that I would be living in northern Virginia for the summer.

"Well, you must go to Truro Church in Fairfax!" he said emphatically. "The Holy Spirit is really moving in that church. John Howe is their new rector, and he's part of this charismatic movement in the denomination that everyone is talking about. I know you're searching for answers, so maybe you'll find some there."

I had thanked him for the information at the time. Although I had no idea what he meant about "the Holy Spirit really moving," I was glad that I hadn't forgotten the name of the church. I found the church's telephone number and called the parish office to check on the services. Besides the regular services, there was a Tuesday morning Bible study.

CHAPTER 11

TUTORED AT TRURO

*The perfection of prayer does not lie within our power; as
the Apostle Paul says, "For we know not what we should
pray for as we ought" (Rom. viii, 26). Consequently it
is just to pray often, to pray always, which falls within
our power as the means of attaining purity of prayer,
which is the mother of all spiritual blessings.*

THE WAY OF A PILGRIM

THIS IS AN IMPORTANT OCCASION, I thought as I got ready on Tuesday.
*What would be appropriate to wear to a morning Bible study at Truro
Church?* I finally settled on a blouse and a denim skirt.

The church in Fairfax was easy to find, and when I went inside,
a kind soul directed me to the room where people were already gathering. An older clergyman with a shock of white hair moved easily
from one person to another, smiling and greeting everyone. *Definitely
a born pastor.* I hesitated, looking around for an empty chair in the
corner. But before I could slip in quietly, the man came over to welcome me with a smile and a hearty handshake.

"I'm Joe Kitts," he said in a delightful British accent. "You're new
to the group. Where do you live?"

I introduced myself. "At the moment, I'm house-sitting in Chevy

Chase for a family while they're away for the summer. But I come from Madison County."

"Hmm. Where is that, pray tell?"

I explained as best I could where it was in reference to Fairfax.

"Now, why are you here?"

"I was attending Wesley Theological Seminary for two semesters."

"And why were you there?"

"There is this church down in the mountains . . ."

Just then a younger clergyman walked into the room carrying some books, which he placed on the podium. His demeanor demanded attention. Everyone immediately settled down. *He must be Reverend Howe.*

The Englishman leaned over and said to me, "I'd like to hear your story. We'll talk about this later."

I smiled and got out my notebook and pen. I had been there only a few minutes and already felt at home. There was something about this church. I promised myself I'd be back the following week.

I could hardly wait for Tuesday to come. I arrived half an hour earlier so I had time to explore the main church before the Bible study began. I peeked inside the narrow nave with its high ceiling; at the front was an altar centered behind a railing. To my surprise, my heart was pounding.

Over the coming weeks I learned the history of the church, which actually began as Truro Parish under the Diocese of London in 1732. In 1843, in the United States, it became Zion Church as a mission at Fairfax Courthouse. During the Civil War the Union army used the church building as a munitions storehouse, and it was destroyed. Zion Church resumed services in 1867 and in 1933 built a chapel and changed the name to Truro. The sanctuary I admired was added in 1959. John Howe had arrived in 1976, two years before my first visit.

When I got to the room where the Bible study met, Joe Kitts was already there. It was still early, so we took the opportunity to get to know each other. Joe mentioned some of his favorite Puritan preachers, including John Bunyan, Richard Baxter, and Thomas Hooker. I recognized those three names but none of the others Joe mentioned.

"You do love old books, don't you?" I said, smiling.

Joe's face lit up. "There are *good* books written today, but I have *lovely* books at home." He proceeded to rattle off titles that meant absolutely nothing to me. Finally Father Kitts detected that I was out of my depth when it came to old English Puritans, so he turned his attention to me. "You mentioned a church in the mountains. Please tell me your story."

As briefly as I could, I told him about my divorce, my move to Graves Mill, Charles's request that I open the shuttered church, and the Bible study.

"Why are you here, then?"

I told him about the night when the man burst into the Bible study and said women shouldn't teach or preach.

"Well, we'll need to do some study about that, won't we?" His smile was apologetic. "There's no time now, but we'll talk about this again. You know the times for Sunday services?"

I nodded, feeling rather guilty. Even though I had thought about attending Truro's Sunday services, I'd been returning to Graves Mill every weekend to pay for the horses' keep and to harvest the garden instead. The produce fed me as well as some of my friends for a whole week. That was important, of course, but I could travel down to Graves Mill on Friday afternoon, spend the night, take care of business all day Saturday, and return to Chevy Chase that evening. Of course I could do that.

I was at Truro for worship the following Sunday, and on Tuesday morning, I brought my Geneva Bible to loan to Father Kitts. He was thrilled. The next week, he invited me to visit him at home, and to meet Freda, his bright-eyed wife.

Their house wasn't far from the church. Joe showed me his library, where row upon row of rich, leather-bound books lined the wall behind his desk. He pulled out volume after volume, expounding on its contents. I listened in awe. Joe was that rare collector who loves the fine editions for their beauty but who treasures the books' contents even more.

Finally, he sat down at his desk and began talking about the passage in 1 Timothy 2 forbidding women to teach men or exercise any authority over them in the church. Then he referenced the verses in 1 Corinthians in which Paul says that women should have their heads covered. By that time, I lost the thread of his argument. I did manage to understand that women had prophesied in the first-century church and had a place in the modern church.

Sensing that I was becoming overwhelmed, Father Kitts led me to the living room to meet Freda. Her sharp brown eyes and fair, freckled complexion suggested that she had once been a redhead, although her hair now was pure white. She mentioned she was trying to recover from a migraine, and when I saw the distress in her brown eyes, I made the visit brief. When we met again at church, I realized she was as lively as her red hair suggested. I had an intuition that we would come to be good friends.

It was already late July, and I had no more idea what I would do in September than I'd had when I arrived in northern Virginia. Still, I was having a wonderful time. The charismatic renewal movement was sweeping across the whole area, and I found myself becoming a "beltway Christian"—someone who traveled from one church meeting to another. Little did I know that this exposure to different worship styles, different preaching styles, and different theologies was exactly the background I needed for the future. I visited Church of the Apostles, participated in evensong at the National Cathedral, and was a regular at Truro's Sunday worship, where I drank in John Howe's teaching and preaching like a thirsty woman finding water in the desert. I had never heard Scripture taught and proclaimed so clearly and persuasively. I heard great organ preludes and sang traditional chant in Episcopal churches. I swayed to guitar-and-drum accompaniments, singing contemporary praise choruses with the enthusiastic worshipers at Church of the Apostles. My seminary textbooks were useful, but the living experiences were preparing me even more for the future, although I wasn't aware of it at the time.

When the house in Chevy Chase was thoroughly clean, I began immersing myself in Christian classics. I had read Brother Lawrence's *Practice of the Presence of God*, but I pulled it out again. I read *The Way of a Pilgrim*, a spiritual classic in the Russian Orthodox tradition. The Pilgrim continually practiced the "Jesus Prayer" in his heart: "Lord Jesus Christ, Savior and Son of God, have mercy on me." Or simply, "Lord Jesus Christ, have mercy on me."

The Pilgrim said that if we do good works because we fear hell, we're simply behaving like slaves. That made sense to me. Furthermore, if we pray continually, hoping for the Kingdom of Heaven, we're bargaining with God. Instead, we are to love God and find our joy and happiness in Him. I began to practice the Jesus Prayer, reading the Psalms morning and night, and as best as I knew how, I tried to thank God for all things.

It is wonderful what giving thanks does for your mind and spirit! I would wake up in the morning, anxious and fearful about the future, but determined to praise God anyway. I would give Him thanks for the bed I was sleeping in, for my slippers, for Dan and Mary Helen, for Tallis, for the sunshine or the rain. I was learning that gratitude is the heart of love. I prayed when I went for my walks in Chevy Chase: "Lord Jesus Christ, Savior and Son of God, thank You for Your mercy," always adding, "Thank You for Your singular mercy. Thank You!"

Through the remainder of the summer, I drove back and forth to Graves Mill. Each week, that hundred-mile trip down into the mountains was a continual reminder that I would need to make some major decisions soon. Fall was coming. Should I apply to American University and finish my PhD in English literature? What was God's will? I reminded Him that I *had* given my life over to His direction in Rome, so I begged for a word to guide my decisions. I spent long afternoon hours at the National Cathedral in prayer, often with Anne Carson. I should have been far more anxious than I was, but somehow I was certain that God would work out the future and all would be well.

The days slipped by and the heavens were silent. Since it was already late for registering for classes at American University, I needed to take action. I had nearly determined to start moving my furniture out of the cottage and into storage when the phone rang early one morning at the house in Chevy Chase. It was Kathleen Rhodes from Graves Mill.

"Kathleen! How on earth did you track me down?" I cried, taken completely by surprise.

"Charles told us that Junior's taking care of your horses, so we got the address and number from him. Listen, C. K. and I are coming up there today. We should get to your place about one o'clock. Will you be there?"

Do I really want to see people from Graves Mill? After what happened, it will hurt. Why not take refuge at the cathedral this afternoon? My panic lasted only a second and I heard myself say calmly, "I'll be here."

I ran the vacuum cleaner furiously, dusted every crevice and corner, and when there was nothing more to clean, walked through the neighborhood studying the architecture to keep myself from thinking too much. One question dogged my footsteps: Why were Kathleen and C. K. coming all the way from Graves Mill?

I got back to the house in plenty of time to start the coffee. When I heard the knock at the front door and opened it, there were Kathleen, C. K., and their daughter Suzy. I invited them in and we sat down at the long dining room table.

"Nice place," C. K. remarked, looking around.

Kathleen wasn't there to admire the Oriental rug under the table. She wasted no time on pleasantries. "We want you to come back to Graves Mill," she said. "You brought us something special. We all appreciated those Bible studies, an' all of us getting together. Graves Mill hasn't had anything like that for a long time."

C. K. cleared his throat, stroked his mustache, and nodded. Suzy's face was pale next to her sleeked-back red hair. "Please come back," she said, her blue eyes very serious. "Don't pay any attention to what happened. Folks will forget about it. We miss Thursday nights."

"Is this your idea, or do you represent the valley?"

"Well, Ruth and Scootie won't come back. But Charles and Mollé'll be there, an' Skip will come. Dolly says that you should come back too. It will be all right, you'll see," Kathleen assured me.

I didn't know what to say. Finally, I found my voice. "I don't know what's right for Graves Mill or for me," I said slowly. "I'll need to think and pray about it. But I'm really glad to see the three of you, and I'm touched that you came all this way."

They stayed a little while longer, regaling me with the latest chapters in Graves Mill's happenings. I listened but thought better of trying to describe to them what I'd been doing. They would have wanted to know why I was attending all those different church services, and in fact, I wasn't sure of the reasons myself. Fortunately, they didn't ask questions, and by the time they finished their second cups of coffee, they were on their way. I spent a restless night—most of it in prayer—and the next day I scheduled an appointment with Father Kitts.

When I arrived at his office, Joe listened to my news, looking as serious as I felt. "So the people want you to come back to Graves Mill?"

"Yes. The Rhodes family came all the way up here—about a hundred miles—to ask me to return."

"I see," he said slowly. "Let's go over to the chapel to pray, shall we?"

I'd never been inside the old chapel. I admired the mullioned windows and scarlet-cushioned pews as we walked down to the front. Joe stopped, motioned me into the pew under the raised colonial-style pulpit, and pulling down the kneeling bench, knelt in prayer. I knelt down too and stared at the Ten Commandments etched on a brown-gold background behind the altar. I stared at the white altar cloth. I tried to pray, but nothing came.

After what seemed like hours Joe opened his eyes, smoothed his hair back, sat back on the pew cushion, and faced me.

"I hear the Lord telling me you should go back," he said.

"Oh." *Go back to Graves Mill? To accusations and cold winters in the drafty little cottage? Well, I would be reunited with Tallis and the horses . . .*

"I am sure the Lord wants you to go back to those people," he said more firmly. "They've called you, and that's a very serious matter, you know."

"Called me?"

"Yes. Twice now. You've been called to minister in Graves Mill, and that's a very precious thing."

"I see." I had heard about God's calling on a person's life, although I didn't completely understand what it meant. But I sensed that the Rhodes family had delivered that message to me. I stared at the Ten Commandments for a few minutes. "I will go," I said quietly.

"Good girl. Let me know how you get on, will you?"

"Thank you so much," I murmured, choking back tears. "Thank you for sharing your books, your time, and for your kindness. I am so grateful!"

"Go with God," he said.

As I drove back to Chevy Chase, I prayed and tried to think through the decision I'd just made. From a practical perspective, returning to Graves Mill to lead a Bible study indefinitely made no sense, but it was necessary for me to go back to the valley whether I stayed there or not. If I didn't stay, it was time to sell the horses, close up the cottage, and apply to a graduate program to finish my doctorate. And if I really intended to realize my dream of raising sheep on the mountain farm, I should arrange for an orderly transition, turning the ministry over to someone else so I could concentrate on things like birthing lambs and sheepshearing. In short, it was time to make some decisions.

Still a voice kept whispering in my heart. *What Father Kitts meant was that you have been called to be a shepherdess to two-legged sheep, not four-legged sheep.* I did my best to ignore that little voice.

The owners of the house where I'd been staying were due to return at the end of August. The last week of the month, I gave the house a good shine; I felt the Holy Spirit's presence alongside me, and it was a joy. I packed my belongings and headed back to the mountains. Later, I received a kind note from the family, thanking me for cleaning their house so thoroughly. "It hasn't been this clean for years." I knew that sometimes it's the little mundane efforts that say the most about our faith and hope. In any case, I was pleased—at least I'd done one thing right!

CHAPTER 12

WHERE IS YOUR TREASURE?

Where is our comfort but in the free, uninvolved,
finally mysterious beauty and grace of this world
that we did not make, that has no price?

WENDELL BERRY

DURING MY LAST SUMMER at Luxmont, I had received an unexpected phone call from a man named Bob Davis representing the Potomac Appalachian Trail Club. He said he would like to visit me to talk about the mountain farm. I had never heard of him or his organization, but I'd hiked parts of the Appalachian Trail and loved it, so I agreed to meet with him. A few days later he came to Luxmont. Even before I could pour him a cup of coffee, he explained that his club was a regional branch of Appalachian Trail clubs. The club had renovated a mountaineer's cabin in one of the hollows on Jones Mountain beginning in 1969, the same year the Baptists closed Graves Chapel. The only way to reach the Harvey Nichol cabin, he said, was via historic footpaths traversing the seven hundred acres of the Big Kinsey tract—my land. Not only were those footpaths on my land, but there was a significant section of the Potomac Appalachian

Trail running across the farm at the top of Jones Mountain and across Bear Church Rock. Would I consider donating an easement on my mountain property to Shenandoah National Park?

I'm sure the question on my face made him hastily explain that an easement is a legal agreement in which a landowner cedes certain rights to the state or an authorized organization. While the owner keeps the land, he or she may agree never to develop the parcel or perhaps, as in this case, to permit foot traffic across a section of the land. The trail easement could be given to the Potomac Club, but in order to protect the land, a larger section had to be included in an easement to the national park. With an easement, the trail would be protected in perpetuity.

Remembering mountain vistas I'd seen from the trail, I cautiously agreed. I wasn't quite sure what establishing an easement would involve, but I knew logging, mining, or development would spoil any hiker's day, and worse, it would damage the mountainside.

After moving to Graves Mill, I had become so busy with the church project, adjusting to my new world, connecting with the community through the Bible study, and commuting to the seminary that I had completely forgotten about the easement discussion with Bob Davis. However, as soon as I returned to the valley from Chevy Chase, he telephoned and we made an appointment to inspect the trails.

It was a lovely early autumn day, perfect for hiking. Mr. Davis, Tallis, and I scrambled nearly three thousand feet up a mountain track to Bear Church, the highest point on the farm. From there, we looked out across the deep, forested valley dropping away below us and beyond that the blue-green backs of the ancient hills stretching out into the hazy distance. I was almost overwhelmed with the magnificent panorama. It was the Shenandoah National Park adjoining my land.

I turned to look back at the Kinsey farm. From that high vantage point, it too was a peaceful wilderness. I didn't want to think of the damage and disruption logging would wreak on that mountainside. "This land must be preserved!" I exclaimed.

As we walked slowly back toward the meadow below, I agreed to begin the process. Mr. Davis invited me to join the Potomac Appalachian Trail Club. My task would be maintaining the section of trail on my property. He said he'd send me the application forms and some materials explaining easements and that he'd return later that fall with others from the club so I could get acquainted with them and with trail maintenance. When he left, I felt smugly philanthropic.

My attitude was typical of my "educated" circle at the time: we supported the Appalachian Trail and the Sierra Club, contributed to the Wildlife Federation, and regarded preservation as one of God's commandments. If it didn't come down on one of the stone tablets, we had a sneaking suspicion that it was because Moses forgot to write it down.

God gave us stewardship over His creation, so I believed preservation and conservation were good and godly aims. Aims are one thing; details are another. Finding the wisest and most effective methods to protect and care for land is not easy. Often, there are equally persuasive arguments for and against a given course of action. Of course, I thought I had all the answers when I arrived in Graves Mill. And yet in this fallen world, what appears to be a perfect plan can have unforeseen consequences.

The following day I contacted Madison County's forestry agent, Lyt Wood, for advice. He agreed to survey the project.

In the mountains it was a given that by the time you'd thought about hanging out laundry, the whole valley knew how many sheets you intended to put in the washing machine. I didn't confide in anyone about my decision except for those two men, but word spread quickly that I was considering a preservation plan for the top of Jones

Mountain. *Preservation* was a bad word, especially among the loggers. Often, "preservation" meant a lot of government regulations, and not all of them were pertinent to the land or circumstances.

More to the point, in Madison County "preservation" generally meant Shenandoah National Park, and there was a long-standing feud between the county residents and the park service. Much of this revolved around hunting—it was a constant irritation when a deer or bear dashed across the line into the protected forests of the park, leaving hunters frustrated and angry. That was aggravating, but in the larger picture, the county had lost about a third of its acreage and taxable real estate when the federal government established the park. As beautiful as the wilderness treasure was, it had come at a cost. Mountain people lost not only their homes but their way of life, resulting in bitter resentments lingering to this day.

So when Honey Bear, a native logger-timberman, heard the "preservation" rumor, he came to Graves Mill to save me from myself.

One morning when I was at the post office, a very large man came in and introduced himself. "Some folks calls me Honey Bear," he said, giving my hand a bone-crushing shake. I bit my lower lip to keep from yelping. I'd heard of him. The gossip was that in a fight he could lay a man on the ground with his little finger. Judging from the width of his shoulders, I thought that was only a slight exaggeration.

"I run the loggin' outfit as is workin' the Fray place," he said in a deep, melodious voice. "I wuz lookin' fer you, wonderin' if we could take a look at the timber on top o' the ol' Kinsey place."

"I don't plan on selling that timber," I replied. I'd already heard from Charles and Scootie Lillard that there were giant trees near the top of the ridge, and I'd made up my mind to preserve them.

"Missus, ye don' unnerstan'," Honey Bear said slowly. "Les go up that-a-way an' take a look. Them big trees atop the ridge, they needs t' be cut!"

"Okay," I replied. "I'll go up there with you." I'd climbed all over the ridge but had never found "them big trees," and I was curious. We agreed to hike up to the ridge the next day.

The next morning dawned cold and drizzly, and I hoped the logger would cancel, but Honey Bear arrived at the cottage at seven thirty. Tallis and I climbed into his pickup, and we were off to the mountain. I prided myself on my knowledge of ecological issues and my "progressive and wise" approach to wilderness, and I regarded the local loggers and their practices with considerable disdain. But I kept my thoughts to myself while Honey Bear expounded on the benefits of removing "wolf trees," very large mature trees with massive crowns that shade the forest floor, preventing younger trees from growing. He explained that it was good practice to thin out timber stands and open up the land with logging trails for fighting forest fires. *You just want to make money*, I thought. In fact, there was considerable wisdom in what he said. I just didn't trust him.

Honey Bear parked the truck in my pasture and we headed up a well-worn game trail following the spine of Bear Hunt Ridge, a steep mountain spur guarding the west side of my farm. I didn't have time to look for deer or bear tracks; I was too busy keeping up with the big logger ahead of me.

We had been climbing for about a half hour when Honey Bear suddenly veered off into the woods, and we scrambled up slopes so steep that we had to climb sideways, digging our boots into the thin soil to keep from sliding down the mountainside. All the while, Honey Bear was talking. "Them wolf trees takes up too much land. Them trees are overripe and needs to come down afore they die from lightnin' hittin' 'em or insects eatin' 'em."

"The best timber has already been logged here," I said, stopping to catch my breath. "The seeds from these old survivors will provide seeds with excellent genes for new trees."

Honey Bear snorted with disgust. "Missus, them trees already done sent all the seeds they's a-goin' t' plant. Wolf trees don' let no others grow, don' ya unnerstand?"

I was still somewhat out of breath so I didn't answer. We continued to climb for a few minutes until Honey Bear changed direction again, following another game trail winding through second-growth forests of oak and poplar. Most of the trees had trunks well over a foot in diameter.

"Them's ready fer cuttin'," Honey Bear announced, pointing to a particularly healthy stand of poplar.

I gave a noncommittal "*hmmm*" as we continued to ascend. Honey Bear clearly knew the mountain, since he'd hunted these forests from the time he was a boy. I had no fear that we'd get lost in the rocks and ravines up there. Not only that, but I trusted his chivalry. In that culture at that time, a big man wouldn't hit or shoot a woman. Besides, since the old logger had approached me at the post office, everyone in Graves Mill knew where I was and who I was with. Public knowledge is like light; it prevents deeds of darkness.

Near the top of the ridge the land dipped into a small bowl, and when we emerged from the second-growth timber into a semi-open space, I caught my breath in amazement. The largest poplar tree I've ever seen stood majestically in the center of the little hollow, stretching its huge limbs toward heaven. Honey Bear was right; the gigantic monarch crowded out all lesser vegetation.

I approached the tree reverently, as if I'd found the Holy Grail. "What a tree!" I exclaimed. "What do you suppose the diameter is?"

"Dunno," he said. "Five—mebbe six feet. Mebbe more."

I ran to the huge trunk and tried to put my arms around it, stretching as hard as I could. Leaning my cheek against the rough bark, I was able to embrace only a fraction of its great girth. Honey Bear took my hand and spread his considerable hulk against the tree. Even joined together, our arms could not begin to encircle the trunk. I drew back, shaking my head. "I've never seen anything like this!" I exclaimed. "Do you think maybe it's the largest live poplar in the United States?"

"I don' think so," Honey Bear replied. "I checked her out once't. There's a bigger one, but I fergit where, though." He waved his hand at the open space around the poplar. "See, missus. That ol' tree's a wolf tree. Time to cut 'er afore the bugs an' th' lightning does the work."

"That tree must have been growing here when George Washington was a boy," I said, ignoring his last comment.

"There's some more. Oaks this time."

I followed Honey Bear perhaps a hundred yards eastward, and once again the heavy second-growth timber gave way to a semi-open space. There, in the center, stood a huge red oak, reigning over all the lesser forest denizens. Again, I caught my breath, unable to comprehend the years represented in that great tree.

"What a monster!" I exclaimed. Once again, I tried to put my arms around the giant trunk, but it was a lost cause too. My reach spanned perhaps a sixth of the tree's girth. With my arms still around the massive trunk, I stared at the almost-bare branches spreading in thick black lines against the gray sky. This tree was truly beautiful, as only an old oak tree can be. And this one was certainly old—a champion.

There were several more red oaks and one huge white oak as well. "How did these trees survive up here?" I asked.

"Th' land was too steep fer the skids to git up th' mountain," he replied.

A hundred yards farther, Honey Bear turned east on the ridgeline where the trail was fairly level and continued the logging history lesson. The West Virginia Timber Company used to pull logs out of the mountains with horse-drawn skids, he said, taking all the virgin timber and clear-cutting the mountainsides. During the 1930s when nearly the entire country was parched by drought, forest fires raged through the mountains, destroying most of the trees the timber company had been unable to harvest. Only these old sentinels had survived! I could barely imagine what the mountains must have been like when the first settlers saw them, but those big trees at the top gave me a glimpse I shall never forget.

We took a different trail down the mountain, and as we passed the remains of a chimney, Honey Bear pointed out several large walnut trees nearby.

"You can tell th' whereabouts of a cabin by th' walnuts. Folks 'ud shuck 'em, an' some of 'em 'ud sprout. An' the farmers liked havin' 'em 'round the house. See that spring there?" I noticed a trickle of water snaking its way out of a pile of rocks.

"If 'n you'd dig a bit, that spring 'ud flow outta there right pretty."

"How did people live up here?"

"These folks done worked for the Kinseys, I reckon, but they grew cabbages an' corn an' hogs. Feller could live pretty good up here in them times."

I stared at the little hollow in the side of the mountain. "But this is so *small*!" I exclaimed. "How did they manage?"

"Don' take much dirt if 'n it's good," the logger replied. "An' if a body knows what t'do."

Farther down, we came upon traces of the logging railroad, one of four that in 1922 had pushed their way into the hollows and lower slopes of Jones Mountain. We followed the railbed down to the narrow meadow on the "other half of the Kinsey place." Honey Bear led the way to a stable that had been used to house the draft horses that pulled the logging skids. A few pieces of heavy tack still hung on nails. I was intrigued with the history this picturesque weather-beaten barn had witnessed.

I would have lingered, but Honey Bear was anxious to get on with talking business while we cut across the meadow to the pickup. He explained that bulldozers could dig trails up the mountainside and then diesel-powered skidders with cables and winches could harvest the giant trees.

"Nobody ain't a-goin' to go chasing up this mountain into them little hollers and see 'em," Honey Bear said. "An' they's not a-goin' t'live forever. Might's well get some good money outta them trunks while the gittin's good. An' there's a right smart amount of good money in them logs if'n they's not holler."

I stared up at the steep mountainside, imagining the damage heavy equipment would wreak on the slopes. It seemed blasphemous. "Lord," I prayed silently, "please help me make the right decision." I already knew the answer, but I dreaded the consequences. *The money is tempting. But where is your treasure?* I asked myself.

Back at the cottage, I thanked the old logger for his time and trouble, then told him I would not sell the trees. Honey Bear was furious, calling me some nasty names. I was sure I had made the right decision, but I had definitely made an enemy. In fact, I'd made an enemy of the entire clan. Somehow, they felt those trees—and the money they represented—should have been theirs by some unde-fined right. But the majesty of those huge, ancient trees hidden up on the mountain would stir my heart with awe for months to come.

When I told Charles about my day with Honey Bear, he said that if I didn't take care, I could be the victim of some timber rustling—loggers sneaking into my forest, cutting the best trees, and leaving the debris behind. Not only that, Charles warned me that even though I'd posted the land with "No Trespassing" signs, I wouldn't be safe alone in my valley; the mountain would be full of hunters, and not all of them would be legally licensed. He advised me to lease the land to the Wolftown Hunt Club in exchange for their help with patrol-ling the territory.

It wasn't long before I began to understand what he meant. One late autumn afternoon I was walking in the Kinsey Valley near my garden when suddenly two hunters appeared out of a very thick early morning fog. Even in the mist, I could see they were city men wearing expensive sportsmen's gear.

"What are you doing here?" I asked, taken by surprise.

"We're hunting. Can't you see?" the taller stranger replied, pointing with one hand to the rifle he carried in the other. "Unfortunately, we're lost. We don't know where we left our truck, and we don't know exactly how to find the road."

"Do you know that this is my property?"

"It is? We don't really know where we are because we're from Maryland. But we were told all the land up here was open to hunting, and we want to bag a bear. I think we came across from over there." He pointed toward my godfather's side of the Kinsey place.

"Who told you that all the land is open to hunting?"

"Why, some big guy—I think they call him Honey Bear. He was hauling logs just up the road—wherever it is. Before the fog settled in."

"Don't you think it would be dangerous to shoot when you can't see twenty yards in front of you? What if you hit a cow? Or me, for that matter? You can't even see the trees from here; the fog is too thick in this valley."

The men looked sheepish. "Never thought of that, lady. Are there cows up here?"

"Yes, sir. There are cows. And even people, as you can see."

The men looked even more sheepish than before. "Ma'am, could you please help us find our truck? Maybe we should just go on home."

I took the hunters to the cottage, and from there, they were able to find their way back to their vehicle. *I'd better take Charles's advice and call the Wolftown Hunt Club. They might be able to help patrol my seven hundred acres.* God had provided a way, and it was wise to accept His provision.

I called the number Charles gave me, and a day or two later I met Milford Shifflett and Bob Yowell, two members of the club. They were good country stock, laconic but obviously pleased with my offer. The club would have exclusive hunting rights, watch for trespassers, and keep an eye on the timber, too. We quickly drew up a contract.

I was glad when it was done, but the arrangement increased the enmity between me and Honey Bear, his family, and the loggers who worked for their company. One day I was walking along the road just above the mountain farm and happened to see some of Honey Bear's men driving a truck full of logs down the mountain. One of the men shook his fist at me.

"Old witch!" he shouted.

I bit my lip, smiled, and waved back, telling myself, *Turn the other cheek.*

Though I knew there were risks, that spring I continued with the preservation plan with Lyt Wood's help. Trees were Lyt's passion, and he enthusiastically began helping me survey and map out an area suitable for permanent preservation.

The land was very steep, riddled with caves and crags frequented by bears and rattlesnakes, so the work always had an edge of excitement and danger. When I wasn't preparing for a Bible study, I was out on the mountain with Lyt. Charles's joints couldn't take that kind of climbing, but he was fascinated and pleased with the project. He told us that at the top of the valley we'd find caves where Hessian deserters from the Revolutionary army had once hidden.

"They hollered out them chestnut logs," Charles said, "an' put 'em full o' leaves to keep warm. You might find some o' them logs yet."

Lyt and I looked but never did find any logs, although Scootie Lillard told me that he had found them not many years before. No doubt by the time Lyt and I explored those cliffs, the logs had become part of the forest floor.

The time spent in the mountains learning the terrain and admiring the trees and the wildlife was almost idyllic, but troubles began almost at once. First, the county attorney called me, wanting to know what I was doing. Of course, gossip had traveled down to the town of Madison, and the newest Light project struck the townspeople as crazy at best and illegal at worst. Easements hadn't been done in the Virginia country areas then, and the attorney thought I might be doing something irregular, maybe even communist, or possibly socialist. I tried to explain, but he went off to research the matter on his own. I was mortified! No one had ever dared to question either my wisdom or political leanings before!

Some of the tension was eased when Anne Carson came to visit me for a few days. Anne, whose beautiful liturgical dancing had inspired me the first time I saw it, loved the out-of-doors and horseback riding. When she heard about Jay and O'Jay, she made a date to come to Graves Mill with her black Lab, Titelus.

We were like two teenagers, giggling and talking until late at night. Titelus and Tallis played happily together, and the horses seemed to like Anne.

One afternoon, we saddled Jay and O'Jay for a ride, even though a storm was threatening from the other side of Bear Church Rock. We rode past the post office, past Rapidan Ranch, and into the wilderness at the edge of the national park. However, as the skies darkened, I could feel O'Jay becoming tense, and I saw that Tallis was uneasy too. He tried a number of times to get under the horses, a sure sign he smelled a thunderstorm. I decided we needed to head back home. Fortunately, we had left Titelus back at the cottage.

"We'd best head home. There's a storm coming! See that black sky over Jones Mountain?"

"You're right. I guess we'd better turn back," Anne said, wheeling Jay around toward Graves Mill.

Jay and O'Jay wanted to gallop to the paddock, but Anne and I reined them in as much as we could. We were concentrating on controlling the horses and keeping an eye on Tallis. When we neared the post office and Mr. Mollé's place, Anne happened to glance up at the cliff overhanging the valley.

"You never told me about that!" she exclaimed.

"Never told you about what?" I asked, trying to keep O'Jay at a trot.

"About that cross on the mountain."

"Huh? Cross on the mountain? What cross?"

"That one!" she almost shouted, holding tightly to Jay's reins with one hand and pointing with the other.

I looked up and nearly fell off O'Jay. There on the cliff, near the top, was a huge rock outcropping, and in the center of it was a big, black cross. A cross! *When had that happened? What did it mean?*

"If you have any doubts about whether God wants you in Graves Mill, look at that cross!" Anne's blue eyes were wide as saucers, and I'm sure mine were too.

We reached the cottage before the storm broke. We even had time to brush down the horses and put the saddles away before the first raindrops fell. The storm passed quickly, and as soon as the thunder subsided, I called Charles. I couldn't wait to ask him if he'd ever seen the cross on the mountainside. No, he'd never noticed it, nor had anyone else I talked to. When did it appear? I don't know, although we guessed that during that summer small trees and brush grew out of the rock crevasses, which from a distance appeared to be a cross slashed in the rocks. After that, several hikers climbed up to investigate, and it was confirmed that no human hand had put it there on the mountainside.

It was fortuitous that Anne had seen the cross when she did, for it wasn't long before serious trouble clouded the horizons and I needed something to remind me that God was in charge of that valley.

CHAPTER 13

THUNDER ON THE MOUNTAIN

In every culture good and evil combine and recombine
in so many ways that even agricultural experts
lose track of all the new hybrids.

CORNELIUS PLANTINGA JR.

WHEN I ARRIVED AT the post office one fall morning shortly after I'd signed the contract with the hunt club, the little building was buzzing with excitement.

"Ranger done kilt a huntin' dog," Charles announced to me before I even had a chance to greet anyone. "Hume's a-gittin' folks t'gether t'go up to th' park."

"Why? What happened?"

"The dogs were chasing a bear up near the park line," Ruth explained. "The bear went into the park, a dog followed, and the ranger shot it."

The crowd in the post office erupted into loud exclamations that the ranger "oughta be shot hisself!" When I scurried off toward the cottage, the men were organizing a visit to park headquarters. They were very angry, and the atmosphere was as threatening as black clouds rolling over the ridge. These were good men, good citizens, but it was an unwritten law here that hunting dogs were valuable and were to be respected.

Because we were very close to Shenandoah National Park, it wasn't unusual for dog packs to lead hunters across the park boundaries when they were chasing a black bear. In this incident the offending ranger was a young man, apparently new to the territory, and when he saw the hunt encroaching on lands he was commissioned to guard, he shot the dog.

I had not been back at the cottage very long when the telephone rang. It was the superintendent at the park headquarters.

"You know there's trouble in Graves Mill?"

"I just heard about it," I replied.

The superintendent said that it was potentially dangerous for the ranger. "He's already gone. We've sent him out west for his safety. The ranger was acting within the law, of course, but Madison County folks aren't going to accept that argument. We've had some threatening calls from the local hunters. Since you've been working on the easement with us, you may be at risk yourself, being in Graves Mill and at the very center of the trouble."

According to the reports I had heard, a delegation—it was more like a mob—appeared at park headquarters demanding to see the ranger. When they learned that he was no longer there, it made them even angrier, though the officials assured them that the ranger would be dealt with "appropriately." The men were frustrated because there seemed no way to avenge the dog's death; their clenched fists had nowhere to land.

Deputy Sheriff Hume Lillard, Scootie's father, knew that I was dealing with the national park for the scenic easement. He had voiced his disapproval one day when I ran into him at the post office, saying I should have nothing to do with the park. Now his sentiments went beyond disapproval to real anger and alarm. Pam called to warn me that Hume had drawn up a petition against the easement and was taking it from house to house for signatures. "Everybody in Graves Mill is signing it," she said. "You'd better stop that easement. The community here will never stand for it."

Park headquarters probably heard about the petition even before I did, so they put the rangers responsible for our section on high alert, knowing that relations between them and the locals was like a lit piece of dynamite with a short fuse.

I was pacing and praying in the cottage when the phone rang again. The park superintendent was calling back.

"Are you still planning to go through with the easement?"

What should I do? I could lose everything I'd worked toward in the Bible study. I would probably lose any friends I had in Graves Mill. I'd be isolated. Was an easement on the mountain worth all this trouble? No, but somehow I knew I had to do this for the Lord. I would trust Him for the outcome.

"Of course I will carry it through," I replied, surprised that I could find my voice.

When I mentioned the petition, the superintendent said, "Yes, we know. That's why I called you. According to our information, the deputy sheriff is outside the law because he's carrying that document from house to house in uniform and wearing a gun. He could be accused of intimidation if in fact that's what he's doing. Do you know what's in that petition?"

"I'm not sure what it says, exactly, except that it's against the easement."

There was a long pause at the other end. "But you intend to continue anyway?"

"Yes," I said, hoping my voice wasn't trembling as much as my knees. "I understand why they're doing this. I understand—at least a little—why they feel as they do. And I'm sorry about the hurt and anger, but I must honor this commitment."

"I will make sure there are a couple of extra rangers in your area. They'll stop by to introduce themselves tomorrow. If you have trouble, call them. Get your will in order. And *don't* set foot on that mountain farm of yours alone!"

I looked at Tallis. We'd miss our afternoon excursions, but the man was right; it wouldn't be prudent to go alone to a place where a stray bullet could just "happen" to put an end to our walk in the woods.

The next day two rangers stopped at the cottage. Although I wondered if their appearance in the community might be like waving a red flag in front of an angry bull, I was glad to see them. They didn't seem particularly anxious, and their calm demeanor gave me comfort and courage. I did call my lawyer, who was incredulous, probably thinking, *What will this woman get herself into next?* He assured me that my affairs were in order.

At the post office, people were still civil to me, but the atmosphere was glacial. Rather than the usual warm greeting, I was met with a curt, "Howdy, ma'am." It wasn't difficult to deduce that the locals considered me stubborn, crazy, and a traitor to them and to their valley. I was certain I was doing what God had called me to do, although I did wonder if He'd ever bring me through this storm on the mountain.

The amazing thing was that about half the people continued to come to the Bible study on Thursday evenings. Of course, it was one way of "keeping an eye on that woman's doings," but I didn't know that. It was also true that the participants had a genuine interest in the gospel and a yearning for community. Our evening gatherings touched and soothed that longing. As for me, I was learning the practical side of forgiveness and "turning the other cheek." Kindness and love gave me a chance to win people over to understanding my hopes for the mountain.

But love wasn't easy, and I was scared most of the time.

Despite my fear, I was determined not to flee the valley a second time. I kept my .44 on the bedpost, just in case "something happened" when I was at the cottage, and I regularly held target practice in the backyard so everyone would know I could shoot straight. I didn't have time to leave the valley, and I didn't want to die a violent death. I had too many projects to finish.

While all this was going on, hunting season was already midcourse when Milford Shifflett came with several men from the Wolftown Hunt Club, bringing me a list of approved members' names. I liked Milford. He was a rather small, wiry man, his weather-beaten face always ready to break into a wry grin. He was also efficient and innovative. Not only did he have a list, he handed me printed permits the size of a business card.

"Now Missy, if'n ye'd fill out one card fer each one o' us, we'd each have a pass, see, an' nobody but those as has a card's t'be in them woods."

I copied a name onto each of the cards, then signed and dated them. As we shook hands all around, the other two men looked at me with grudging respect. I could tell from their expressions that they were surprised that I would support hunting, considering the rumors they'd heard.

I had lived long enough among farmers eking out a living at the edge of the park to understand that hunting was essential for healthy bear and deer populations. Selective hunting thinned out the wildlife for the benefit of everyone. When nature was in balance, it actually prevented disease and famine. Supporting these men who understood the land was the wisest stewardship I knew.

The Bible study group met at the cottage to celebrate Christmas. I was at the piano in the back corner playing Christmas carols when

Diane Rhodes tapped me on the shoulder. When I turned around, I couldn't believe what I saw—the room was full of hunters, perhaps twenty-five of them! They had come to say thank-you and to wish us a merry Christmas. I had made some enemies in the community. But if I had made enemies, the Lord had provided an army of friends. In fact, there was barely room for them to stand in the cottage, but we hurried to pour eggnog for them all (somehow, there was enough!), and when I went to bed that night, I knew it was indeed a very merry Christmas.

Just before hunting season the following year, the Wolftown Hunt Club had a woodcutting day when all the men showed up to cut, split, and stack my winter's wood supply. Thanks to our leasing agreement, I found myself a respected part of the community as I never could have been otherwise. God brings good out of evil; He can even redeem our mistakes for the good of His Kingdom. If Honey Bear hadn't given me a firsthand look at the sentinels guarding the top of the mountain, I would never have come to know and love the Shiffletts, the Yowells, and many of the hunters who traversed my half of the Kinsey place in pursuit of bear, deer, and wild turkeys.

The deputy sheriff delivered the petition to me, but since it had no legal force, I read it, put it away in a file, and continued working with Lyt Wood on plans for the easement boundaries. We kept a close watch for timber rustling but never saw even a sign of trespassing.

CHAPTER 14

"BLESSED ARE YOU POOR . . ."

*A life is a definite range of activities and responses. The spiritually
born exhibit a life deriving from an invisible spiritual reality
and its powers. In natural terms one cannot explain what is
happening with them. . . . But just as with the invisible wind
and its effects, we recognize the presence of God's Kingdom
in people by its effects in and around them.*

DALLAS WILLARD

IF JOE KITTS HADN'T TOLD me the Lord was calling me back to Graves
Mill, I would never have had the courage to return. Even with that
assurance, the days ahead weren't easy. My work with the park and
plans for the easement were only one problem; opinions in the valley
were still divided as to whether a woman should be leading a Bible
study, let alone teaching men, even as a missionary. The attendance
at the Bible study remained quite static. The Lillards never did return
to our meetings, but Charles, Mr. Mollé, Skip, Pam, and Rich came
faithfully. C. K. and Kathleen Rhodes were there too, with occasional visits from their daughters, Suzy and Diane, when they were
available. Diane was at college now, and Suzy was a busy teenager.
Skip, Pam, and Rich showed up just about every week, while Dolly's
attendance became more sporadic, although she frequently stopped
by the cottage for coffee. After Graves Chapel closed in 1969, Dolly

had joined the Baptist church in Wolftown, which had become her spiritual community.

Several others eventually joined us. Ron and Patti Bunce became part of the fellowship when Suzy Rhodes began dating their son Steven. Patti invited Jean Passierb, a friend and colleague in the Madison County schools, to come. Rich may have invited Earl the Pearl (as we called him) because he arrived soon after he took the farm manager's position at Rapidan Ranch, a spread up beyond the post office and adjacent to the national park. Earl, a very earnest young man, had just graduated from agricultural college.

Patti, Ron, and Jean lived several miles downriver from most of us. The Bunces came from charismatic backgrounds, and Jean was a Roman Catholic and not "country folk," which made the discussions lively. Patti began bringing her Autoharp and would lead us in praise and worship before we dug into God's Word. Her passionate love for Jesus inspired me to prepare more diligently. The Scriptures came alive for me in a deeper way than ever before. The Lord seemed to be present in my little study as I worked. At times, I'd look out the window at the old church and schoolhouse, thinking I would catch a glimpse of Him rounding a corner.

I attempted to overcome my natural shyness and began to reach out to more of the local people, spending more time in the village of Wolftown, about six miles downriver. It was scarcely more than a fork in the road with two stores, but it did have three churches: Methodist, Baptist, and Pentecostal. The stores were old-fashioned general stores and were often a welcome alternative to a trip into the town of Madison. In the winter, the older men gathered around the wood-burning stoves to read the papers, tell stories, and exchange news. I could buy nails, boots, canned goods, and work socks, and even leave my dry cleaning for pickup at the general store. Gradually, I came to know more about the local people and their stories.

As in Graves Mill, many of the families had been there for generations—if not in Wolftown itself, then in the surrounding countryside. There were certainly economic differences between households that caused social barriers, but even more apparent was the line between those whose families had been there for generations and the newly arrived like myself. Rich, Pam, and Mr. Mollé were among these latecomers, and so were most of the residents in the development close to the wilderness area appropriately named Lost Valley. Most of them were seasonal residents, and it was several years before I came to know many of them, but because of Pam's food co-op, I did meet some of the back-to-nature transplants.

Pam usually picked up the Wolftown–Graves Mill co-op bulk orders for both of us, but sometimes she would ask me to help distribute orders throughout the valley. One day she asked me to deliver flour, beans, cheese, nuts, and brown rice to a "good earth" family living in an old house back in a hollow near Wolftown.

In the sixties and seventies, people were leaving cities and suburbs and flocking to the country to escape alienation, the breakdown of communities, and the destruction of the environment, hoping to find the "something" that was missing from their lives. This was one such family.

When I arrived at their address, I picked my way among the young cabbages in a large vegetable garden that took up nearly the entire front yard, sending chickens clucking and scurrying in all directions. I balanced bags of flour, beans, and oatmeal and a big slab of cheddar precariously in my arms so that I could knock on the weather-beaten front door. A petite, dark-haired woman in jeans opened it and ushered me into a country kitchen where a big wood range dominated the space. I deposited my armload of food essentials on a crude wooden counter. The woman thanked me, smiled, and motioned for me to sit at the oilcloth-draped kitchen table.

"The bread is almost finished rising," she said. It was obvious she wanted to talk. "Our parents don't understand why we're here. They want us to come back to the 'real world.' But it's not the real world, you know. It's all appearances and consumption, a rat race run by the military-industrial establishment."

Between peeks at the bread dough, she told me that both she and her husband had college degrees, but they had known Pam and Rich and admired their determination to live an "essential life like Thoreau." When they had visited the Quemieres, they'd found this old vacant farmhouse and had immediately decided to rent it and move to the mountains.

"We want something better for our children," she said, looking wistfully out the window at the neighboring mountain range. I nodded.

Just then her baby cried and my hostess got up to tend him. *She's clearly well-educated,* I thought, *but is she prepared for this kind of life?* I looked around at the kitchen. I recognized the washboard and guessed that the laundry tubs were outside in a lean-to. The old farmhouse's frame seemed sturdy enough, but even my amateur eye could see that when winter came, every gust blowing off the mountains would roar through the gaps around the windows. I was certain there was no insulation in the walls—that would have been unusual in an old farmhouse—and I guessed that those cold winds would find their way into the crawl space under the house and blow up between the old floorboards. I thought of what Honey Bear had said about the generations who'd lived in mountain cabins. In those times long ago, farmers didn't have or expect to have as many things as we do now. *This is a summer's adventure for them.* A few minutes later when the baby was quiet again, the woman returned to the kitchen.

She checked the dough once more, and seeing that it had finished rising, she pulled out a big breadboard, slapped it over the oilcloth, and began to knead small handfuls of whole wheat flour into the dough. "I've even learned to make whole wheat pie crust," she said proudly. "I've learned so much . . ."

Her husband worked on one of the local farms. "It's very commercial," she said with disdain, "but it does bring in some money and we need that—for beans and rice and flour and cloth to make clothes," she explained.

I invited her to our Bible study, but she merely stared blankly at me. "We're not into religion," she replied flatly.

A little voice in the back of my mind whispered, *Your whole way of life is an attempt at religion, dear heart.* But I didn't say anything to her. Perhaps I should have tried to help her understand. Could I have touched her heart? I don't know. I left shortly after that, and as I climbed into my pickup and drove down the rutted track, I said softly to no one in particular, "They want something real. If they only knew they're searching for something only God can give them! If they only knew they're trying to find it through their own efforts. It won't work. It just won't work. If they would just come up to Graves Mill and learn country ways from Charles and the old-timers, they might have a chance, but they're trying to do it alone. It just won't work, not on any level, spiritual or agricultural."

It didn't work. Pam told me that winter that when the winds came howling down the mountains, the gusts blew through the chinks in that little house just as I knew they would, and the young woman and her baby became ill. Finally in desperation, the family left the valley to rejoin her parents in the city. Pam never mentioned them again. I felt a sinking sense of failure and loss. Could I have reached them somehow? What could I have done? Perhaps nothing.

Becoming a part of a community takes effort, sympathy, purpose, and love. I had certainly been learning how true that was. Would that family have wanted to embrace this world in the mountains?

Would they have come to treasure the people for their idiosyncrasies and stubborn endurance? I don't know. Graves Mill was no longer a viable old-fashioned community. The economic links were broken and the connections between households were very fragile at best. Those factors made being an outsider challenging. For me, the family's exit strengthened my resolve to reach out even more.

Initially, I tried making rounds on horseback. This had the double advantage of giving O'Jay a run in the early mornings and letting me get a good look at what the farmers were doing in their fields. However, O'Jay scared babies and small children—especially Tilah. O'Jay had a fiery disposition and didn't stand still very well.

One day on my way home from a run up toward the national park, I looked across the river and saw that Pam was hanging out laundry. I turned O'Jay's nose to the river ford and rode down the dusty farm track to see my friend.

She was startled, but glad to see me. Tilah, who was playing beside her, took one look at the horse and began to wail. O'Jay bolted toward the clothesline, and I managed to duck just in time. I reined in the horse, apologized profusely, and prayed a quick thank-you to the Lord that He spared me from being decapitated. From that time on, I decided that I would use the pickup for parish visits. It was fine to dream about being an old-time circuit-riding preacher; it was another thing to avoid death by clothesline or meeting one of Honey Bear's big logging rigs barreling down the narrow road. As Nehemiah might have put it, the Lord's hand was with me.

Pam, Rich, the "good earth" contingent, and the Graves Mill farmers were not the only residents up there in the mountains. There were renters and squatters, too. Jimmy Leighton Johnson and his wife lived in a shack perched in a little niche in the ridge several miles down the road, downriver, next to the McDanolds's farm. Jimmy was black, courtly, and well spoken. He had been raised by the Deales, a white family. I learned that he could play the piano and that he'd had a hard life, working for a pittance wherever he could. One thing was clear: Jimmy didn't really fit into either the white or the black world.

Big Jim McDaniel lived in the other direction, up toward Thoroughfare Mountain at the edge of the national park and the Virginia Game Commission lands. He and his neighbor were mountain-bred. The first time I saw Big Jim, I was still living at Luxmont but had come out in my Jeep to explore the hollows. Big Jim was sitting on his porch with his dog beside him, a rifle across his knees. I drove past as quickly as I could without running off the road.

I finally met him before my first winter in Graves Mill. It was nearly December, and the little woodpile I'd inherited with the cottage had quickly disappeared in the cavernous fireplace until only four or five big hunks of sycamore were left. I tried to split one with my axe, but the wood's tight grain only made the blade bounce off the surface. Thankfully, I had purchased a good Stihl chain saw, so trembling with apprehension, I got the thing running.

As I prepared to attack one of the three-foot-wide sycamore rounds, I heard a noise behind me. Three men were lined up on my porch steps like buzzards on a limb, tittering with amusement—Mr. Mollé, Charles, and Big Jim. I was deeply humiliated. None of them offered to help me. Between gales of laughter, they told me who to call to deliver wood. I was distressed, but stoic. I looked at them and thought, *I'm glad you find this amusing. If I have to be the butt of a joke, okay. But I do hope it helps build the Kingdom!* When they finally stopped laughing, they headed toward the post office.

My comedic situation turned into a mutual blessing for me and Big Jim. Once he had seen my ineptitude with a chain saw, Big Jim made a point to stop by the cottage once a day to see if I had any odd jobs for him to do. I paid him a little more than minimum wage—five dollars an hour in those days—which he happily accepted. He needed the money as well as the encouragement that doing something for others brings to the soul. Whenever I found a fallen tree on the mountain farm, Big Jim would cut it into firewood for me. Thanks to him, I had a pile of locust logs to last the winter. He also tuned up my lawnmower and changed the oil in my truck. I could do most of the things Big Jim did, but he did them much more skillfully, so I was glad for his assistance.

As we got to know each other, it became apparent that Big Jim and his nearest neighbor were longtime adversaries. Like Jim's, the neighbor's house was close to the edge of the wilderness. It had so many cracks in the siding and around the windows that I was quite sure on cold days that the old man who lived inside had to be shivering like a patient with ague. Big Jim's shack, just a short way up the road, was more spacious, with a kitchen lean-to, a couple of bedrooms, and even a dining room. Jim was very proud of it, especially because it was luxurious compared to his enemy's.

I was thrilled when Big Jim joined the Bible study. Of course, his neighbor would have nothing to do with us—I surmised he had an allergy to church. I did invite the old mountaineer when I saw him at the Wolftown general store, but he merely grunted and turned away. People said that the old man was partial to moonshine. Some of the others in the Bible study and I did what we could to help the old mountaineer, but given his habits and Big Jim's animosity toward him, that wasn't easy.

I continued to think I knew a lot more than the valley folks did; after all, I was more sophisticated than they were. But I was slowly accepting a hard truth: I had been rich but now I wasn't, and one of my challenges was learning to accept my "place" in this culture. When I had been the "lady of Luxmont," everyone deferred to me. In the mountains, however, I discovered I couldn't expect the deference a big plantation owner expects. While there was a certain chivalric code in Graves Mill, that didn't mean that women were exempt from doing rough work. Big Jim was one of my best teachers.

Christian hospitality in this particular social setting was a conundrum for me. I had learned early on in my own family that if someone comes to your door at mealtime, he or she is to be invited in, given a place at the table, and included in whatever festivities are planned. I had always attempted to hold to that rule, and because Jesus said we were to include the poor, I had always tried to include, even at Luxmont parties, those who could not return the hospitality. Dan, Mary Helen, and I ate our noon meals together, though at first that had required some insistence on my part. The couple was initially afraid and uneasy, being accustomed to segregated dining, but it wasn't long before all three of us enjoyed exchanging news, reviewing the morning's work, or telling jokes.

In Graves Mill, visitors were a constant. Generally, if they arrived at mealtime and you asked them if they wanted to join you at the table, they'd politely refuse. "Oh no, thanks. I didn't mean to interrupt you-all's dinner. I just needed to ask you 'bout . . ."

But not Big Jim. He drove up and down the road several times a day keeping an eye on all the houses. As I soon learned, he had an uncanny ability of knowing when someone had guests for dinner. He'd knock on the door, and instead of apologizing for the interruption, he'd come in, see the table with food, and say, "Don't mind if I do," proceeding to eat mounds of whatever was offered. If a second helping wasn't immediately forthcoming, he would ask for it. When Big Jim was there, I was always worried that I would run out of food for the rest of my guests. He'd gulp down masses of my best gourmet creations, food I thought should be savored. Big Jim treated crème brûlée as if it were mashed potatoes. It took all my patience and self-control to keep a smile on my face each time he "invited" himself to dinner. He would give me a nearly toothless grin in appreciation; those empty gums with two yellowed canine teeth weren't exactly pretty. Being hospitable to Jim while attempting to remember that I was doing it "as unto the Lord" deepened my prayer life exponentially. I was learning how impossible it is to love others without a lot of help from the Holy Spirit.

Dolly was another drop-in visitor at dinnertime. She could see my driveway from her kitchen window, and if she noticed an unfamiliar car, she'd be at my door just when we were ready to bless the food. If I invited friends for dinner, I could be almost certain I'd have at least two extra guests at my table. Dolly and Big Jim would entertain themselves and my guests with anecdotes of valley history. I found myself waiting on everyone there, silent and resentful, unable to enjoy any intimate conversation with friends during dinner or even after. There were times when I would mutter a prayer in the kitchen, "Lord, couldn't I—just once—enjoy my friends from outside the valley myself?"

But as time passed, I noticed Big Jim was looking neater than when we first met; on most days he was clean shaven. His mouth still looked awful, but he stood up straighter and looked people in the eye when he talked. *You're working in Big Jim's life in spite of me, Lord. Thank You for using even my reluctant generosity.* I was beginning to love these people I had struggled to accept. When I loved them, I found I loved my Lord even more.

One evening as my friend Heidi and her husband, Tom, were saying good-bye after dinner, she remarked, "We had a wonderful time, Jeannie. Thanks so much for dinner and the fun. Of course, we didn't get to talk to you, but we certainly enjoyed being part of your life here. There's such a nice atmosphere in your house. We love being here."

The Lord has interesting ways of sanctifying us. My regular

drop-in guests were forcing me to learn patience and forbearance, but most of all, they were teaching me something about love. I was no match for their canny intelligence—they could outwit me every time—but something was happening to them as well, something good and healthy.

If I have anyone to thank for demonstrating godly love not by what he said but through who he was, it is Elzie.

I didn't see Elzie often. He lived at the edge of Wolftown in a little house he shared with his mentally challenged sister, Polly. Elzie had been accidentally shot when he was a teenager, so he walked with a pronounced limp. He seemed bright, but he'd never learned to read. When I came to Graves Mill, Elzie was retired from his job in Madison, some eight miles away, but he had more than enough to do caring for Polly.

I remember the first time I paid them a visit to deliver some extra groceries. I maneuvered my pickup carefully up a deeply rutted track, climbing a fairly steep incline. After about ten feet, the terrain flattened out a bit and I saw a neat little clearing, with an outhouse at one end of it and a small, weathered shack at the other. Smoke was curling up from the chimney, so I knew someone was home.

I balanced the box of groceries on my shoulder, knocked on the door, and heard uneven footsteps inside. The door opened slowly, but when Elzie saw me, he welcomed me warmly.

"Come on in, do," he said. "The Lord bless you, the Lord bless you."

I followed him into the room, which seemed to serve as kitchen, dining room, and sitting room. I spied a wooden table, scrubbed and clean, and set the box down.

"Thank 'ee, thank 'ee," Elzie said. "Jus' have a seat there while I puts these things by." He pointed to a chair where I sat while he hobbled around, putting the flour, sugar, and potatoes away. Looking around, I marveled at how clean everything was. There was a wood-burning range, but every trace of ash or wood chip had been whisked away. The walls were carefully lined with flattened cardboard boxes, nailed between the studs to keep the drafts at bay. Every inch of the pine floor had been scrubbed until the boards were almost white. "How do you get your floor so clean?" I asked.

Elzie smiled. "Sand does good, missus."

Polly was sitting at the table too. I smiled at her and she smiled back, showing her rotten teeth. Then with the delight of a curious child, she began pulling out everything in the box I had brought. She chortled with delight at each item. For some reason, I'd been inspired to include a tiny teddy bear, and Polly grabbed it, hugging it while making little grunts of joy. Now and then, she looked at me from beneath a mop of stringy gray hair. She had unusual eyes, the irises an almost eerie gold color. I was a little afraid of Polly because from time to time her smile would suddenly turn into an angry frown for no apparent reason. Elzie seemed to understand her, though, and a word from him dispelled her glowering looks.

Every other sentence, Elzie quoted Scripture, and when I complimented him on his knowledge of Scripture, he explained that he'd memorized the Bible from hearing his mother read it to him. Indeed he had! I don't know whether he knew the entire Bible or "merely" the New Testament, but I'd never met anyone so deeply steeped in the Scriptures. He led me into the little parlor room adjoining the kitchen to show me a shiny tape recorder and cassettes the local Pentecostal church had given him. He was so proud of that recorder! He would listen to the Bible on the cassettes when he cleaned and cooked, but I don't think he really needed the tapes to remind him of the verses he loved. When I looked into his eyes, I knew he lived them. Even though Elzie's life was difficult, he was content. I could see it in his face.

"Jesus's always here," he said. "He gives all we need. He's good. He's good."

I thought about my seminary training, about my expectations for ministry. Instead of being "pastor" or "spiritual counselor" and listening sympathetically to his trials, I was learning from Elzie, treated to living Scripture.

As I negotiated the track back to the main road, I couldn't stop thinking about Elzie. "I've heard of St. Anthony living in the desert," I said to myself, "and I've heard of St. Francis, and do you know, I think I've just met one of their number."

Given the chance, would I have changed places with Elzie? No. Like most of us, I prefer to admire great sanctity in other people.

CHAPTER 15

"I WANT THAT CHANDELIER!"

A community identifies itself by an understood mutuality
of interest. But it lives and acts by the common virtues of
trust, goodwill, forbearance, self-restraint, compassion, and
forgiveness. . . . Such a community has the power—not
invariably, but as a rule—to enforce decency without litigation.

WENDELL BERRY

MAJOR PROJECTS SELDOM proceed exactly as we expect. We have our ideas, but God has His timing and often tests our determination along the path toward the consummation of an undertaking. Then, too, because we "see through a glass, darkly," the plans we think were exactly what we've been called to do turn out to be more complicated and more expansive than we ever dreamed. It was turning out that way with Graves Chapel. Back when Charles and his friends began the work, I thought opening the church was going to be a relatively simple matter of repairs and resolve. As it turned out, however, the task brought more people together than I could ever have expected and expanded our ministry far beyond any horizons I could have imagined.

That's the way God often works. What seems to be a major obstacle turns out to be a blessing if we move forward in faith. It's a one-day-at-a-time program, though. God provides for that particular day, that particular problem. When another insurmountable challenge appears, if we are willing to be patient and persevere, God will show up again in unexpected ways.

During my months in northern Virginia, away from Graves Mill, I had seen that the Holy Spirit is very much alive and active in the world. I had seen remarkable healings that medicine could not explain. I had watched lives significantly changed. One northern Virginia family I had known well as secular agnostics became on-fire Christians when they sat under John Howe's preaching. Having witnessed these things, I studied diligently, and now more than ever, the Scriptures came alive to me and grabbed my heart and mind. In Graves Mill I was certain that if I could preach and teach the Bible in simple English that everyone could understand, without jargon or theological terms, there would be a great revival in the hamlet and far beyond. I really did want to do it for Jesus! It hurt my heart to think what everyone was missing!

I had heard wonderful teachers during the charismatic movement within the Episcopal church, and it seemed to me that the local country preachers—at least those I'd heard since I'd lived in rural Virginia—focused on doctrines rather than the Word. The preachers talked about justification, inerrancy, and postmillennialism. Entire books had been written on the meaning of each of these words; they were complex theological concepts that scholars never seemed to get tired of discussing. What I didn't understand was that while the average churchgoers weren't moved by these defining doctrines, they still found comfort in their exposition. I didn't know what every preacher learns sooner or later: that no matter how clearly an argument may be stated, there will be those who "hearing, they do not hear." After all, I had been one of the deaf among them.

That fall I was convinced that if God's truth could be presented clearly, everyone would believe, people's hearts would be ignited, and their love for God would spread like wildfire through the country-side. I was sure that I could be the agent of that revival. (Even then, humility was not among my outstanding virtues!) When the Bible study reconvened, I acted on that dream and recommended that we form a nondenominational fellowship. All we needed, after all, was the Bible. Ours would be first-century Christianity, and there would be a magnificent Great Awakening. (Of course, after the revival, I'd get on with that sheep ranch.)

As keen as I was in facilitating a great move of the Spirit, Charles was more practical. He was impatient to "git that old church *open*," and this time I agreed with him. So in the very early spring of 1979, we sent Big Jim to the church to repair some of the window frames.

Big Jim seldom moved very quickly unless he was mad, so he spent quite a long time poking the floors and sills, and in the process he discovered termite damage. He quickly deduced that he needn't work any longer, threw down his tools, and appeared at my door insisting that no more could be done—the building was "ruint." I followed him back to the church, and when I saw the sill and floorboards that looked more like a sponge than good oak and pine, I agreed with him.

That's the end of it, I thought with some relief. Leading a church was a daunting prospect anyway, and the state of the building released me from my agreement. It was one thing to dream about leading a revival or a Great Awakening in the valley; it was another to figure out what to do with a country church! Besides, I had an uneasy suspicion that perhaps what I'd learned in my church and community class might be right. How could a little country church survive in the modern world? It took money and resources to support a church. We didn't have either of these. We didn't have enough people left in Graves Mill to form a "real" congregation. Maybe this was God's sign that enough was enough.

I called Charles to tell him the news. There was a grunt at the other end of the line. "I'll mosey on down there an' take a look," he said crisply.

He was there within a few minutes. He inspected the damage, then climbed into his old pickup without saying a word and roared off down the road.

I knew Charles considered Big Jim lazy and "shiffless," and I suspect he thought I was naive, and he wasn't about to see his dream vanish so quickly on the basis of our opinions. He promptly collected most of the able-bodied men in the valley, particularly the former Baptists, to inspect the building. Their verdict was completely different from Big Jim's and mine—the damage *could* be repaired. We called an exterminator to halt the chewing, and under Charles's watchful eye, the floor and several support beams were replaced or repaired. The project proceeded fairly quickly because Big Jim wasn't working alone; the other men worked alongside him. The mountain man became much more productive than when he was left to himself.

No sooner had we finished the floor repairs than Mr. Gerstein, the gentleman lawyer who had purchased most of Dolly Seekford's farm some years before, appeared one sunny afternoon. He and his wife had a chalet high up on the side of the ridge above Dolly's house. I was in the church when he arrived, sweeping out the sawdust Big Jim had left after the floor repairs. I had just decided that the only way to clean the old strips of red carpet would be to carry them outside and beat them on the grass when Mr. Gerstein walked through the chapel's side door.

He was a trim, rather stylish man with graying hair, the sort of fellow who delights in English tweeds. He had a pleasant voice and was always gracious. I was pleased to see him but also puzzled. Since he and his wife were weekenders, we seldom saw them, even in town. But here he was, obviously with something on his mind.

After a few innocuous pleasantries, he dropped his bombshell. "Did you know that I own this church?" he asked.

I was too startled to reply.

"It's this way," he explained patiently. "When I bought the farm from Dolly, I bought the reversion clause along with it."

"What on earth is a reversion clause?" I asked, completely at a loss.

Like a true lawyer, he launched into a lengthy explanation. When Dolly's forebears, the Estes family, deeded the land to the Baptist church, they inserted a clause saying that should the church ever close, the land would revert to the Estes heirs—in this case, Dolly.

"The church closed in April 1969," Mr. Gerstein declared, "and when I bought the farm, I bought the right to the chapel and its land."

"Does Dolly understand this?"

"I don't think she does," Mr. Gerstein admitted reluctantly. "It didn't matter before, but now that you're trying to open the church again, you should know that this land is the access from the road into that field." He pointed to the land immediately behind the church. "I hope that in the future I can sell a lot for a house or build there myself. So you need to stop your plans to open this church."

"I'll tell Charles and the rest of the folk what you've said," I replied slowly, still in shock.

Mr. Gerstein took a couple of steps toward the door but walked back and stood under the elaborate gas light fixture in the center of the ceiling. Looking up, he pointed emphatically with his finger. "And I want that chandelier!" he exclaimed.

When he was gone, I sat down in one of the old pews for a few minutes and prayed, "Lord, what now? Is this the end of Graves Chapel? And that chandelier—it seems so wrong to take it out of this room."

I hurried down to the cottage and telephoned Dolly. She was furious.

A few minutes later, she called me back. "We're havin' a meetin'," she said tersely.

The "we" she was referring to were Charles and Deputy Sheriff Hume Lillard, the two remaining Baptist trustees of Graves Chapel, and herself, the chapel treasurer. Charles gave me a full report later. After conferring, they declared that the reversion clause in the deed was not presently effective because the church was *inactive*, not closed. Dolly was still treasurer, and she still held about six hundred dollars in the treasury.

A day or two later, near sunset, I walked to the church to pray. For the first time since I'd moved into the valley, I realized the significance of the work and the struggles and sacrifices it had cost the families to build that little church. I'd heard about the egg money the women had tithed, the "God's acre" the men planted. I had lived among them long enough to begin to understand, just a little, what that meant. The egg money could have purchased new curtains or a new bonnet. God's acre's produce could have meant a little more for a family lacking the luxuries of indoor plumbing or central heating. It might have meant a new roof for the cabin. But first they built the church, paid their portion to the circuit, and paid the preacher. Then in 1954, the money purchased cement and other materials to erect a parish hall.

Somehow, Mr. Gerstein's claim to the church brought that little world into focus for me with a clarity I'd been missing. I began to pray out loud, and as the words came out, the tears rolled down my cheeks, unheeded. In fact, I didn't know I was weeping. "Lord, I didn't want to be here. I don't see how I can do what Charles and the old-time trustees and deacons have asked me to do. I haven't the talents or the money or the time. But please, Lord, answer their needs. Honor their sacrifices. Please, Lord, use me according to Your will, but please, please, don't let them down! And Lord, somehow, help me to love Mr. Gerstein!"

Suddenly I heard a noise outside. When I realized I had been crying, I hastily dried my eyes just as Dolly walked past the window toward the front door.

Once inside, she nodded at me and walked slowly past the pews, her fingers lovingly brushing each one, as she made her way up front beside me. Neither of us said anything as we looked out over the empty seats. I guessed Dolly was remembering the Sunday mornings when the room was filled with people she had known and loved.

"We tried to keep it open," she said softly, "but the women couldn't get along. We'd just built the Sunday school rooms at the back, and they couldn't agree what color to paint them. After that, fewer and fewer people came and we couldn't pay our 'portionment to the circuit. The last pastor, he tried hard, but he was only here once every six weeks. He even said he'd come for nothin', but we didn't have enough people to keep it open. We didn't really close it down, though. We just stopped having services. Charles has always kept the yard neat and there's not a window broke, even though the church is right beside the road."

She turned and walked up and down the aisles for a minute. "I had a dream," she said, "maybe what you-all would call a vision . . ." Her voice trailed off, then she continued.

"One day, I was at home and looked down here. I used to just hate it, lookin' down here and seein' the old place dark. But one evenin' I looked down here and there was this beautiful tree in bloom. All pink, it was. And the lights were blazin' in the windows. I don't know if it was a dream . . ."

"I believe it was a vision," I said gently. "Thank you for telling me, Dolly." I hugged her. Somehow, I knew it wasn't just a dream; it was a promise.

Even though Dolly's vision encouraged me, I was still anxious about the final outcome. What would happen if Mr. Gerstein really did

claim the church? Did that mean I could start that sheep farm? Did
I have enough money to build a bridge across the Kinsey Run and to
cut a good road into the valley? Several days later, as we usually did,
Tallis and I walked up to the farm. It was a peaceful afternoon, ideal
for thinking. As we rounded the bend in the road, I smelled smoke.
There was no house close by, so the smoke wasn't coming from a
chimney, and in those hills, forest fires were always a terrifying prospect. It wasn't wise to take any chances, so I followed my nose past
my farm gate and soon spied burning bushes—and not like the one
Moses encountered in the wilderness! These shrubs were definitely
being consumed. My heart caught in my throat. Pushing on a little
farther, I saw a blond, well-built young man struggling desperately
to keep the fire from spreading.

"What are you doing?" I shouted. "Do you know what a fire can
do in these hills?"

"It's okay. Everything's under control," he said determinedly. "I'm
Paul Oesterreicher, and I was just trying to clear out some of the
brush." He explained that he was from northern Virginia and had
bought a lot across the road from the Kinsey place.

"I think we need to call the fire department," I said, trying to keep
from sounding too alarmed.

"It will be all right. Here, take a shovel." Reluctantly I took the
spade, and while we struggled to beat out sparks and dig firebreaks,
Paul told me more about himself.

"I organize teen vacation excursions. In the winter we go on ski
trips, and in the summer we go camping and hiking in the mountains. Most of the teens who participate are from the city, so it's a real
adventure for them. I purchased this land in order to set up a base
camp in the Graves Mill valley."

I introduced myself and told him that I had been asked to get
Graves Chapel open. "We have a Bible study on Thursday evenings,
and the people who come are the beginning of a congregation.

Since we're from a number of different backgrounds, we'll be a non-denominational fellowship. "

Paul had noticed the church and had hoped it might be a place where he could bring campers and hikers to worship on Sundays. "I'm so glad to meet you, even if it's not under the most ideal circumstances. I'm Catholic, but the teens in my groups come from various church backgrounds, too, so your church would be great! Would you consider being our chaplain? And when did you say the church will be open?"

I explained the most recent difficulty with Mr. Gerstein, but Paul shrugged and said, "Have faith. God won't let you down. And keep me posted. I'll bring a group of kids down here to help with the cleanup and repairs. They would love that."

Teens! From northern Virginia! The ministry of Graves Chapel had suddenly expanded exponentially in one conversation. What was God doing? Was this possible?

"Thank you," I said. "But right now we can use help with this fire. Can I call the fire department now?"

Thus began our friendship. Paul eventually came with a group to work on the chapel. Even though I had had my doubts about how much a teenage repair crew could accomplish, I was pleasantly surprised and grateful. Whenever Paul was in the area, he'd stop by to see me, sharing his frustrations about his church, his finances, and the various teenagers he led on the hiking trips through the Blue Ridge. Most of them had never been in the wilderness before. As I listened to Paul, I thought about all the things that could go wrong. *Suppose one of the teens was bitten by a rattlesnake? What would I do in that situation? What would I say to the parents?* I shook my head in amazement that this young man had the courage (or blind faith) to take responsibility for the lives of all those kids. I could never do it. I told Paul that I was glad God called him to his work, and me to mine. Though I didn't see it at the time, Paul's example was teaching me indirectly about God's marvelous protection and providence.

In the meantime, the telephones were buzzing up and down the valley. Charles stopped by the cottage every day or so to inform me about events as they unfolded. Hume Lillard, Dolly, and Charles made sure that everyone called every relative, down to their thirty-second cousin, Baptist or not, Christian or not, to tell them to come to a community meeting to show "that Mr. Gerstein" that he didn't own the chapel—never had and never would.

"We's a-goin' t' pack that ol' church fer that there meetin'," Charles exclaimed, "an' all them Estes heirs is a-comin' too."

The momentous day of the meeting finally arrived. We'd continued to work on the repairs because Dolly, Charles, and Hume were convinced that right was on their side—and all the Baptists thought so too. I laid aside my customary blue jeans and put on a dress, trying to look as dignified as possible as I walked to the old church. The yard was full of cars, and there were cars and trucks parked along the roadside. The appeal to the community and to former members had borne fruit.

My heart was thumping when I sat down in the back of the church. The room was crowded. What would happen? Would Mr. Gerstein triumph? I didn't know. I only knew that in the last few weeks, I'd learned to care, really care, what happened. I remembered Dolly's tears and her vision of lights and a blooming tree. I thought about Charles's years of silent hope, a hope that kept him mowing the churchyard even though no congregation met there during those ten years. I recalled Big Jim pausing from the repairs one day and standing in front of the old pulpit. "I accepted Jesus as m' Savior right *here*," he exclaimed, stamping his foot. "I done got baptized in th' river, too, an' ain't *nobody* a-goin' t'take m'church! Just you see!"

Mr. Gerstein was a lawyer, but the Baptists had lawyers too, and I saw them conferring with Hume, Dolly, and Charles. As I watched, the crowd grew until there were more people than seats. A number of the men leaned against the walls or sat on the windowsills. Finally the three stood up and faced the gathering. Hume and Charles motioned for everyone to be quiet. When the talking and shuffling subsided, Dolly took charge.

"The minutes say that Graves Chapel did not close," she began. "It became inactive, that's all. There's still six hundred dollars in the treasury to prove it. So Mr. Gerstein has no right to this church. The reversion clause he's talkin' about is for when the church closes. It never closed, an' Charles has kept the yard mowed."

There was a buzz, and the crowd erupted into excited commentary. Hume and Charles tried to keep order, but there were lawyers arguing, people arguing, and everybody sweating as the sun began to beat down on the old tin roof. It wasn't that warm, but the emotional temperature was quite high. As the arguments proceeded, it was clear that if Mr. Gerstein pressed his case, he would forever be Graves Mill's bad guy. He backed down.

Charles, Hume, and Dolly then asked the Baptists and the Estes heirs to approve my work in Graves Chapel. I could scarcely believe my ears when I heard, "And all in favor of giving the money in the treasury to Mrs. Light's congregation for repairs to Graves Chapel, please say aye." There was a resounding aye and not a single nay.

Looking back, I think it is doubtful that a new congregation under my leadership would have enjoyed much if any support and approval from the old-time congregation, from the Estes heirs, or from the country community if Mr. Gerstein hadn't claimed the chapel. However, faced with the prospect of losing the property or giving the old place another chance at life, they were united and hearty in their support.

Before the meeting concluded, our little band of Bible study members was given the use of Graves Chapel for ninety-nine years. We had suddenly become a congregation with a church and a treasury.

I struggled to grasp the implications of what was happening around me. Was I ready for this? Well, God seemed to think so. I'd have to trust Him. I took a deep breath. *Thank You, Lord. At least You heard my prayers that all the work and love and sacrifice the community has invested in Graves Chapel would not be lost to a legal entanglement.* It seemed God was taking me at my word too. After all, I did tell Him He could use me as He saw fit!

The meeting finally broke up. I shook hands with dozens of people I'd never seen before, smiling until my face hurt.

The next morning, I was at the chapel sweeping when Mr. Gerstein appeared in the doorway. I took a deep breath and braced myself for whatever he was about to say.

"I'm just on my way to the post office," he said, "and I thought I'd stop by. You know, in spite of what happened yesterday, I do own this building."

I choked back the words that sprang up to my throat. "The Baptists don't think that's true," I said slowly.

"It doesn't matter what they think. I have a legal right to this church."

I stared at him, unable to think of an appropriate reply that he might actually hear or accept. Besides, under the law, he was probably right.

"If I exercise my legal rights to this building and the land, I will make enemies of everyone in the valley and of all the Estes heirs, including Dolly," he continued. "I have no intention of being in that position. I want to be friendly with my neighbors here. So I will lease this church to you for a dollar a year."

I stared, openmouthed.

"You don't even need to pay me the dollar," he said with a slight smile. "I won't collect that rent. I just wanted you to know." Then he turned and was gone.

At the time, I discounted his statement, and as the months and years rolled by, I forgot all about it. However, some twenty years later, I learned that he had gone down to the courthouse and recorded his verbal agreement, without, of course, my signature. Nevertheless, from that time on, he was our loyal and faithful ally. He did not come to Bible studies or services, but he clearly supported our efforts. He was a good man, and though it meant sacrificing his road frontage and access to the fields behind the church, he wanted to be part of the community and wanted to do the right thing. There are few people in this old world whose mettle is gold of such good quality.

Once the matter of the reversion clause was cleared, there was a flurry of activity. Olga came down for our workday that spring, and Paul brought his troupe of teens. We caulked windows, cleaned floors, and beat ten years' worth of dust and dirt out of the old red carpet runners. While she was working, Olga kept everyone laughing with her funny commentaries. The local women laid out a marvelous picnic lunch under the trees. There was fried chicken, of course, and ham biscuits, pickles, and watermelon. The whole scene was so hectic, I made a lame excuse and took refuge in the cottage long enough to catch my breath. After the quiet of the hills, all of the activity was more stimulation than I could absorb without a break.

We were suddenly a recognized body of pilgrims, and with recognition comes responsibility. We quickly decided that the first order of business was to put kerosene in the fuel tank so that the old stoves could heat the chapel when the winds turned cold in November. Next we hired a local man to paint the exterior of the chapel. The old building looked quite respectable when he finished.

There was a little money left after we had taken care of these priorities, so with everyone's approval I pursued my dream of having the piano tuned before the first service. I called a piano tuner in Harrisonburg, asking if he could bring the big old upright back somewhere closer on key.

"How long you say that church was closed?"

"Ten years," I said.

The voice at the other end of the line was dismissive. "I don't think there's much point in my coming up there. It will be a waste of time and money. I'm certain the moths have eaten the felts off the hammers and the mice have finished off the strings. Mice'll sharpen their teeth on strings, you know."

Somehow, I was sure the piano was all right. I didn't know it, but my faith was growing. If the Lord God had managed to clear the way thus far, surely He wouldn't abandon us now! "Well, come and have a look," I pleaded. "If it's hopeless, we'll pay for your travel anyway."

"It's your money," he said.

When the piano tuner arrived, he reiterated his opinion that this was a useless exercise, and then he opened the piano to confirm his suspicions.

A few minutes later, he scratched his head and turned to me, incredulous. "I can't believe this! The felts are fine and not a string is damaged. I've never seen anything like this! Makes you believe in angels," he exclaimed.

"Exactly," I replied.

It would not be the last time that a small miracle at Graves Chapel would touch a stranger's heart. The piano was tuned and the piano tuner left, still muttering in amazement. I was as amazed as he was, although I'm sure he wasn't nearly as grateful.

The Bible study group was excited as we began to plan for the first service in the church. Everyone was involved with cleaning, polishing the old pews, and washing windows. Pam Quemiere brought Tilah to play on the floor while we scrubbed the windows and removed the excess putty and paint spills left by the workers. The most amazing worker was Mr. Mollé. He had continued to come to the Bible study and was very involved in the restoration of the church.

One evening when we were working, I mentioned that we needed a cross in the sanctuary. "We need a *rough* old cross," he said slowly. "Jesus' cross wasn't pretty, so we need a weathered one to remind us. I could make one out of some old barn siding."

"That's a wonderful idea," I replied, hiding my surprise that he would volunteer to do this. Not long after, Mr. Mollé appeared on the cottage porch with a five-foot-tall cross constructed from rough boards. He had skillfully notched them together and beveled the edges. We walked up to the church and drove some nails into the wall at the front to hold it in place above and behind the pulpit, Baptist fashion.

When the cleanup was almost finished, I reminded the group that we had to decide a date and time for beginning our Sunday services. *This shouldn't take long.* I was wrong. Setting the date wasn't a problem, but deciding a service time sparked several intense discussions. Most of the women thought we should worship at the traditional "holy hour" of eleven o'clock on Sunday mornings, but the men were hesitant. "I got chores t'do in the mornin's," Charles protested. "And we'd like to be here, but we're Lutherans and we go to Mt. Nebo on Sunday mornings," Kathleen Rhodes added. "We can't be here at eleven, but four o'clock would be perfect."

The men murmured their agreement. "If'n you has services at four, we'll come," the men promised. Since I was still attending services at Pastor Hall's church myself, the question of our afternoon service hour was settled. I was relieved that I didn't need to leave old friends and familiar places and that I would even have the occasional opportunity to travel to Fairfax to hear John Howe at Truro.

The men kept their word. Sometimes there'd be a tractor in the church lot on Sunday afternoons, especially during haying season. Sometimes the men in the back row were clad in well-worn work clothes. But they came.

The first service was a momentous occasion for the little congregation, and they wanted to celebrate in some special way. "Let's process with the cross from my house to the church," I suggested. We were small in number but hugely enthusiastic. In April 1979, exactly ten years after the church's last meeting had taken place, we held our first new service in Graves Chapel. Skip McDanolds carried the big cross on his shoulders as we walked from the cottage up the road to the church, singing and rejoicing. I do not remember what I said that afternoon, but I know Kathleen Rhodes played the newly tuned piano and Charles took a seat in what became his corner. There were probably no more than a dozen of us that first Sunday, but when I looked at their happy smiles, to my eyes that little band of pilgrims resembled a multitude.

CHAPTER 16

GROWING TOGETHER

God's written word is full of mystery; His word
accomplished on earth is none the less so.

JEAN-PIERRE DE CAUSSADE

THE FUROR OVER my work with Lyt Wood and the National Park
Service, and my efforts to place some of my land under easement,
had subsided somewhat by the time we began services at the chapel.
I had stopped trying to defend the project because I knew anything
I might say would fall on deaf ears. As far as Graves Mill was concerned, the Potomac Appalachian Trail was an unnecessary intru-
sion into their world. My relationship with most of the residents
remained somewhat strained. But one spring morning, the US government intruded in a way no one had anticipated.

From my kitchen window, I saw the mail truck coming upriver
that particular day, so I waited a few minutes to allow time for the
mail sacks to be exchanged before walking over to the post office.
Everyone knew that when Ruth Lillard was upset she generally had

little to say, but each one of us inside the post office could feel deep trouble in the air.

I broached the subject. "What's up?"

"The Postal Service wants to close our post office," she replied.

"That would be terrible." She turned to get my mail from the box, but when she reappeared at the grill, I saw that she was pale.

"That *is* terrible! Why would they do that? This is the center of the community."

"We're just a little place, so Charlottesville wants to cut costs. We don't bring 'em lots of revenue—we don't sell lots of stamps, and we don't have a lot of volume passing through. So they want to close us down."

"I wouldn't think Graves Mill would cost the United States Postal Service *that* much!" I said. "Besides, surely it would cost as much or more to deliver mail to every man and woman in these hollows. Something must be done, but what?"

I turned and looked around the room at the mounted deer antlers, the slightly curled black-and-white photos of the hunt, the ladder-back chairs. The place smelled faintly of pipe smoke, damp winter mackinaws, and kerosene. It was an institution, a definitive statement of who and what we were. Graves Mill was a tiny place, but we had a zip code, which was the world's admission that our community actually existed in space and time. That mattered. It signified that we had a history and we were a recognized destination.

No, the post office must not be consigned to oblivion.

Before Ruth could answer me, Charles's truck roared into the gravel apron outside, and a moment later he burst into the dim little room.

"Heard they's a-plannin' t'shut us down, th' b— . . . ," he exclaimed. I think he intended to add some colorful words to that announcement, but when Charles saw me, he bit off his sentence.

"That's what the letter says," Ruth replied.

"What can we do?" I asked again.

"You can write to the Postal Service and to your congressman and senator," she said.

"Do you have the addresses? I can do that, and I'll encourage everyone else to write too. I'll even take dictation," I exclaimed.

Ruth almost smiled. "That might help," she said and handed Charles his mail. He stomped over to the ladder-back nearest the stove and plopped himself down. He knew it wouldn't be long before Art Mollé made his way down to pick up his mail. A few minutes later, Art lumbered inside. Charles yelled the news into his neighbor's nearly deaf ears. (Art had started building wooden chairs and gift items to sell at craft shows, and over the last few months, the loud noises from saws and drills had affected his hearing.)

Pam arrived and heard what was happening, and suddenly everyone seemed to be talking at once. Each person had an opinion on what our strategy should be, but Ruth kept repeating that we all needed to write letters. As soon as I returned home, I wrote to the US Postal Service in Charlottesville as well as to our representative and senator, emphasizing how critical the Graves Mill post office was to the community. I prayed that the pleas would be effective. Others wrote letters too, though no one accepted my offer to take dictation.

While the post office drama was unfolding, Lent and Passover were fast approaching. I thought it would be a good educational experience for everyone if we celebrated Passover with a seder supper and liturgy. I had a few copies of the service and knew something about the corresponding special menu. Two weeks before Easter, I proposed celebrating Passover on Holy Thursday.

Many in the Bible study group had heard of seder suppers, but no one had ever participated in one. Those who hadn't heard of it didn't want to admit their ignorance. Everyone was curious.

"How's you a-goin' t'do this?" Charles wanted to know.

"Well," I began carefully, "I thought maybe we could borrow some folding tables and use the pews for seats."

"I reckon I can get tables from our church in Rochelle," C. K. said. "They're not doing anything on that Thursday so far's I know. Skip, could you help me go an' get 'em?"

Skip nodded and I was glad that the project was set in motion. When I mentioned the menu, Kathleen said that she would bring a plate of boiled eggs, and Pam said she'd take care of the parsley. "I'll roast a leg of lamb so we'll have the bone, and I'll also make *charoset*," I added.

The unusual combination of food items required some explanation. "The egg is a symbol of mourning. It reminds us of the Temple in Jerusalem, which is no longer standing, where no sacrifices are offered anymore. But since the egg has no beginning and no end, it is also a symbol of hope. God's grace is not dependent on the Temple sacrifices."

The faces in front of me were awestruck. "Never thought that 'bout a *egg*!" someone murmured.

"The *charoset*," I continued, "is a mixture of applesauce, cinnamon, honey, and nuts. It is to remind us of the bricks with straw the Israelites were forced to make in Egypt. And the parsley, a bitter herb, is used because their slavery was bitter in Egypt. We will dip it in salt water because life for them was often bathed in tears."

"What we doin' this fer? We ain't in Egypt!" Big Jim looked angry and frustrated.

I took a deep breath. "We do it," I began slowly, "to remind ourselves that we were once slaves to sin, but we have been set free and we're on our way to the Promised Land, just like those Jews were set free from Pharaoh."

That explanation made matters worse, because slavery was a sensitive subject. Big Jim's expression looked like a thundercloud. I tried again.

"Well, what I mean by slavery is that we want to be good but we can't really manage it, can we? We keep on doing things we know we shouldn't. That's slavery to sin. Paul talked about it in Romans chapter 7." Heads nodded and Big Jim's frown subsided.

A little voice in the back of my mind whispered that I didn't really know much about slavery. At that point, I hadn't really come to know the sons of slavery in the valley well enough to know their suffering. At Luxmont I knew Dan and Mary Helen, yes, and their family. I knew something about slavery's history in the South, but when the word came up, I most often thought of it in theological terms. It was difficult for me to grasp that slavery applies to most anything in life that holds a person in bondage—habits, places, addictions—and that it's lived out in our attitudes and in our communal relationships. We see through a glass, darkly, as the Scriptures say.

During my weekly trip to town for groceries, I made copies of the service for everyone, and the following week we chose readers for the various parts. On Thursday morning, Kathleen called to tell me that the folding tables had been delivered to the church. I set out with clean rags, a pail of water, and a set of my white tablecloths. The men had set up the tables in a line under the windows looking out on the road. The spring sunshine streamed into the room, reflecting off the white walls and tin ceiling. *Peace in the valley*, I thought as I approached an old table the Baptists had used to hold the Communion trays and offering plates. It was beneath the looming lectern where countless Baptist sermons had sounded forth.

After I washed off the table, I threw a white cloth over it to make it appear more like an altar and also to hide a drawer knob. The drawer held the Sunday school record books, a pair of string gloves someone had left behind, some pencil stubs, and a pair of rusty scissors, but because I didn't know what to do with these things, I'd left them undisturbed. I set out a wine goblet and candles.

I hadn't troubled to tell everyone that there would be four cups of wine consumed during the service. It never occurred to me that this might present a problem. In the world from which I'd come, good wine, like good bread, was almost a staple. I set out tiny bathroom-sized Dixie cups for the wine along with plastic forks, spoons, and eight-ounce cups for water as well as a copy of the service for each participant. C. K. and Rich were going to help me lead the festivities, and I had made extra copies in case we needed them. I had found matzo at the international foods store in Charlottesville. I placed them beside the candles and stepped back to survey the scene. The white tablecloths looked beautifully pure, and the morning light brushed the piano's old oak case with a honeyed kindness.

Why was I doing this? Mostly, it was an intellectual exercise. I enjoyed making the connections between the Passover service and modern Communion practices. I was discovering that I loved to teach, and when it came right down to it, my motive was nothing more than the joy of knowing the symbolism and sharing that knowledge. However, somehow I sensed that this little band of souls would eventually become a local manifestation of the church and that sharing this background might help us find our way toward Easter, toward the meaning of Resurrection, and the Eucharist. Or so I hoped.

That evening about a dozen of the Bible study members gathered around the white linen, and I took my place at the little table under the pulpit. As I looked at each one of them, I silently thanked God for bringing us all together. There were C. K. and Kathleen, who were carrying the weight of the old home place, a farm that had been handed down for generations. At the end of the twentieth century, it no longer produced a living for their family so C. K. worked in Charlottesville, threading his way out of the valley Monday through

Friday. Pam and Rich were there, refugees from the world that supported C. K., two souls looking for a lost time that had offered simplicity and wholeness. They didn't realize that C. K.'s life was a warning that such a time was truly lost and they would never find it. There was Charles, in Graves Mill all his life, but ill at ease with a world in which the old general stores were closing in favor of supermarkets. And Big Jim, who was never at home anywhere because the clans had dispersed when the national park took their lands. And there was Skip. His family's farm had been squeezed out of existence when the shopping centers took over northern Virginia. Like me, he was a transplant, and though he was clearly a member of the community, he would always be an outsider because he didn't grow up in the shadow of old Jones Mountain. Mr. Mollé was another outsider.

The economic ties that had held people together when the old church was built were gone. The culture was gone. All we had in common that evening was a little church in the valley, our studies in the Scriptures, and a hope that somehow these two things would make a difference.

We were all, in our different ways and from our different contexts, hoping for the Promised Land. I lifted a piece of matzo and broke it. "This is the bread of affliction, which our ancestors ate in the land of Egypt," I began. "All who are hungry, come and eat. All who are needy, come and celebrate Passover with us. Now we celebrate it here. Next year, may we celebrate Passover in Jerusalem. Now we are slaves. Next year may we be truly free."

Pam asked the first question from the script, "Why is this night different from all other nights?" C. K. answered, "Once we were slaves in Egypt, but the Lord in His goodness and mercy brought us out of that land with a mighty hand and an outstretched arm."

So we told one another the story of that first Passover and we drank the tiny cups of wine and I flourished the lamb bone explaining that a Lamb had died that we might live. We ate eggs and dipped parsley in salt water. We nibbled the "bricks" while I explained that it was this meal that Jesus ate with His disciples on that last night before going to the cross, and that the Exodus story is our story too. We recited the traditional responsive readings. Little Tilah played on the old moth-eaten carpet while we cracked matzos and I struggled to make the connections between our bondage and Christ's redemption. Tilah played, but her brother's tiny body lay in a little churchyard a few miles away. Were we free? Perhaps, but we were not in Jerusalem yet.

No one protested about the four glasses of wine, and although the cups were tiny, I noticed that the younger men drank more than was strictly necessary for liturgical purposes. *Didn't they understand that we are in a church? Didn't they understand the word "sanctuary"?* Nevertheless, I thought the event went quite well, and while Pam and Kathleen helped me clean up crumbs and wilted parsley, I said, "I think we should make this an annual celebration at the church." I should have known that others in the community might not be as enthusiastic about what had taken place in the chapel.

The next morning I arrived at the post office to find Ruth standing on the porch, hands on her hips and eyes blazing.

"I understand you served *wine* in our church last evenin'!" she exploded.

I braced myself. "We had a Passover service," I replied carefully.

"You served *wine!*" she exclaimed. "Jesus didn't drink *wine!*"

"But He did," I replied slowly. "It's right there in the Bible. Jesus took the cup of wine and said, 'This is my blood of the New Covenant . . .'"

"That's not the right translation," she shot back. "It's grape juice, not wine."

"But it is the right translation," I said slowly. "I can read Greek, and the original language says 'wine.'"

"My Jesus wouldn't drink *wine*," Ruth insisted. "Besides, wine was different in those days. It wasn't strong like it is now."

I shrugged. "Maybe it was different." I didn't mention that I'd read somewhere that the alcohol content was somewhat higher in Jesus' time than it is today, and I decided not to trouble her with the historical fact that early Baptists had used a common cup of wine at Communion.

Ruth felt she had triumphed and once again said, "My Jesus wouldn't drink *wine*." Suddenly her eyes filled with tears and she told me a personal story I had never heard, of addiction, sorrow, and loss in her family.

No, I thought, *your Jesus wouldn't drink wine. Our Savior is gentle and merciful, and I don't believe He cares whether there's grape juice or Manischewitz in the Communion cups.*

Obviously, there were going to be some considerable theological challenges awaiting us on the road ahead, and they weren't all related to the issue of women in the ministry. I hadn't even resolved that matter in my mind, and here was a new difficulty. I'd forgotten that Baptists use only grape juice in their Communion services. Furthermore, when I was honest with myself, I had to admit that though the seder was *intended* to be a sacred celebration, the local incarnation of it hadn't been entirely reverent considering the amount of wine consumed. Maybe God was trying to tell me something through Ruth Lillard's complaint.

I was slowly coming to understand that a nondenominational church emulating first-century Christianity wasn't exactly a simple project. Such decisions as wine versus grape juice for Communion or methods of baptism demanded a choice between several doctrines. We live in the historical stream, and we're a long way downriver from Paul's time in Corinth or Ephesus. Because it was impossible to begin with a clean slate, "nondenominational" was very likely going to mean setting up one's own denomination by culling doctrines and practices from the various backgrounds of the congregation. In the meantime, the better part of wisdom seemed to be to use grape juice for public occasions.

There was a certain amount of snickering at the post office the week after our Passover seder. I ignored it and turned the conversation to the projected closing of the Graves Mill post office. As I listened to various opinions, suddenly I had an idea. "I know a reporter at the *New York Times*. I'll give him a call and tell him what's going on. Maybe he can help." The next thing we knew, he arrived in Graves Mill. I didn't see him when he came, although Ruth told me that he had visited the post office.

On May 20, 1979, an article appeared in the newspaper, complete with a photograph of the tiny building sitting at the foot of Jones Mountain. As I recall, no one in Graves Mill subscribed to the *Times*, but Wolftown was buzzing with the news and most of us rushed to the general store to buy the paper. The story generated a lot of excitement and our congressmen finally interceded on our behalf, so the US Postal Service changed its plans. Ruth received an official letter saying that the Graves Mill post office would continue service in the valley. Ruth had her job. We had our community center and post office, and Graves Mill was still on the world's map.

"Look at this," Ruth exclaimed proudly one morning when I came for my mail. "Just look at this!"

I peered over her shoulder at the scrapbook I didn't know she kept. The Associated Press had picked up the *Times* article, so it was featured in numerous newspapers across the country and even in Europe. Readers loved the tiny building in the mountain community and had written to say so. Ruth had received dozens of letters she'd preserved in the scrapbook, but this one was exceptional because it came from Germany and included the article from their paper with the photo of our tiny post office. "We're famous!" Ruth was ecstatic. "They know about Graves Mill even in Germany."

We all breathed a sigh of relief that the immediate threat to close the post office was behind us. I was grateful that at least for the time being, the valley people seemed to have forgotten about the scenic easement for the national park and the Passover service. People greeted me warmly again at the post office, and I hoped the truce would help strengthen and build the little congregation.

Almost every day during those first years, unless I was on the mountain working with Lyt on the land survey, I would walk the half mile up the road to my farm. It was quiet there, and I could mull over events and concerns without being interrupted by the telephone or unexpected callers. Some days I dug thistles out of the pastures; sometimes I sat on a rock above Kinsey Run and prayed while Tallis dashed up and down the farm track. But always I pondered and worried about economics and ecclesiology. How could I start the farm? How could I afford to build a house up in the valley? What did God really want me to do about the chapel? Was I really called to minister? And if God had called me to minister, what sort of minister would I be?

My main source of income from the divorce settlement had been coming in monthly installments. The checks grew smaller as the principal was paid off and less interest was included. Because I needed the money for each month's needs, there wasn't any left over to invest for the future. When the payments were finished, I would be land-poor unless I could get the farm going soon and make some sort of living from the mountain acres. I recognized that the Graves Mill congregation clearly wasn't large enough or prosperous enough to pay a pastor a living wage. How could it grow? How could we reach out to the wider world? What could I do? There were no immediate answers, so I concentrated on giving thanks for the glorious meadow there, for the crystal stream dashing over the rocks, and for the blue crest of the steep ridge against the sky. I was learning that I couldn't solve the problems of an unknown future, but I could attempt to live fully in the present.

It never ceases to astonish me that when I finally give up on my inept efforts to sort out my problems, the Lord reveals a new direction. Anne Carson had visited Graves Mill in the spring, and through the summer we kept in touch by telephone. Anne and Olga were good friends; in fact, Olga had introduced us at American University. When Olga told Anne that we were now holding services at Graves Chapel, she had an idea.

Anne and I were having an ordinary conversation one summer day when out of the blue she said, "Our liturgical dance troupe could come and present a program in Graves Mill." I nearly dropped the telephone receiver.

"Dance? Graves Mill?" I stammered.

"Why not? We could come down on Saturday afternoon and practice and then have the dance service on Sunday. Wouldn't that be *fantastic*?"

My initial reaction was that indeed it would be fantastic—as in fantastical—but Anne was so excited that I finally agreed. When we hung up the phone, I went outside and sat on the porch steps to think and pray over this new development.

I had never seen liturgical dancing before I went to seminary. It wasn't as common in the late seventies as it is now. My first encounter with this form of worshipful ballet had touched me deeply when I saw it. The troupe's choreography had brought a visual component to Bach's *Jesu, Joy of Man's Desiring*.

As I remembered the joy I felt watching that performance, my enthusiasm began to grow about introducing such a lovely worship service in Graves Mill. Perhaps it would touch off that revival I hoped to see. It might even bring so many new people to the chapel that we would become a "real" congregation. Such is the making of dreams.

Unfortunately, when I accepted Anne's proposal I did it without a single thought about the local residents and their attitudes.

I had forgotten how difficult it might be to explain the proposed event to people who'd never seen a ballet, let alone *dancing* in any church. The local Baptists thought Moses had forgotten to write down an eleventh commandment forbidding alcohol, card games, cigarettes, and yes, dancing. I was still smarting from the confrontations after our seder supper, and now I was planning to bring this "outrageous" service to Graves Mill! When it was time to announce this event to the congregation, I suddenly realized the implications of what I'd done and braced myself for the reactions.

I customarily gave the announcements before I began the homily, so midway through the service the following Sunday afternoon, I began listing the coming events, including the prospective dance service. I didn't dare look at Charles in his "Amen corner" at the back of the church. My knees felt unusually weak, and I hoped my skirts hid them so no one would see them shaking.

There was a pause when I finished but not for more than a few seconds. "What you talkin' 'bout?" Charles bellowed. "You talkin' 'bout them wimmin what puts their bare legs over their heads an' don't wear nothin' but one o' them ruffles? That what you mean?" I was certain he was ready to make big trouble.

"Not exactly, Charles," I replied, trying to sound matter of fact. "They wear something called leotards—long stockings. Their legs aren't bare."

"Might's well be," Charles grunted. "An' you're bringin' them folks down here to th' *church?*"

"Well, yes," I said, remembering Ruth's explosion after Passover. "It really *is* Christian worship, Charles. Honest it is!"

Charles looked around the church. All heads were turned toward him, and everyone seemed to be smiling. He could see as well as I could that if he insisted on opposing the idea, he wouldn't get any support from anyone else because everyone was curious to see what this was all about.

He guffawed. "Well, I gotta see this, I do. Some doin's this'll be, for sure." I breathed a sigh of relief.

The valley was buzzing, per usual, and after I put a notice in the local paper, the county joined the gossip and conjecture. I was too busy to notice. I had a Bible study to prepare as well as the house to clean before and after our gathering. The church needed a good shine, too, and although others came to help, my presence was expected.

Finally the dancers arrived. Anne knew the area already and loved it. Her friend Holly, who had been with the Frankfurt Opera Ballet, was equally enthusiastic. We spent Saturday afternoon on the mountain farm, wandering through the open meadow and dabbling our feet in the run, and before we returned to Graves Mill, we picked armloads of golden coreopsis, which had grown wild in the mountain garden. Zinnias, marigolds, bachelor's buttons, and the coreopsis were thriving unattended, untouched by the rabbits who were more interested in vegetables than flowers any day.

On the day of the performance, the "cultured tier" from Madison County came, curious and amazed that the tiny mountain church was so *avant-garde*. The Frays came, proud as could be, along with some of their friends. Charles was so impressed with the ballet and with the crowd it brought to the church that he didn't even chortle during the dance, though afterward he confessed that he wasn't at all certain how liturgical ballet related to good Baptist preaching. He was relieved, I think, that the dancers wore long, filmy skirts over their leotards.

I hoped desperately that our congregation would grow exponentially after our special performance, but the following Sunday, the same

small troop filed into the pews. Charles took his usual place at the
back. Mr. Mollé lowered himself into his customary pew next to the
window. All the same faces looked back at me from the pews. My
heart sank. What could change this?

Then Charles invited Dawsey Tanner to our services. Newcomers
were always immediately obvious in a small country church. I greeted
the toothless little man before the service began—he might have
weighed eighty-five pounds after a sumptuous meal—and learned that
he lived in Wolftown. Dawsey played the guitar and mouth organ.

"Both at the same time," he insisted. "Next Sunday, if you likes,
I'll play for you'all."

"He's really somethin'. You should hear him!" Kathleen chimed
in. "Dawsey, we'd just love to have you play for us. Wonderful!"

Dolly was at church that Sunday, and she piped up, "Dawsy used
to play on the radio."

"I had a reg'ler program," the little man explained. "I played all
over the country."

I smiled, but I had my doubts. We already enjoyed Pam Quemiere's
lovely voice, and the Rhodes sisters' duet. Did we need another guitar? And besides, Kathleen was a fine pianist and so was her daughter
Diane. I just kept smiling.

"Perhaps you could play for us at the beginning of the service,"
I suggested. "Could you begin about a quarter of four?"

"I'll do that," the little man replied. I watched the tiny figure
hurry out of the church. *He's hardly bigger than a guitar case himself,*
I thought.

The next Sunday, Dawsey arrived early, found an old chair in
the parish hall, and placed it carefully in front of the pulpit platform. He unpacked his guitar, and from somewhere produced a wire
contraption he hung around his neck. He slipped his harmonica
into the contraption, and holding the guitar firmly across his knees,
began to play a medley of old-time hymns with a definitely country

flavor. I recognized "Onward Christian Soldiers" and "I Love to Tell the Story," among others. There were some songs I didn't recognize, such country favorites as "Gospel Railroad," but I saw immediately that Dawsey was delighted to be among us and that his music was perfectly suited to Big Jim, Charles, and the younger people as well.

"Well, Lord," I said, alone after the service, praying before our old rugged cross. "You tell us to bring the best we have. Dawsey does that, and we know it when we hear his offering. He's really talented. I guess, Lord, that art doesn't always mean high culture, does it? So we bring what we have to worship You."

It seemed to me that I heard Him say, "Bring the best you have."

After that, we attempted to include creative works such as art, music, and ballet in our worship services. It wasn't always "high" or classical culture we offered God; in fact, it was quite a mixture. Those who wished to bring a song, a hymn, a painting, or a poem felt comfortably at home, and the country singers rubbed elbows with Kathleen's renditions of Bach and Handel. Theologian Francis Schaeffer was right: as far back as the Tabernacle, God had revealed to His followers the joy of offering our best and our most beautiful works to Him for His glory, and He delights when we attempt to follow in that tradition.

Ours was a comfortable, down-home community, and gradually new faces appeared in the congregation. I was learning that people will visit a church for special services but it's rare for visitors to attend regularly afterward. New members come into a community because someone in the church family brings them and because when they arrive, they feel at home. Special services are just that: a service to the wider world that often draws attention to the church. But people stay because they want to be part of the family.

CHAPTER 17

CLEARING THE WAY

And so our good Lord answered to all the questions and doubts
which I could raise, saying most comfortingly in this fashion:
I will make all things well, I shall make all things well, I may
make all things well and I can make all things well; and you
will see that yourself, that all things will be well.

JULIAN OF NORWICH

AS THE DAYS AND WEEKS PASSED, I fretted about my financial situation, adding up my assets with fear and trepidation. I was deeply enmeshed in the community and particularly in the development of the little church in Graves Mill. I had given my word that I would revive the inactive church, I had accepted the endorsement from the former Baptist congregation, and our little band had spent the money from their treasury. My neighbors and friends were relying on my faithfulness. I was committed.

But the reality was that the congregation could not provide much personal financial support to me, and I began to see that I was indeed land-poor. I didn't have money to invest or the promise of a secure income. What were my choices? I could sell the mountain farm. That might provide enough for investments. But what then? Most likely, I would move away from Graves Mill. If I were to remain in the valley, I simply had to find a way to earn a living—or so I thought. It was already clear to me that I had neither the time nor the money to develop the mountain farm. Graves Mill was proving to be a full-time job.

Questions and possibilities for the future tumbled around in my head during the late winter of 1980 as I climbed Jones Mountain behind the park surveyor. The Shenandoah National Park had accepted the proposal for the easement Lyt Wood had drawn up, and the final step in the process was an official survey of roughly two hundred acres. The giant trees were in that tract.

The park superintendent had called to tell me that their surveyor was coming that Monday, so I was waiting outside the church when the park service truck pulled in beside me. The surveyor, in the standard brown park uniform, jumped out of the truck and exclaimed, "You're the church lady, aren't you? Well, I don't believe in any of that and I don't want to hear about it. If you'll remember that, we'll get on fine."

I swallowed hard. "I understand. I'll be praying, but I won't trouble you by talking about it."

"Fine!" he replied. "Now let's get to work."

We rumbled up the farm track as far as Canterbury Hollow, about halfway up the mountain. From that point, the road was impassible, so we parked and scrambled up the remains of the old track to the ridge's rim. Locating the corners and line at the top of the ridge was relatively easy because the land had been surveyed at the time of the divorce settlement and Lyt had marked it again when we laid out the proposed easement. Since the Potomac Appalachian Trail ran through the area, there was no brush and the hiking wasn't particularly strenuous. That section of the survey required only a day or two to complete. The difficult and dangerous work would be laying out and marking the lower lines across a very steep, rocky section of the mountainside where the rock face was home to bears and rattlesnakes and, of course, a refuge for occasional poachers and rustlers. Lyt and I had surveyed the line and had flagged it, but this final survey required more attention to detail.

My main task was to help locate the flags and markers Lyt and I had placed along the projected lines and to certify that these were where I wanted the final easement boundary to be located. As we worked, the surveyor told me a little about himself. He lived in a condo, he said, because after hiking through the wilderness all day, the last thing he wanted to do in his time off was yard work or gardening. So after his days in the open, he went home to the city.

One day when we were eating our sandwiches, he confided that his first wife had committed suicide. He came home and found her dead in the swimming pool. I tried to ask a couple of questions, but he would say no more except that this was the reason he didn't believe in God. Praying silently, I offered my sympathy, but he shrugged and rose to his feet.

"We're going to be working through rattlesnake territory now, you know. Matter of fact, I'm really surprised we haven't seen any snakes before this. There's been plenty of opportunity. Today's a perfect day for snakes—warm sun, leaves piled up. The first one over a log often stirs up the rattler and the person behind gets bit. You want to go first or second?"

"I'll follow you," I replied. "And I'll pray all the time. I know this cliff is famous for rattlers."

He set off ahead of me, keeping up a good pace across the relatively level stretches. I stayed a good six feet behind him, both to pray and to have plenty of room in case he did stir up a rattler. We had traversed perhaps half of the cliff face when I saw him step over a log and just miss stepping on a very large coil of rattler!

"SNAKE!" I screamed. "You just stepped over a rattlesnake! Get out of the way!"

The surveyor turned around, his face white as a snowdrop. He saw the snake and stood frozen in the track we'd been following. Fortunately, the snake was rather torpid, and after waving its head back and forth a time or two, it slithered off down the ridge.

I cautiously approached and stood beside the shaken surveyor.

"I was so *stupid*!" he exclaimed, mopping his brow. "I know better than to step across a log without looking, but it was such a small log, I didn't think . . . Were you praying?"

"Yes," I replied, "I was praying."

"You must have been!" he replied. "It's absolutely amazing that the rattler didn't strike. And that you saw it in time to stop."

"It was pure grace," I replied.

"Well, you just keep praying!" he exclaimed. "After this, if either of us gets bit, the other one returns to the truck and goes for help. Remember, don't move about, hear? That will make things worse. Okay?"

For the rest of the time we were together we never saw another snake, and by the time we finished the work I can't say the surveyor was converted, but for the remaining days he even asked me to pray for our safety on the mountainside. Sometimes we sow seeds and others reap the harvest. At least the man had enough faith to believe in my prayers, and I have a notion that the Lord put that deadly reptile there for our mutual benefit.

Finally, the work outdoors was completed, the maps drawn, and all the legal paperwork finished. I made sure the documents were reviewed by my lawyer as well as by park service officials. When that process was finished, there was a quiet celebration at park head-quarters in September 1981. Lyt and I accepted the superintendent's thanks while we shared cookies and coffee with park rangers. Needless to say, there were no newspaper reporters present. All of us understood the necessity of keeping the whole affair very quiet.

Amazingly, there were no repercussions down in the valley. The community had forgotten about my dealings with the park; they were more focused on plowing, sowing, harvesting, cattle prices, and corn prices. God was gracious and my world remained quiet. Little did I guess that in twenty years, conservation easements would be common and prestigious charitable donations, or that Madison County's quarrels with the park service would become less hostile over time. Meanwhile, I hiked along the trails at the top of the ridge, doing my part to keep them clear from brush and new undergrowth.

While we were finishing the particulars of the easement, I decided to apply to Virginia Theological Seminary in Alexandria. After all, I led a budding congregation and thought perhaps I could become a deaconess. In the early twentieth century, there had been a string of Episcopal missions in the Blue Ridge Mountains, places where deaconesses brought the gospel, administered basic first aid, and helped people learn to use sewing machines. The deaconesses also ran a "clothing bureau" where the mountain folks could get secondhand garments. In fact, Big Jim confided that he got his first shoes from the Middle River deaconesses. I felt that I was following in their footsteps, and since they had been Episcopalians it seemed reasonable to me to attend an Episcopal seminary.

I was incredibly naive. I didn't know the requirements for establishing a mission—either the unwritten rules or the written ones—and I didn't have any exposure to diocesan politics. It simply didn't occur to me that under Episcopal diocesan policy, the location of future missions was decided in the diocesan offices and then priests were deployed to build them. Inevitably, these missions were established in new and growing city suburbs where the population was sufficiently large and affluent to pay for a building and to support a priest and his family. I'd learned that model in seminary, of course, but somehow I thought we could be an exception. I didn't realize that churches were not expected to spring up spontaneously under lay leadership, and especially not small rural congregations of poor and middle-class families. The thinking at the time was that these should be eliminated, not inaugurated.

I didn't understand the politics of the ordination process either; I didn't realize that devotion to our Lord was hardly the only consideration when selecting future clergy and leaders. What I did learn, very quickly, was that I could not be accepted as long as I continued to serve at Graves Chapel. I knew from my discussions years before that pursuing postulancy for holy orders took a year to complete, but I thought I might be able to commute to the seminary as I had done at Wesley. Since I wasn't planning to be a priest or a pastor, I thought I could earn a master's in theology and become a deaconess. However, those were the days before long-distance learning, and when I contacted the seminary offices, I heard the message in no uncertain terms: leave Graves Chapel or close it down, because you can't study here off campus. I sensed that the real unstated message was, "Close down that church! It's too small, too rural, and too impractical."

"Lord, isn't there some way I can do things right?" I whispered. "Couldn't I please be like normal church leaders?" No answer came. Since there were no candidates standing in line to take over the ministry in Graves Mill, I knew I was honor-bound to continue the work. I had lived there for almost three years, and I knew my commitment to these individuals was deeper than merely honoring a promise. I was not a hired shepherd. I genuinely loved those whom God had placed in my charge. Yes, God would provide for them—I knew that—but I could not leave the sheep without a shepherd. And when I was really honest with myself before the Lord, I had to admit that I needed them, too. I knew that I was growing closer to Jesus as I worked with the people, listening to their pains and triumphs, and as we studied the Scriptures together. It really was a two-way process. Reluctantly, I put the admissions forms and course catalogs away in my files. At least for the time being, it was clear that was not an option.

My immediate concern, however, was funds. I knew the payments arranged in the divorce settlement would end soon. I was no closer to a farm operation than I had been when I moved to Graves Mill, and the chapel wasn't likely to pay a living wage for years to come, if ever. We weren't really organized, and contributions were still not tax deductible. I had not moved forward on that legality simply because we hadn't made a decision about the kind of church we would be. I prayed desperately for guidance, especially when Tallis and I walked up to the mountain farm.

"Lord," I would cry, "I am Your servant. You have provided for me all this way, far beyond what I ever expected. Please help me now. Show me the way! I know You are my Father and that You care for Graves Mill. Please show me the way!"

I tried to rest in the Lord and leave it all in His hands, but most nights I tossed and turned in my bed, and every muscle in my back was as tense as a fiddle string.

And then God sent an unexpected answer to my prayers one day while Lyt and I were double-checking the boundaries for the conservation easement. After working for a while, Lyt paused and looked over the forested slopes of Jones Mountain. "You should consider selective timber cutting," he said. I was startled. That was not something I would have expected Lyt to say. We'd been so deeply involved in discussing conservation policies for the mountain that logging had never occurred to me as a possibility on the farm.

"It won't harm the slopes below your designated preservation area," he said, "and it may actually encourage new growth so that the wood lot will continue for generations to come. If you use selective cutting practices, there will be plenty of trees to keep the mountainside from eroding. As you know, I hate to see any tree fall victim to a saw, but this is good management. You should think about it."

Because he was a government employee, he couldn't help me with the commercial arrangements, but he recommended a man named Gary Younkin to mark the trees for cutting and negotiate with logging companies.

I did contact Gary, and for some weeks I scrambled through hollows and briars, following him and his dogs. The timberman loved working in Kinsey Hollow. The land was sufficiently extensive that his canine friends could run loose beside him without fear of getting near any farmers' flocks or homes. We made two marks on each tree selected for cutting. Gary used a special paint and sprayed one mark on the trunk at roughly chest height, and a second mark on the tree just above the ground. With this system, I could see at a glance if any tree had been removed other than those we'd chosen. It was a time-consuming effort but well worth the trouble. Timber rustling would be risky for any rogue logger to attempt.

As we scrambled over rocks and logs that autumn, I learned to identify trees by their shape and bark; I also learned the topography and character of the land as I never could have done otherwise, and I had the satisfaction of knowing that to the best of my knowledge, I was caring for the land even as it cared for me. Most of all, I understood just a little more of God's magnificent creation as well as His intimate care for the small events of our daily journey.

By December 31, 1981, I had signed a contract for timber sales, and at least for the moment my concerns about paying for my daily bread were somewhat eased. I should have known better than to worry so much, but I'm a slow learner. God always provided, but when there was a looming crisis, I often wondered if He'd come through *this time*. He always did, and never in ways I expected.

We had begun services in April 1979 after cleaning up the chapel's sanctuary enough to be presentable, but the parish hall was deteriorating and the basement still harbored that nasty pool full of submerged, rotting theater seats. The air in the annex was fetid with mold and mildew. Through late summer and autumn, I struggled with the choices before me. How could I continue to live in Graves Mill, leading that little church? Was that God's will for my life? The flocks of sheep I had dreamed of tending were stampeding away out of the hollows.

How could anything significant come out of Graves Chapel? We were just a tiny band of people, and most of us were single, divorced, or widowed. C. K. and Kathleen were a solid family, but they actually belonged to Mt. Nebo Lutheran Church downriver. For the most part, we were a wounded lot, including me. Big Jim and Charles were both older and single; Big Jim was divorced, and Charles had been separated from his wife long before I came. Mr. Mollé was divorced too. I had done a survey for my parish statistics class and knew that about 80 percent of the valley residents were elderly single people. What could God possibly do with us?

And then one morning Big Jim came thumping up on the cottage porch. He pounded on the door, and when I opened it, he was grinning from ear to ear. "I done uncovered them drains," he almost shouted, "an' the water's runnin' out o' the basement. Drains is workin' jus' fine. You come see."

I followed him to the church and through the parish hall to the basement door. "'Tain't safe, goin' down them stairs," he reminded me, "but you kin see from here."

I sat down on the threshold, peering into the dimness at the bottom of the stairs. As my eyes adjusted, I could see that the floor was wet, but for the first time I could see cement instead of water. "Jim, that's wonderful. Really!"

"Come on t'other way," he commanded, so I followed him outside and down the outside steps. The congregation had replaced the missing door leading into the basement, and Big Jim had kept the drain at the bottom of the outside stairs open so the rains were no longer flooding the lower level. Originally, the Baptist congregation had planned to put an awning over the stairs. Charles, Big Jim, and C. K. discussed the idea and decided that it would never survive the winds sweeping down through the valley. Instead, they asked Steve Bunce, Suzy Rhodes's boyfriend, to build a roof over the stairs. Thanks to the improvements, for some weeks Jim had reported that there was considerably less water in the basement than when I first viewed the murky mess. It was still a murky mess, though—that is, until that morning.

Big Jim's chest actually swelled with pride. "I done poked around them drains," he said, "an' all on a sudden, they's this *gug-gug-gug*, an' that there water, she just went down. An' it's runnin' inter ol' Kinsey Run, jus' the way she uster do. Them drainpipes is doin' jus' fine. 'Twas all that there mess in th' cellar what was stoppin' things."

I complimented him heartily, and we went to work sweeping out the basement. Then we opened the windows and left the place to dry out for a few days. When we came back to inspect the floor, the surface of the cement was pitted, soft, and crumbling. Since it had been under water so long, and acidic water at that, the floor had deteriorated.

"We's goin' t'need some ce-ment in here," Big Jim said, assuming that as a matter of course we would make the necessary repairs. "An' we's a-goin' t'need a new stove. It's spring now, but winter's a-comin'."

He was correct about the stove. The old wood heater was so badly rusted that the firebox was clearly unsafe, and yes, winter would come. However, I lacked Big Jim's confidence that we could actually restore the basement. The cinder-block walls were a nasty gray, and the wooden steps from the upstairs hallway down to this lower level were rickety and about as thin as a spider's web. It would take work, materials, and money to make the place even marginally habitable.

Big Jim was not going to let his triumph go unnoticed. I went back to the cottage to prepare for the week's Bible study, but Big Jim sped off in his old station wagon to spread his news. It wasn't long before C. K. and Charles appeared to inspect the basement floor.

A dry basement floor was only the beginning. Whenever our present world shifts a bit, new conditions and possibilities appear. Charles called a cement dealer for an estimate, and before I knew what was happening, the men gathered at the chapel and set to work. They carefully cleaned the floor and made sure the drains were clear. On the appointed day, a cement truck lumbered up the road, angled in beside the basement stairs, and with a roar and a grind, poured the gray mixture onto the old floor. As the cement crew raked and smoothed it, every man in the valley who was available came over and watched. It was quite an event. I stayed in the background, knowing that a woman's advice was quite unnecessary. That was fine with me because if anything went wrong in the future, it wouldn't be my fault!

There was enough cement left in the load to fill a form at the edge of the parish hall porch, creating a new and needed step between the platform and the ground. Charles proudly signed the step and dated it.

When the cement had hardened, the whole parish set to work building new interior steps and sealing and painting the cinder-block walls and the floor. Someone found a secondhand wood-burning stove, and the men installed the black hulk. It was the crowning moment for a job well done. For the first time in more than a decade, the parish hall was habitable. I took heart in this miracle unfolding before my eyes. God's economy provided for a low-cost reconstruction of the parish hall; surely He would provide for me, His servant!

The previous year, our second Thanksgiving together had been hosted by Skip's parents at their farmhouse. The inclement weather had kept the crowd small. This year there was no question where the festivities would take place. The whole valley was astir with excitement. At last, the Graves Chapel parish hall's doors would reopen to welcome everyone into the building built for celebrations such as this, the first of many Thanksgivings to come.

As I recall, we borrowed tables and chairs from the Lutheran Church in Rochelle, and Charles promised a haunch of venison for the women to cook. Somebody managed to shoot a wild turkey and sent it to me, the designated cook. I didn't relish the assignment. Tenderizing a wild turkey is a trick the pioneers may have known well, but aside from parboiling the bird before putting it in the oven and then smothering it with bacon slabs while it roasted, I had no idea what to do. Worse yet, one of the hunters contributed a haunch of bear meat for the dinner. Aside from grinding it to a hamburger-like consistency and adding sausage, I was clueless how to prepare it. In fact, I was somewhat overwhelmed with the prospect of making sure any of those meats were edible at Thanksgiving dinner. But in the midst of all my worries, the phone rang. It was a gentleman from the wildlife club in Orange County.

"We understand that you have venison and bear meat," he said. "We're planning a banquet, and we'll be glad to trade you beef prime rib, pound for pound, for the venison and bear."

I could hardly believe my ears. "I'll ask about it," I replied. "I think I can get you a wild turkey, too."

"That would be wonderful!" he exclaimed.

I called Charles and the others, and there were whoops of delight when they heard the news.

Charles was as proud of that parish hall basement as if he'd built it single-handedly. He'd stop by the church every morning on his way to the post office, just to make sure we were "doin' right" and that all the preparations for dinner were coming along according to plan. Somehow, we'd acquired a wood supply for the new stove, and we had a couple of rocking chairs, one on each side. Charles claimed the best one and Big Jim boldly claimed the second. The two would sit and rock and argue or tell yarns for half an hour, and the rumble of their voices resonating made the place come alive and seem quite homey.

Big Jim became a fixture beside the stove. He faithfully kept it stoked with good locust logs, and if I came downstairs, he loved to talk about the old days when the forest was full of game and the McDaniels lived up in the hollows.

"Ye ain't got no idee," he'd say. "In them days, we'd jus' go out an' get a catch o' trout fer breakfas'. Plenty o' fish in the crik in them days. An' you shoulda see'd the apples we done shipped down t' Gordonsville. Sent 'em over th' water on a boat, I unnerstan'. An' cabbages . . . law, we grew 'em this big!" He'd space his hands about two feet apart. "'Twas good livin' in them times."

One of the hunt club leaders whose family had come from the hollow's clans told me that Shenandoah National Park's takeover of the land was the best thing that could have happened to the mountaineers.

"We all lived from the chestnut trees, you see," he said. "The pigs ran wild in the woods and got fat on the chestnuts. We built cabins and fences from the chestnut logs. The women even made flour from chestnuts when the wheat and corn crops didn't do well. When the chestnut blight came and wiped out the American chestnut forest, the clans were in big trouble. Then when the drought hit in the thirties, what the blight didn't kill, the forest fires finished. And times had changed. People needed schooling, more than could be had in those hollows."

I thought it better not to mention that conversation to Big Jim. In his mind, the mountain ridges were still as pristine as they had been when the first ships sailed into Jamestown. Yes, he agreed that the hills had been ravaged with the chestnut blight and forest fires, but he also believed that if the clans had been left to themselves, all would have been well. Who needed all that "schoolin' an' stuff"?

I knew that the government takeover of the mountain people's land had not been kind and gentle. Some of the mountaineers were moved out bodily, their cabins burned to prevent them from returning. The loss of their homes and culture was traumatic for the mountain people, and for some families it required several generations before they adapted to the wider world. Some, like Big Jim, never really did adapt. Shenandoah National Park is a national treasure, but it was costly in more ways than one.

When Thanksgiving Day finally came, Charles arrived mid-afternoon to sit and rock. The feast would be an hour or so later, so I scurried around with preparations. I had retrieved my big linen tablecloths from the trunks stored in the parish hall Sunday school room and had carefully draped them across the folding tables. I was delighted with the elegant result. We needed a place for the big coffeepot, though, so I brought my card table to the church and positioned it in a corner near the stove, careful to allow plenty of room for the rocking chairs. I covered it with my best lace-edged linen cloth. The coffeepot looked quite lovely sitting there.

"Only the finest will do for You, Lord," I whispered as I smoothed out the beautiful linens from Luxmont, nevertheless thinking about the laundry and ironing ahead of me when the festivities were over. I was beginning to understand why Dolly had volunteered to host the feast on only one occasion.

Earlier that day I had carried my big cooler to the parish hall, along with four or five water jugs and a gallon of lemonade. The newly-sealed cinder-block walls were a shining creamy white, and the whole place smelled of new paint. Remembering my first tour of Graves Chapel with Charles, I could hardly believe this transformation. Truly, it was a singular grace!

While I kept busy, Charles was happily relaying bits of gossip to which I paid scant attention. People would begin arriving in about half an hour, so I started the coffee. We heard footsteps on the outside stairs and someone fumbling at the basement door. Big Jim came stumbling into the basement, his face more ruddy than usual and his eyes slightly bloodshot. Charles and I both froze in astonishment as Big Jim came weaving toward the stove. Before either one of us could find our wits to intervene, the old mountaineer stumbled against the card table. I had the presence of mind to grab the table and coffeepot to keep them from capsizing completely, but there were huge coffee stains on the beautiful white linen cloth. I think Charles grabbed Jim's shirttail to guide him into the rocking chair, where the big man collapsed.

"You are DRUNK!" Charles exclaimed. "Some *Christian* you be! An' on a day like t'day. What in tarnation got int' ye, man?"

Big Jim hung his head, utterly shamed. "I dunno wha' happen," he muttered. "I done stopped by a couple o' places an' they give me some custard. I dinna knowed t'was spiked. Miz Light, I'se sorry. I'se so sorry."

Charles guffawed and I couldn't help smiling. We both knew what had transpired. Jim had made the rounds, visiting every house up and down the valley. The local "custard" was eggnog, of course, and in some houses it would be generously laced with brandy or moonshine. Moonshine, if it were the "best" of local distilling, was smooth as silk, and Big Jim could not have guessed exactly how much he was imbibing.

"Have some coffee," I commanded, pouring him a big cup. "And no, you're not getting any cream in it."

For once, he was obedient and gulped it down. "Now get up from that chair, Jim, and walk around outside in the air. It's cold enough to clear your head."

Charles nodded and we watched while Big Jim carefully hoisted himself from the rocker and slowly retraced his steps. I began mopping up the spilled coffee. I didn't have another fancy linen to replace the stained cover, so I found some white towels and redid the table. *You're right, Lord. This is much more appropriate than the lacy cover! Ahh, vanity. Pruning never ends.* Sometimes the Lord asks us to pay a different honor to Him than we had initially intended.

By the time the first cars pulled up beside the old church, Big Jim was nearly himself again—at least he could walk in a straight line. From that day on, we never again saw him the slightest bit tipsy.

Kathleen arrived carrying a covered dish, with C. K. right behind her. Rich and Pam were there; Skip and his parents came, bringing more food. Charles was holding court from his rocking chair beside the stove. One after the other, the valley people arrived. For the third year, Olga joined us, this time with her husband. As I looked over the assembled company enjoying one another and their dinner, I was content.

That Thanksgiving, we dined on mouthwatering beef while the Orange County folk had plenty of bear, venison, and wild turkey on their plates. I never did ask any of them if their entrées were tender. *De gustibus non est disputandum.* ("In matters of taste, there can be no disputes.") Certainly there was no disputing that the Lord had provided a rich feast for us all.

CHAPTER 18

"O LITTLE TOWN OF BETHLEHEM"

O little town of Bethlehem, how still we see thee lie! . . .
The hopes and fears of all the years are met in thee tonight.

PHILLIPS BROOKS

SOON AFTER THAT first service in April 1979, we began holding
regular Sunday worship in the old church, using the 1928 *Book of
Common Prayer*. Before we began, I spent hours worrying that a
guided prayer service would trigger rebellion in the ranks, but to my
surprise, King James English seemed familiar to the old-timers. As
Charles put it, "It sounds jus' like the Bible" and "It must be all right
because it sounds holy." We had a few grumbles about the Apostles'
Creed ("What we need creeds fer? All we needs is th' Bible!"), but
otherwise, the transition to formal worship on Sundays happened
without any ruffled feathers in the flock.

However, as summer ebbed into fall, the days grew shorter, and
by 5:00 p.m., when I would be saying the benediction at the chapel,
there was so little natural light coming through the windows that
people could barely make out the words in their hymnals. Winter

was definitely coming, and it was clear we needed more illumination than the fading daylight if we were to continue services through Christmas. What could we do for light?

One Sunday afternoon after everyone had gone home, I sat in a back pew watching the deepening shadows move across the room. I looked up and focused on the old chandelier hanging at the center of the room. Of course! That was the answer!

When we had cleaned and made repairs that spring, I had removed the broken glass globes from the old gas chandelier. The fixture had four "arms" with plates at the end of each one, designed to hold the carbide gas lamps. It looked as if the plates were large enough to hold kerosene lamps. In those days, electricity wasn't very reliable in Madison County. Whenever there was a storm, we always expected there would be an outage, so I wasn't surprised to find a selection of kerosene lamps at the Madison General Store. There were some with tall chimneys, some with handles, and to my delight, there were four fat little lamps with glass oil wells and short chimneys, the same size as the globes I had taken down. I was certain these would fit exactly into the chandelier.

The lamps were inexpensive, so happy as a cow in clover, I carried them back to the chapel. I climbed up on the pew underneath the chandelier and set a lamp at the end of one arm. It looked as if it were custom made for this chandelier, and singing "Hallelujah, Thine the glory!" I liberated the remaining three lamps from their boxes, filled all four bowls with kerosene, and slipped them into place.

When dusk fell, I lit the wicks. To my dismay, the little circle of light barely touched the far corners of the church. Doubtless the old carbide gas lamps had been much brighter than the feeble rays of these oil lamps. The kerosene lights were so dim, you couldn't see the words in the hymnal unless you happened to be directly underneath the chandelier. *If we had more oil lamps, maybe that would help,* I thought. *But there is only one chandelier.*

The next week, I was looking for something at the Wolftown store, and to my amazement, I spied some small pewter lamps almost the same shape and size as the glass fixtures in the chandelier—and these were fitted with wall brackets! It was as if the Good Lord's providence had especially ordered just those lamps for our use. I brought them back to the church and hung them between the windows. If the pioneers could manage with oil lamps, so could we!

In its heyday, the chapel had been wired for electricity. The white globes I'd noticed on my first visit hung like ghosts from the tin ceiling. After we paid our bills for fuel to feed the old kerosene heaters on either side of the church, we had no money left over for electricity.

We had never taken up an offering during a service. I'd read a number of testimonies and "Holy Spirit" accounts of how the Spirit moved hearts so that ministry needs were miraculously met. Why did we need to take up an offering? Surely if we prayed, God would supply all our needs. I remembered a little mountain chapel I'd visited in Italy. There was an offering box beside the door where visitors left their love gifts. Why couldn't we do the same thing? If we did that, all giving would be completely anonymous, a gift to the Lord. No one would feel pushed to give to God; everything would be completely "from the heart by the Spirit."

At the next Bible study meeting, I broached the idea to Mr. Mollé. "Could you," I began, "make us a little box for love offerings?"

"Huh? Wassat?" I thought he didn't understand me.

"Could you make a little box for the church, a box for love offerings?" I repeated several decibels higher. By then, everyone was looking at me.

"Love offerings?" Mr. Mollé shouted back. "What's love offerings?"

From the blank looks I saw on almost every face, I realized that they had no idea what I was talking about. "I mean money," I explained. "I thought we could put a little box beside the church door so people could leave donations for us."

"Oh! I see," Mr. Mollé said, rubbing his ear. "I could do that." And he did. A few days later, he brought a handsome little birchwood box about eight inches square to the chapel. It had a hinged lid pierced with a slot large enough to accept bills and coins. The lid, fastened by a small hasp, was secured by a little padlock. Any thief could have broken the box's hinges with a good jerk, and for that matter, the hasp could have been popped out with a very small screwdriver, possibly even a hat pin. However, it was a pretty little box, and I was completely confident that God's angels would keep the donations safe.

The angels did their job, or perhaps there was so little in the offering box that so far as we knew, no thief ever wanted to take anything. We'd occasionally find a dollar bill or a few coins in the box, but that was all.

So there was no money for electricity. Now that we had oil lamps, the shades needed washing after every service. Without running water at the church, keeping them clear became a major production. I carried them to the cottage and back after every service because no one wanted that work. In fact, even sweeping and dusting the church soon fell to me. Occasionally some of the other women volunteered to help, but they didn't enjoy beating rugs and using a dust mop, so most weeks I did it myself. It wasn't fun, but I reminded myself that this was the way the old-timers did it. Brother Lawrence glorified God while peeling potatoes, so I sang hymns and gave thanks for my dust mop. I tried to be stoic, but I did long for the cheerful *whirrrrr* of a vacuum cleaner every once in a while.

One November Sunday evening after I finished the sermon, Charles cleared his throat loudly, signaling a speech.

"I'm a-gittin' th' lights turned on this week," he announced. "Can't half see in here, an' I'm sick o' squintin'. I'm payin' th' bill, too."

I could scarcely believe my ears. Charles? He was not normally known for his generosity, and in fact, his farm didn't bring him a lot of spare cash. However, he loved that old church, and he knew what needed to happen next whether I did or not.

"Oh my goodness!" I exclaimed. "Oh my! Thank you so much, Charles!" We all thanked him profusely with applause. I had visions of a vacuum cleaner dancing through my head.

But Christmas was on the calendar, and now that lights blazed from the chapel every Sunday, the women began to talk about a Christmas tree.

"Now, wouldn't that be *nice*," Kathleen Rhodes said several times. The men understood what had to be done to keep the peace on their hearths, so Charles, Rich, Skip, Big Jim, and I all decided we'd go up to my mountain farm to get a tree. I knew we'd have no trouble finding something about six feet high, but almost as soon as we passed through the gate, the men began to argue over who could find the biggest and most perfect tree. We passed any number of respectable pines, but if Big Jim liked a tree, it didn't suit Charles. If Skip approved a tree, Rich wouldn't have it. Finally they found a big cedar, and perhaps because the day was waning, they decided this one would do. We could barely get it into Skip's big pickup; the tree extended several feet over the tailgate. The men secured it in the bed of the truck with ropes. I had no idea how they intended to get the thing into the chapel and I'm not sure they did either, but I did know better than to ask that question.

The tree raising became quite a production. First, it was necessary to cut off several feet and trim the branches before the men were able to push the tree through the door. Then it was still too tall to stand upright so they sawed off more of the trunk and trimmed more branches. There was much pondering and pounding while they braced the tree with two-by-fours. But at last, there it was, standing on the left of the pulpit (displacing four or five pews) and touching the ceiling about fifteen feet above the floor. The menfolk were jubilant. The women had lots of sawdust to clean up, but nobody really cared. Their vacuum cleaners roared.

I contributed half a dozen strings of lights left over from Christmases at Luxmont. Somehow, it was a fitting resurrection for the decorations. Later, though, when Charles got the electric bill, he was furious and said he'd had enough of *that* foolishness, and he took back his offer to pay another month's bill. Eventually everyone voted to start taking up an offering so we could pay our expenses.

Early in December, Pam and I spent an enjoyable afternoon cutting boxwood and running cedar. While we discussed possibilities for a Christmas program, we hung boxwood and pine swags from the kerosene lamp brackets along the walls and made a large boxwood wreath to hang at the back of the chapel. We draped the chandelier with running cedar, and I found some little cornhusk angels to hang from it. When we finished, it looked as if the heavenly host floated above the congregation.

But what could we do for a program? How could we bring something special to Graves Mill that honored the birth of Christ? For me, Christmas programs meant Handel's *Messiah* and glorious choral offerings. That wasn't possible with our small group. Suddenly I had an inspiration. I'd heard the old service of Lessons and Carols when I was in London one Christmas, and I had a recording of King's College Chapel's 1964 festival. I knew that the service originated at Truro Cathedral, so I felt a sentimental connection. I had loved the people at Truro Church in Fairfax and retained fond memories of London. I pulled out the record. There was a booklet containing all six lessons with the carols interspersed between them.

"Thank You, Lord," I murmured. There was our Christmas program, complete with introductions to the lessons and accompanying prayers.

At the next Bible study, I broached the plan for the service. Skip could lead the lessons, but we'd need to adapt the carols to our abilities and experiences. Kathleen Rhodes would play the piano for us, and with help from Big Jim and Earl the Pearl, we moved my harpsichord to the chapel for the occasion. I had my mother's violin and intended to play that on Christmas Eve as an interlude in the Graves Chapel version of Lessons and Carols. C. K. would sing "O Holy Night." The weeks before Christmas were hectic but joyful with practices and anticipation. Everyone was enthusiastic. We were certain it would be the most glorious of all Christmases in Graves Mill.

Once the tree was up and the Christmas program planned, the younger folks decided it would be great to go caroling before Christmas. One young man volunteered to drive his pickup, and on the designated night, six or so of us climbed into the truck bed filled with hay bales for us to sit on. It was a cold but beautiful moonlit evening. Suzy Rhodes rode in the truck cab with her guitar to keep her fingers and the guitar strings warm for playing. C. K. and Kathleen followed us in their car.

We had some small poinsettias to deliver to the elderly in the valley, a list of carols, and some song sheets. At each house, we sang lustily and were very well received. However, before long, I saw one of our young men drinking a bottle of brandy. I couldn't believe it. What was the matter with him? Didn't he realize that this was a Christian mission? That we were on the Lord's business? Apparently not.

I drew him aside when we reached the next stop and told him that his behavior was not appropriate. He merely laughed at me, and there was nothing I could do to stop him other than insisting that we return to the church at once. This was not the way things were supposed to happen! Where was the conviction? This man was part of our Bible study; why didn't the Word cut through his heart and change his behavior? I was grateful that we had only one more house to visit.

It occurred to me that preaching the gospel clearly so that everyone could understand might be a laudable goal, but I had a long way to go to reach it. I was learning that the distance between God's Word and the heart is very often further than I'd ever anticipated. In fact, the distance between the Word and my own heart has been a surprisingly long journey, one that will take my entire life to navigate.

Just before Christmas, Dolly came down to the church on her way to town.

"I've just got a minute," she said, "but I wanted you to know I looked out my kitchen window last night and saw the lights burnin' down here. My dream really has come true!" I think I saw tears welling up in the corners of her eyes.

When she left, I sat staring at the flank of Jones Mountain visible from the window in my little study in the back corner of the parish hall. Maybe God did have a plan. It seemed that way even if I didn't understand it. If He had a plan, maybe everything would be all right.

With the church decorated, the Bible study group decided that a living nativity would be a great draw to advertise Christmas at Graves Chapel. Skip volunteered the family donkey, and Earl loaned us a red calf. A few days before Christmas, the donkey and calf were tethered beside the chapel. The men found a wooden box for a manger, which they placed on sawhorses with a drop light inside it. The box was deep enough to hide the lightbulb, and in the dusk no one could see the electrical cord. The light from the "manger" illuminated calf, donkey, and the wall of hay bales behind them. People from all over the county drove up to see the scene, including Joe Fray.

He shook his head thoughtfully as he stood beside me, looking at the nativity. "We miss you," he said, "but I can see you're really busy here."

I nodded, a little sad. I missed Joe and Mary Temple and Christmas in Madison, but I was needed in Graves Mill.

On Christmas Eve, I went up to the church in the late afternoon to light the kerosene lamps and to pray. As I lit the big chandelier festooned with running cedar, it seemed as if all the prayers of all the years, all the hopes and fears of the valley, hovered over the sanctuary. I sat looking at Mr. Mollé's hand-hewn cross for a long time until to my wondering eyes, a faint halo shone at the edges of the wooden beams. It may have been visible only to the eyes of my heart, but it was visible, a special Christmas gift that banished the lingering nostalgia for my lost world. I knew the Lord was there, and that was all that mattered.

I plugged in the Christmas tree lights, and one by one the little band of worshipers filed into the church. I stood up to offer the old Bidding Prayer.

"Beloved in Christ, we come by this service to prepare ourselves to hear again the message of the angels, and to go in heart and mind to Bethlehem, and to see the loving-kindness of our God, and the Babe lying in a manger . . ."

I heard a soft *baaaa* outside. Yes, we did seem to be close to Bethlehem.

The service went smoothly, and as I listened I was glad there was no preaching. It was unnecessary—the lessons told the amazing story of salvation through the Word itself. We heard God announce in the Garden of Eden that the seed of woman would bruise the serpent's head, and we rejoiced to hear Isaiah foretell Christ's birth and Kingdom. And then the angel Gabriel came to visit the Virgin Mary. C. K. was in good voice, and Skip read the lessons unusually well. Every face seemed to shine with Christmas joy when Skip read "she brought forth her firstborn son, and wrapped him in swaddling clothes, and laid him in a manger; because there was no room for them in the inn."

When Skip finished, Kathleen quietly moved from the piano bench to sit at the harpsichord and I stood next to her with my violin. The delicate tones of the instruments took us back to a different time and seemed to offer us the possibility of a gentler world. The congregation sang softly. "O little town of Bethlehem, how still we see thee lie! . . ."

Bang! Hee-haw! Baw! Bang! Aww! Hee-haw! Bang! Bang! Waww!

The noise from outside was deafening. Something was banging against the chapel walls. Charles, Skip, and Rich rushed outside, with the rest of us not far behind. The red calf was standing, legs braced, eyes wildly staring over its bloodied nose. The hay bales were scattered and the donkey continued to bray while the red calf let fly a kick or two. They were as far apart as their tethers would allow, clearly in battle positions. It was obvious that the donkey had bitten the calf's nose.

The service ended abruptly before we heard the exhortation from the Gospel of John that we should love one another. I prayed the traditional prayer: "May He who by His incarnation gathered into one things earthly and heavenly, grant you the fullness of inward peace and goodwill."

Really! All things gathered into one? Things earthly and heavenly?

Earl and Skip quickly loaded their animals to take them home.

I went back into the empty church. It had been such a beautiful idea—ruined with a fight between the animals. All my hopes and dreams for bringing real culture, something fine and historic and beautiful to Graves Mill had ended in comedy. Somehow that seemed worse than tragedy at the moment. I was tempted to cry, but suddenly, as if I'd heard a little voice whisper, it occurred to me that this must have been how it was that first Christmas Eve. There were donkeys and calves and sheep, and they do bray and kick and bleat. It's the nature of beasts. I smiled to myself. Perhaps we'd come closer to the real Christmas than we'd guessed. I stepped outside. The stars were bright over Jones Mountain, and although the animals were gone, the light shining from the Christmas manger was undimmed.

Every year thereafter, we held the service of Lessons and Carols on Christmas Eve, but we never attempted a living barnyard nativity again. It may have been very first-century, but I cannot say that I regretted the omission.

When Christmas was past, Big Jim took the tree, cut away the branches, and at my direction fashioned the trunk into a big cross. Jesus' Passion—His journey to the cross—really began at the Nativity so it was fitting that the Christmas tree should become a cross.

The following spring, on Palm Sunday, we all marched into the church waving palm branches and singing, "Hosanna in the highest!" Then one by one, each of us laid our branch at the foot of the Christmas cross, and each in turn picked up a hammer and drove a nail into the rough cedar. As we pounded, we all understood: He died for *us*. I know tears filled my eyes each time I did this. And I know I wasn't the only one.

When the next December came, once again the men vied with one another to find the best and biggest tree on the mountain farm. This time it took most of the afternoon to find the candidate. It was more massive than the previous year's cedar. After a slow trip down the mountain in Skip's truck, they unloaded it on the chapel's front lawn. C. K. looked at the tree and then the chapel's roofline.

"We'll never get that tree inside," he announced. "We'd better stand it up out here between the doors."

And so they did exactly that. We managed to find four or five strings of outdoor Christmas tree lights, and when these were judiciously arranged, I brought an extension cord from the cottage and we lit the tree. Everyone cheered, certain that we had outdone ourselves. The real confirmation came at sundown. I walked up to the church with Tallis at my heels and plugged in the lights. The effect was stunning! The chapel stood on a rise at the bend of the road, and when the Christmas tree lights began to beam, their soft radiance seemed to change the character of the whole valley. They were a beacon of welcome and hope, and a promise of joy shining out between the doors of that old church. The impossible had come to pass, and I knew it was not by might, nor by power, but by His Spirit that those lights were burning bright.

Christ was there, and His feet were beautiful on the mountain.

MIRACLES DO HAPPEN

Blessed is the man that walketh not in the counsel of the ungodly, nor
standeth in the way of sinners, nor sitteth in the seat of the scornful.

PSALM 1:1, KJV

THE YEARS THAT FOLLOWED were anything but quiet. One denomination after another told us that we should close Graves Chapel because it was too small and too rural to survive and prosper, but thanks to Clarence Chambers, a lay reader who had done missionary service in the Blue Ridge, Emmanuel Episcopal Church in Rapidan agreed to sponsor me. I was confirmed in the Episcopal church in 1980 and shortly afterward I was licensed as a lay reader. The chapel congregation voted to become an Episcopal mission and we had our first Communion service in 1982, including a dedication and blessing of the church and parish hall. In February 1983, Bishop Hall of the Diocese of Virginia licensed me as a lay missioner (a lay missionary and an unordained deaconess) for Graves Chapel.

All the stories surrounding those events would take another book to tell. I was convinced that my work in the mountains was to get the church open, to build up the congregation, and to spread the gospel. But did you ever notice that in Jesus' parable of the sheep and the goats, the sheep are just as clueless as the goats?

In Matthew 25, Jesus tells us that when the Son of Man comes in glory, He'll separate the sheep from the goats. The sheep will be on His right and the goats on His left. He will tell the sheep that a place is prepared for them because they fed Him when He was hungry, clothed Him when He was naked, and took Him in when He was a stranger. And the sheep will say, "Huh? When did we see You hungry? When did we clothe You or take You in?" And the goats are cursed and cast out because they didn't feed Him, clothe Him, or take Him in when He was a stranger. They know no more than the sheep.

That's why we need a Shepherd. We're called to love—to reach out to the hungry, the lonely, the sick, and the broken—but we often forget to do so. And then the Shepherd reminds us.

My 1977 visit to the young girl with a broken neck was a harbinger of things to come. Many of the households on the edge of the national park were poor, and because we were in that area, social services often called me to visit someone in need. Eventually we at Graves Chapel would open a thrift shop and maintain a small food pantry, but that was later. In the first two years after I became a lay reader, new faces appeared in the pews—some from the local population, some from among the mountain's weekenders.

Just after Easter 1982, I recognized Jimmy Leighton Johnson sitting in a back pew, the first time he had come to our church since it had reopened. I greeted him warmly.

"I'm so glad you could join us today, Mr. Johnson," I said, extending my hand.

He pumped it up and down. "I used to come here, years back," he replied. "Brings back memories, it do. Glad you got it goin' again, Miz Light."

We didn't see Jimmy often in church, but I would stop by his house occasionally on my way to or from Wolftown. Gradually I got to know him better and learned about his difficult life. I encouraged him and his wife, Lavinia, to come to our services, but they didn't have an automobile and didn't want to inconvenience anyone to transport them.

One October evening at Bible study, Skip McDanolds announced that Jimmy Leighton was going to lose his house.

"*What?*" everyone asked at once.

"The man who owns the place is sick of Jimmy," Skip explained. "He never fixes anything, he probably doesn't pay any rent, and the owner wants him out of there. He's got an eviction notice."

"I think it's a rotten shame!" Kathleen exploded. "The owner could at least let Jimmy alone. Jim and Lavinia don't have that many years left. They're both ailing. Why couldn't they be left in peace? Where can they go?"

"Jim doesn't know what they'll do," Skip replied. "Poor old guy— I guess he's scared to death. He can't afford to rent an apartment in Madison, and he certainly couldn't afford to rent a regular house. The thing is, he's lived in that place for over forty years, and besides, he and Lavinia both have diabetes and Lord knows what other problems. They're helpless."

"Is there anything *we* can do for them?" I asked.

C. K. cleared his throat. "D'you think we could get together enough money to buy a trailer? We could put it on a corner of my farm, there by the road, and at least the Johnsons would have a place to live."

"We'd need permission for that, providing we can even find a trailer for Mr. and Mrs. Johnson," Patti Bunce replied. "These days the county has all these ordinances against trailers. We'd need an exception. And what about a septic field? I don't think the county would allow a privy unless there's one already in place. The supervisors really do not like trailers, and they'll do anything to keep them out."

C. K. frowned, his bushy white eyebrows fusing into a hedge over his nose. "We can try it," he growled.

I bit my tongue and kept quiet. I was one of those county people who had been very vocal about the need for land conservation, strict zoning laws, and regulations prohibiting trailers in the county. It had never occurred to me that the poor might have no other option.

My thoughts kept racing as we prayed for the family. I was grateful when Patti got out her Autoharp to lead us in praise songs, effectively ending the discussion. The participants were less attentive than normal at the Bible study, and I noticed that the conversations over coffee afterward were unusually intense. I could sympathize; I knew we were facing a challenge, and I didn't know how it could be resolved.

I don't recall whether it was at the next meeting that C. K. told us the county officials had refused permission for any trailer on Graves Mill Road, but it was very soon after we learned of Jim's predicament.

Matters dragged along until April 1983. Somehow, perhaps because of sheer resistance, Jimmy had managed to cling to the little shack beside the road until early spring. We all talked about the problem, but we didn't know what to do about it. We continued to pray for a solution and to discuss the situation.

Someone would come up with a possible answer to the problem and then would report back that it turned out to be a dead end. Finally Skip suggested that we all go to the upcoming county planning commission meeting in Madison and talk to them about Jimmy and Lavinia.

The entire congregation plus eight or ten other people from the area gathered at the county building that night. The officials were in closed session when we arrived, so we camped in the hallway outside the auditorium for the next half hour.

For me, it was strange and surreal to be there. I'd taught poetry and English classes in that building for the University of Virginia. Several years after I resigned my position, the university closed its extension in Madison, and the county took over the facilities for offices, using the auditorium for public meetings. As I looked at the people crouched on the hallway floor and leaning against the walls, I realized what a diverse group we were. Some could barely read. Big Jim could sign his name, but that was about as much as he knew. He often held his prayer book upside down. Others had college educations. Some were poor. Some were middle class. What a strange journey it had been from my early days of teaching in the county to that moment!

Finally the big doors opened and we all trooped inside. The planning commissioners sat behind a desk on the raised platform at the head of the auditorium. We sat down and waited until the floor was open for discussion.

One person after another stood up to plead Jimmy's case, often passionately. But at the end of the meeting, the commissioners refused to bend the rules. "If we grant an exception to you, we'd set a precedent and we'd be forced to allow more trailers to sit anywhere in the county." The commission chairman asked if there was any way this "hardship case" could be alleviated without putting a trailer on the land. Carleton Deale, whose family had raised Jimmy Leighton, spoke for all of us, explaining that we'd checked into every alternative but Jimmy failed to qualify for any aid.

There was a buzz among the planning commission members, but finally Alvin Lohr, the vice-chairman, said, "We're sorry, but the answer is no. There just isn't enough evidence to convince me that this is a hardship case."

We couldn't believe our ears. At seventy-four, Jimmy suffered from high blood pressure, gout, osteoarthritis, and diabetes. Lavinia had recurring skin infections—probably from poor hygiene—anemia, and diabetes that required daily insulin shots. And this wasn't a "hardship case"? What did a hardship case look like, anyway?

All of us were discouraged as we turned to leave. When I glanced at the committee members' faces, they didn't look very cheerful either. They understood that this incident wouldn't play well in the county. Leaving a poor man on the side of the road for the sake of aesthetics and "good land use" obviously made them bad guys. I suspected they were imagining numerous sermons thundering from county pulpits the coming Sunday. I think most of us spent a restless night. I know I did.

The following week at our next Bible study meeting, we had a surprise visitor. We had moved our gathering from the cottage to the parish hall, and that night Pentecostal pastor Claude McDaniel walked in through the outside basement door. He took off his hat, smoothed his hair, and refused the chair I offered him. He bent his head for a moment, undoubtedly in prayer, and then cleared his throat.

"I spoke with Earl Estes today," he began. "You-all know that little resettlement house at the fork of the road just this side of Earl's house?"

We nodded.

"The poor old man who lived there just died," Claude continued. "The house is in really bad shape. He was blind, you see, and the outside privy fell apart so he used the dining room for a facility. The rest of the house isn't much better than the dining room, and Earl intended to bulldoze it, but I've persuaded him to let it stand if you folks will help my congregation clean it up and make it a decent place for Jimmy and Lavinia Leighton."

We all sat there stunned. Not only was this an unexpected answer to prayer for the Johnsons, but it had come at a cost—the suffering of the poor old blind man.

Then, in what seemed at first a non sequitur, Claude said, "I've been reading the Psalms lately, especially the first psalm. 'Blessed is the man that walketh not in the counsel of the ungodly, nor standeth in the way of sinners, nor sitteth in the seat of the scornful . . .'" he quoted slowly. "Now, have you sat in the seat of the scornful? I have. I've looked with scorn on other men when the psalmist tells us that we must meditate on the law of the Lord day and night. If we look at His law, there's no room for scorn." He broke off, leaving us to make the applications.

There was silence. Then C. K. cleared his throat. "We'll do it," he said. "We'll help build the house."

"The flooring company will donate some materials," Claude replied. "Other businesses will help too. We'll start work tomorrow, if you agree."

Every man and woman in the room said a resounding "Yes!" as one soul.

We had until June 1 to get everything done, which was little more than a month away. The men would rebuild and make repairs to the little saltbox house, and the women volunteered to paint.

Claude's congregation couldn't pay him an adequate salary, so he supported his family by building and repairing houses as well as doing electrical work. As a result, he had contacts all over the county for lumber, wiring, and miscellaneous materials, which were generously donated. Word spread, as it does in rural areas, and I suspect the commissioners worked behind the scenes to make sure we had what we needed.

One of them may have nudged the county newspaper to run a story about our renovation efforts. I happened to be on site when the reporter arrived, so my picture appeared on the front page of the Madison paper. It was not a very flattering shot, since I was wearing an old rusty-black, too-big jacket. I would have been mortified three years before to have had such a photo taken, let alone published, but now I didn't care. What did dressing stylishly matter, so long as Jimmy had a house?

That day at the resettlement house, the parish women and I were working in a cleanup effort. It was very unpleasant work. My stomach was roiling with indigestion—not because of anything I'd eaten, but because my conscience was struggling with many questions as I looked at the surroundings.

I had been digging and shoveling human excrement from the little dining room's floor. As I worked, I remembered that I'd driven past the place dozens of times in the years since I'd moved to Graves Mill. I'd known an old man lived there. I'd heard he was blind. I'd never stopped to see him because there had been no call to do so and no nudge in my heart. What was wrong with me? And what about God? Why did He allow that poor old man to die in squalor—alone and unloved?

I knew one reason: the hardness of our hearts. It was tempting to think, *That old man was black. The Rock Hall Church is where those folks go—he was their responsibility. They should have done something!* It was easy to say to myself, *Why didn't the people in Wolftown do something? They knew this old man! Why didn't Earl Estes intervene? This house is on his land!*

To this day, I still don't have answers. I never found out whether any of the churches had attempted to reach the poor old soul—may he rest in peace! I don't know the man's history or what sort of person he was. What I do remember, what is still etched on my heart, is Claude's word to us all that evening in the parish hall basement: "Blessed is the man that walketh not in the counsel of the ungodly, . . . nor sitteth in the seat of the scornful."

I do know that God's ways are not mine but He is love. This tragedy changed us as a community. We knew, whether we articulated it or not, that there had been a failure in love and that we had all played a part in it. We wanted to make amends in some way, and the county's response was almost overwhelming. Larry and Betty Baker wrote, "Many people have prayed concerning the Johnsons. The Lord really did answer. He is there in all things." Jim Carpenter, the owner of the local lumber company, gave us a generous credit at the store. He wrote, "The kind of work you are doing for the Johnsons is the kind Jesus appreciates. . . . P.S. Of all my donations, I feel like this will top the list. After all, Jesus was very dedicated to the poor." I cried when I read that one because I had a sense that the Lord truly was pleased.

The planning commission chairman sent a generous donation too, and Clyde Deale wrote from Georgia, "I am pleased to be able to contribute, as Jim Johnson has been like another uncle to me all of my life."

And so the floors were sanded or replaced, and new linoleum seemed to appear almost of its own accord. When it came time to paint that little house inside and out, there was no shortage of either paint or labor. For once, despite our differences in wealth, status, and perspectives, we acted as a community. I even took Jimmy down to Hebron Lutheran Church, where he shared some of his history and played the piano for people who were born and raised in a segregated world, who would not have dreamed twenty years before that they'd be listening to an old black man play and speak right there in their historic church. The county had come a long way from the days when Jimmy's kin sat in the slave galleries above the white parishioners.

I dare not give pat answers to the questions this incident raised, questions about suffering, selfishness, privation, guilt, and racism. There are always more threads in the tapestry than we can either see or count. I do know that the old man who lived at the fork in Wolftown Road did not die in vain, because God used his suffering to soften people's hearts.

As we were finishing up the resettlement house, Earl Estes worked out a legal document giving the Johnsons the right to live there until their deaths, guaranteeing that our work would not be in vain. It wasn't.

We moved the Johnsons to their new location and when we visited them, it was a joy to see the floors shining, the windows sparkling, and each surface clean and neat, as only love and pride could make it. God can and does use even people like us to bring light into the darkness.

I was in Graves Mill fifteen years, and even though it wasn't easy, it was a singular favor. I remained a laywoman but eventually became president of the county clergy association. Oddly enough, because I wasn't a priest or a pastor, I could reach out more effectively to these good men and women than if I had been ordained in a particular denomination. Graves Chapel hosted a silent retreat for the clergy each year, which was a special time of prayer and reflection for us all.

During those years in Graves Mill, I was privileged to be part of a history that had almost vanished. Living in the mountain hamlet was, in many ways, a step back in time to a simpler world. For a spoiled woman like myself, the reductions were the best soul medicine I could possibly have received. Furthermore, the little hamlet remembered what it means to be a community, a rare commodity in our busy, impersonal twenty-first-century world. To have been part of that community's renaissance, to have seen the cross on the mountain, to have known Charles, Dolly, Big Jim, and all the others—what a gift!

But the best gift of all was walking with the Lord and watching Him supply what we needed. There was no one else to whom I could turn for help. I did not know what I was doing. I was miserably ill-equipped for the work, but He knew what was needed, and He took care of the details, every step of the way. I think we come to know God better not in the extraordinary miracles, but in the simple, daily duties. If we have but eyes to see and a heart to receive, He provides for us, too, just as He provided for the little church.

I never did keep sheep on the Kinsey place. I was not the shepherd. But He was. He is. He keeps the sheep. He even kept me. And He, the Shepherd, let me work beside Him on that mountain.

Acknowledgments

BEAUTIFUL ON THE MOUNTAIN came into being after Charlene Fu Aikman read parts of my story and said, "You really should write a book!" Friends and fellow parishioners had been saying that for years because I had used many of the stories as sermon and teaching illustrations. However, Charlene was adamant and agreed to edit some of the manuscript. I am deeply indebted to her excellent suggestions and fastidious work with the early chapters of the text and to her husband, David Aikman, for his encouragement, good advice, and support throughout the writing and publishing process.

Douglas Graves, the local historian and a descendant of the Graves family for whom Graves Mill was named, patiently reviewed each chapter, checking for errors in dates, genealogies, and geography. I am very grateful for his kindness and interest. His history of Graves Chapel can be found on the Internet at http://graveschapelva .blogspot.com/2009/08/chapel.html.

My friends at Truro Anglican Church in Fairfax, Virginia, have gone above and beyond the call of duty, keeping me, the book, and Tyndale Momentum in their daily prayers. Their encouragement has been more precious than silver.

Last but not least, I am especially grateful to the Tyndale Momentum team for their patience, wisdom, and diligent efforts to help me make *Beautiful on the Mountain* as fine a book as possible and for their courage in publishing a first-time author. Special thanks are due to Sharon Leavitt, Bonne Steffen, Katie Fearnley, Sarah Atkinson, and Jan Long Harris, who've given generously of their time and expertise to help me navigate the publishing process.

It is my hope and prayer that you, the reader, enjoyed your visit to Graves Mill and that as you relived my adventures, you found encouragement and hope in God's amazing love and providence for all His people.

Notes

xiii   Historical . . . *does not refer only to the bare, plain facts*: Raniero Cantalamessa, *Beatitudes: Eight Steps to Happiness,* (Cincinnati: St. Anthony Messenger Press, 2009), 50.

1   *It cannot be stated definitely what the call of God is to*: Oswald Chambers, *My Utmost for His Highest* (Westwood, NJ: Barbour and Co., Inc., 1963), 159.

17   *faith comes by hearing the Word*: See Romans 10:17.

19   *God moves in a mysterious way His wonders to perform*: William Cowper, "God Moves in a Mysterious Way"

23   *Jehovah Jireh, meaning "The Lord Will Provide"*: See Genesis 22:14.

35   *His purposes will ripen fast, unfolding every hour*: William Cowper, "God Moves in a Mysterious Way."

51   *As long as the most important thing in your life*: Robert Farrar Capon, *The Parables of Grace* (Grand Rapids: William B. Eerdmans, 1989), 67.

67   *A face I cannot see, a voice that by faith alone*: Frederick
     Buechner, *The Alphabet of Grace* (New York: Seabury
     Press, 1981), 82.

84   *"Now when Jesus was born in Bethlehem of Judaea in the
     days of Herod the king"*: Matthew 2:1-2, KJV

85   *"And the soldiers led him away into the hall"* :
     Mark 15:16-17, 19, KJV

85   *"He who did not spare His own Son"*: Romans 8:32, NKJV

87   *I think that as long as we can feel things we walk by
     feeling*: Father Andrew, *The Life and Letters of Father
     Andrew, S.D.C.*, ed. Kathleen E. Burne (London:
     A. R. Mowbray & Co., Ltd., 1953), 241.

96   *"in the world but not of it"*: Romans 12:2 (emphasis added).

103 *Don't worry about what you ought to do. Worry about loving.*:
     Carlo Carretto, *Letters from the Desert* (New York:
     Orbis Books, 1972), 25.

117 *Real answers are answers to real questions. Death is a real
     question.*: Peter J. Kreeft, *Love Is Stronger Than Death*
     (San Francisco: Harper and Row, 1979), 23.

118 *About suffering they were never wrong*: W. H. Auden, "Musée
     des Beaux Arts," *Selected Poems*, ed. Edward Mendelson
     (New York: Vintage, 2007), 87.

123 *"God is our refuge and strength"*: Psalm 46:1-2, KJV

123 *"Man born of woman is of few days and full of trouble":*
Job 14:1-2

131 *"He Will Carry the Lambs":* Isaiah 40:11

131 *At its heart most theology, like most fiction, is essentially
autobiography.:* Frederick Buechner, *The Alphabet of
Grace* (New York: Seabury Press, 1981), 3.

131 *Keep your eyes fixed on Jesus:* See Hebrews 12:2.

138 *You promised to give Your angels charge over us:*
See Psalm 91:11.

143 *"No discipline is enjoyable while it is happening—it's painful!":*
Hebrews 12:11, NLT

145 *"Whatever you do, do all to the glory of God":*
1 Corinthians 10:31, NASB

145 *"I am the true vine, and My Father is the vinedresser":*
John 15:1-2, NKJV

155 *The perfection of prayer does not lie within our power:*
The Way of a Pilgrim, trans. R. M. French (New York:
Seabury Press, 1965), 8.

158 *the passage in 1 Timothy 2 forbidding women to teach men:*
See 1 Timothy 2:11-15.

158 *Paul says that women should have their heads covered:*
See 1 Corinthians 11:2-16.

165   *Where is our comfort but in the free, uninvolved, finally mysterious beauty*: Wendell Berry, *What Are People For?* (Berkley, CA: Counterpoint, 2010), 140.

179   *In every culture good and evil combine and recombine in so many ways*: Cornelius Plantinga Jr., *Not the Way It's Supposed to Be: A Breviary of Sin* (Grand Rapids: William B. Eerdmans, 1995), 73.

185   *"Blessed Are You Poor . . ."*: Luke 6:20, NKJV

185   *A life is a definite range of activities and responses.*: Dallas Willard, *In Search of Guidance* (San Francisco: HarperSanFrancisco, 1993), 158.

190   *the Lord's hand was with me*: Nehemiah 2:8, 18

194   *"as unto the Lord"*: Colossians 3:23, ASV

199   *A community identifies itself by an understood mutuality of interest.*: Wendell Berry, *Sex, Economy, Freedom, and Community* (New York and San Francisco: Pantheon Books, 1993), 120.

199   *"see through a glass, darkly"*: 1 Corinthians 13:12, KJV

200   *"hearing, they do not hear"*: Matthew 13:13

215   *God's written word is full of mystery*: Jean-Pierre de Caussade, *The Sacrament of the Present Moment*, trans., Kitty Muggeridge (San Francisco: Harper and Row, 1989), 65.

231   *And so our good Lord answered to all the questions and doubts which I could raise*: Julian of Norwich, *Showings* (Short Text), trans. Edmund Colledge, O.S.A. and James Walsh, S.J. (New York: Paulist Press, 1978), 151.

247   *O little town of Bethlehem, how still we see thee lie*: Phillips Brooks, 1868.

255   *the seed of woman would bruise the serpent's head*: See Genesis 3:15.

255   *Isaiah foretell Christ's birth and Kingdom*: See Isaiah 7:14; 9:2-7.

255   *the angel Gabriel came to visit the Virgin Mary*: See Luke 1:26-38.

255   *"she brought forth her firstborn son"*: Luke 2:7, KJV

256   *love one another*: See John 13:34.

257   *"Hosanna in the highest!"*: Mark 11:10, NASB

258   *not by might, nor by power, but by His Spirit*: See Zechariah 4:6.

258   *His feet were beautiful on the mountain*: See Isaiah 52:7.

259   *"Blessed is the man that walketh not in the counsel of the ungodly"*: Psalm 1:1, KJV

260   *In Matthew 25, Jesus tells us . . . He'll separate the sheep from the goats*: See Matthew 25:31-46.

271   *more precious than silver*: See Proverbs 16:16.

Back cover *God calls us to go where there is no path*: Adapted
from the words of Ralph Waldo Emerson: "Do
not follow where the path may lead, go instead
where there is no path and leave a trail." Quoted
in Bob Kelly, *Worth Repeating* (Grand Rapids:
Kregel, 2003), 108.

About the Author

Jeannie and Tallis

JEANNIE LIGHT grew up hearing colorful adventure stories about her great-grandfather, a circuit-riding pioneer preacher on the Michigan frontier. Although she admired him, she had no desire to follow in his footsteps; her ambition was to be a writer. She earned a BA in English literature from Kalamazoo College and as a Woodrow Wilson scholar, received an MA from the University of Virginia. She worked as a journalist, teacher, and farmer until she was called to revive a dormant country church in the Blue Ridge Mountains, where she served for fifteen years as a lay missionary.

In 1985 Jeannie became a member of Truro Anglican Church, Fairfax, and since her resignation from Graves Chapel in 1993, she has ministered at Truro in various capacities as a layperson, including leading bimonthly services at the Fairfax Nursing Center and teaching a Bible study. She lives in Louisa, Virginia.

Online Discussion *guide*

TAKE *your* TYNDALE READING
EXPERIENCE *to the* NEXT LEVEL

A FREE discussion guide for this book
is available at bookclubhub.net, perfect
for sparking conversations in your book
group or for digging deeper into the text
on your own.

www.bookclubhub.net

*You'll also find free discussion guides for
other Tyndale books, e-newsletters, e-mail
devotionals, virtual book tours, and more!*

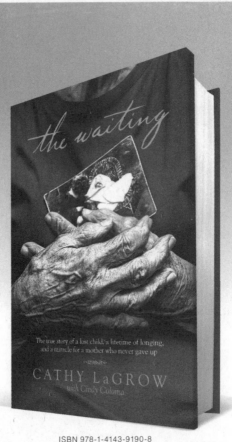

ISBN 978-1-4143-9190-8

In 1928, an innocent young woman was assaulted and raped. A baby was given up for adoption. And nearly eighty years and a lifetime later, a mother's secret, impossible prayer for her daughter was finally answered. *The Waiting* is an unforgettable true story that will touch your heart and make you believe in love's enduring legacy, and in the power of prayer.

"REBECCA'S HARROWING ACCOUNT SERVES AS AN INSPIRATION TO US ALL."

—Dr. Tim LaHaye, author of the *Left Behind* series

ISBN 978-1-4143-2659-7

Rebecca never felt safe as a child. In 1969, her family moved to Sellerstown, North Carolina, where her father was eagerly welcomed in his new role as pastor. But glaring at him from pew number seven was a man obsessed with controlling the church, and he would stop at nothing to get his way. Even in the face of terror and violence, Rebecca's father stood his ground—until one night when an armed man burst into the Nichols family home . . . and Rebecca's life was shattered. If anyone had a reason to seek revenge, it would be Rebecca, but *The Devil in Pew Number Seven* tells a different story—one of incredible forgiveness and freedom.

CP0751